Brush Men & Vigilam

❖

NUMBER ONE:
Sam Rayburn Series on Rural Life
James A. Grimshaw, Jr., General Editor

Brush Men & Vigilantes

CIVIL WAR DISSENT IN TEXAS

David Pickering and Judy Falls

Foreword by Richard B. McCaslin

TEXAS A&M UNIVERSITY PRESS
College Station

The paper used in this book meets the minimum requirements
of the American National Standard for Permanence
of Paper for Printed Library Materials, z39.48–1984.
Binding materials have been chosen for durability.

Excerpts from *Brokenburn: The Journal of Kate Stone, 1861–1868*,
edited by John Q. Anderson, reprinted by permission of
Louisiana State University Press.
Copyright © 1955, 1972 by John Q. Anderson.

Library of Congress Cataloging-in-Publication Data

Pickering, David, B. 1939.
    Brush men and vigilantes : Civil War dissent in Texas /
David Pickering and Judy Falls—1st ed.
        p. cm.—(Sam Rayburn series on rural life ; no. 1)
    Includes bibliographical references and index.
    ISBN 0-89096-923-X (cloth); ISBN 1-58544-395-6 (pbk.)
    1. Texas—History—Civil War, 1861–1865—Social aspects.
2. Unionists (United States Civil War)—Sulphur River Watershed
(Tex. and Ark.)—History—19th century.   3. Vigilantes—Sulphur
River Watershed (Tex. and Ark.)—History—19th century.   4. Sulphur
River Watershed (Tex. and Ark.)—Social conditions—19th century.
5. Sulphur River Watershed (Tex. and Ark.)—Economic conditions—
19th century.   6. Violence—Sulphur River Watershed (Tex. and Ark.)—
History—19th century.   7. United States—History—Civil War, 1861–1865
—Social aspects.   I. Falls, Judy, 1947–   II. Title.   III. Series.
E580.P54   2000
973.7'1—dc21   99-04593

In Charles Frazier's novel *Cold Mountain,* rogue Confederates slaughter several "outliers" who had been hiding out in the North Carolina back country, trying to avoid getting caught up in the Civil War. But one outlier—or "brush man," as Texans of the time would have called him—survives. After being taken to town and jailed, he feels a need and an obligation to tell what happened and calls down to people on the street from the window of his cell, shouting out the story of his friends' deaths. It is in the same spirit of need and obligation that the authors dedicate this book to the following, most of whom were brush men who died at the hands of vigilantes: Joseph D. Campbell, Frank Chamblee, Horace DeArman, Pleasant R. Fitzgerald, Austin H. Glenn, Thomas Greenwood, James E. Hemby, Jonathan Hemby, Henry T. Howard, James K. Howard, Thomas Howard, Cicero Franklin Millsaps, James Monroe Millsaps, Thomas Randolph, a man named Newman, and one called "Trace Chain" Smith.

CONTENTS

List of Illustrations   ix

Series Editor's Foreword   xi

Foreword, by Richard B. McCaslin   xiii

Preface   xvii

Acknowledgments   xxi

Chapter

❧─◆─❧

1. Where North Met South:
The Sulphur Forks Watershed Counties of Northeast Texas   3

2. The Hanging of the Hembys and Howards, 1862   28

3. Hangings in Hunt and Hopkins Counties, 1863   68

4. "Blessed with Peace!": War's Bitter Aftermath   102

5. Forgetting   137

Notes   145

Bibliography   191

Index   203

ILLUSTRATIONS

James Wesley Hemby   *page* 32
E. L. Dohoney   36
Micajah Lewis Armstrong   37
Martin D. Hart   70

Maps

Northeast Texas, 1860   *page* 4
Southern Migration Routes to Texas   6
Major Migration Routes to Texas   7
Sulphur Forks Watershed Counties, 1860   19
Martin Hart's Civil War   74
Jack Helm, South Texas, and the Sutton-Taylor Feud   130

SERIES EDITOR'S FOREWORD

Brush Men and Vigilantes: Civil War Dissent in Texas inaugurates the Sam Rayburn Series on Rural Life, a series established on the Texas A&M University-Commerce campus under the auspices of the Texas A&M University Press book-publishing program. Designed to be diverse in scope of topics, the series focuses on northeast Texas and the surrounding region. The late David Pickering and his coauthor Judy Falls have written an enlightening and well-documented account of nineteenth-century political and social history in Fannin, Lamar, Hunt, Hopkins, and Delta Counties in northeast Texas.

Who were these brush men? Who were the vigilantes who sought to administer "justice" to those men who chose not to side with the Confederacy? Pickering and Falls spent five years researching county documents, other public sources, and family records to identify them and to record their history. Like Inman in Charles Frazier's *Cold Mountain* and Adam Rosenzweig in Robert Penn Warren's *Wilderness,* the Hembys and the Howards and others have a story to tell. Their history, too, is tied to the South's history and to the institution of slavery; the fear of a slave uprising led, in part, to the vigilante "safety" groups. Prejudice was also an underlying factor. Pickering and Falls ably set the place and time preceding the Civil War in the Sulphur Forks watershed area, an area that did not have a majority of slave-owners. The effects were the same, however: those who supported slavery versus those who opposed secession. Conflict was inevitable, and the authors lead into those conflicts with measured step and an insightful introduction. Those men who opposed the war and did not go to Mexico or north sought refuge in the thickets and bottomlands of the Sulphur Forks watershed; these men were the "brush men."

From the broader perspective of the "Texas Troubles," Pickering and Falls have selected specific incidents on which to report. The events leading to the hanging of three Howards and two Hembys in 1862 are articulated with objectivity and clarity, revealing further the split between the anti-secessionists and the pro-slavery factions and the dominance of the Southern sympathizers in this region. Clearly life was difficult, made more so with the political stress of the time; and sentiments wavered even among the slaveholders. The violent Texas that James A. Michener portrayed in his epic novel, *Texas*, finds ample support in Pickering and Falls's work. Other accounts follow, attesting to the authors' thoroughness and perseverance in obtaining family documents with statements of varying opinions on events surrounding other vigilante killings, such as that of Frank Chamblee.

David Pickering and Judy Falls have brought forth this previously unpublished material in a lively style and with a precise eye for historical detail. Judy Falls, cousin of David Pickering, teaches English at Cooper High School. David Pickering had a long career at the *Corpus Christi Caller-Times* before succumbing to skin cancer just after this book was accepted for publication. Their personal interest in these events in history, their individual talents in research and writing, and their intellectual integrity in presenting the facts that they discovered contribute significantly to this final product, which provides a firm basis for understanding and for future work in this area, a region which is now highlighted in the Sam Rayburn Series on Rural Life publications.

—*James A. Grimshaw, Jr.*
General Editor

FOREWORD

It remains one of the great tragedies of Southern history that the Confederacy, which was created to shield individuals from a potentially destructive national government, proved unwilling or unable to protect its citizens from each other. Confederates in almost every Southern state zealously attacked and even killed their neighbors in an attempt to eradicate dissent against the new regime or simply to settle old grudges. To establish an image of a unified South as part of the popular mythology of the Lost Cause, many of these affairs were deliberately forgotten, or the facts were skewed to present the victims as criminals and their attackers as heroic defenders of law and order. Time has allowed passions to settle, and careful scholars have provided more accurate accounts of some such events in an attempt to recreate a truer picture of the embattled Confederacy. This work represents yet another step in that laudable undertaking.

The South's collective amnesia regarding wartime violence has been enhanced in Texas by twentieth-century residents who ignore the state's Southern and Confederate history. Instead, they focus on the achievements of the postbellum cattle kingdom and oil boom. This may be due to the painful sense of defeat and loss associated with the earlier period, while for most modern Texans the later era supports a more positive self-image. Texas was definitely part of the cotton and slave economy that dominated the South before the Civil War, and it became one of the original Confederate states in 1861. Thousands of Texans fought for the Confederacy on almost every front. Many were killed in combat or died of disease, while those who came home remained staunchly proud of their service.

Both the cattle kingdom and the cotton kingdom have their dark side, though, and those seeking to understand either must explore the positive and negative aspects of each. While most Texans who fought in the Civil War did so for the Confederacy, a substantial number remained loyal to the old Union. Some of the latter joined Federal units, but many had no opportunity to do so and stayed at home. There they were joined by those who believed that family or business ties outweighed any national allegiance, by others who had gone to war but returned disillusioned, and by more unscrupulous characters faithful to no one but themselves. The imposition of a military draft by the besieged Confederacy made outlaws of all these dissenters, just as elsewhere in the South. The result was a violent backlash in Texas and other Southern states against any who were perceived as threats to the new order.

The ferocious efforts of Texans to eliminate dissent created for the state an image as the "dark corner of the Confederacy." An ugly label originally applied to the northeastern counties by a young lady in her wartime diary, these words were embraced by later scholars who resurrected a disturbing aspect of Confederate Texas. Texas partisans and vigilantes hanged dissenters on the Trinity River, slaughtered German Unionists along the Nueces River, and lynched Federal recruits by the Rio Grande. For this, the many assailants were generally applauded in Texas and throughout the South. The victims were portrayed as ruffians whose elimination was good for Texas and the Confederacy. These events, like those in other Southern states, were almost forgotten after the war. Then inquisitive historians picked up the bits of stories preserved by local oracles. Weaving these pieces into a narrative whole with the aid of voluminous records, these literary reconstructionists contributed greatly to a new understanding of Confederate Texas.

David Pickering and Judy Falls take their place in the ranks of Texas' literary reconstructionists with this fine study of the violence that took place in Hunt and Hopkins Counties during the Civil War and afterward. They have painstakingly recreated the economic and social framework of the region before the war, and clearly show how prewar tensions led to wartime atrocities. The circumstances that plagued Hunt and Hopkins Counties are those that created clashes in many other Southern states, especially the conflict between slaveholders and nonslaveholders. The usually unspoken rivalry between these two groups was forced to the surface by the events of the war. Men had to take a position and act upon it. As Pickering and Falls show, sometimes these choices had tragic consequences, not only for the men who made them, but for their families and even descendants in future generations. The Civil War for Hunt and Hopkins Counties did not begin in 1861, nor did it end in 1865. Such perspectives, explored here by Pickering and Falls, can be applied everywhere in the Confederacy.

It is hard for present-day Americans to understand how events such as the lynchings in Hunt and Hopkins Counties during and after the Civil

War could occur. They live in secure homes, protected by omnipresent police and military forces, and reassured by a well-established welfare state that they will not starve. In the Civil War South, there were no police, the military was faltering, the regime was under siege, and almost everyone lived hand to mouth. If crops failed or slaves rebelled, the government could offer little or no assistance. In this social and economic pressure cooker, as the authors indicate, tempers were short and tolerance for those who might be disruptive was minimal. Excesses in defense of law and order were not considered vices. Old friends became enemies, and blood was spilled. That which was done could not be undone, and victims denounced as criminals had to remain so in order to justify what happened. This human impulse to seek validation ultimately made the task of Lost Cause apologists easier, and the research of Pickering and Falls more difficult and valuable.

I had the honor of meeting David Pickering and becoming a colleague in this project. He was a remarkable individual, and it is a shame he did not live to see his work published. Judy Falls has also honored me by continuing our association as she completed the task she and David began. Texas history will be much richer by this work, and by the contributions Judy makes in the future.

—*Richard B. McCaslin*
High Point University

PREFACE

Young kinfolk were chasing fireflies through the park at our family reunion in Cooper, Texas, on an August evening in 1993 when my nine-years-younger cousin Judy Falls told me that a couple of Hembys had been hanged in our home area during the Civil War. Judy had written a college paper on the hangings years before but only mentioned them to me after I told her I was searching for information about my great-grandparents, John F. and Mary Elizabeth Evans Hemby. Both disappeared from the record during the Civil War, leaving their daughter Clarissa, my grandmother, to be raised by relatives.

After I left the reunion, there followed a year-long search, in libraries and elsewhere, for information about two Hembys and three Howards of unknown first name who were put to death in 1862 or 1863—perhaps in the spring, possibly on Christmas Day, maybe for deserting the Confederate army, possibly for hiding out in thickets and terrorizing their neighbors, maybe by act of official court-martial, possibly by a mob—with the single, modest goal of learning: Was my great-granddaddy one of those men?

The answer, as it turned out, was "No." My great-grandfather, who was related to the hanged Hembys and may even have been their brother, survived them for at least a few months, according to land records unearthed in the course of research. What became of him later still isn't clear. He may have been the "J. Hamby" who "died of sickness" while serving with the Confederate Ninth Texas Cavalry Regiment, or he and my great-grandmother may have fled to the North in fear of the vigilantes who hanged their kin. In the course of learning this much, however, I stumbled onto other information of enormous interest: unmined historical material about the Hembys and Howards who were hanged, as well as stories about the hangings of at least nine other men.

At this point, Judy agreed to join me, as lead researcher, in what had ceased to be a genealogical search and become an exciting endeavor in historical discovery. It's a project that eventually expanded to cover a lot of ground, including the peopling of northeast Texas' Sulphur Forks watershed counties with a volatile mixture of slaveless Upper Southerners and slaveholding Lower Southerners during the early 1800s; the flight of numerous men into the "brush" during the Civil War; the hanging (by vigilantes, in February, 1862, we finally learned) of the Hembys and Howards, who were pro-Union civilians; the hangings in 1863 of men named Campbell, DeArman, Fitzgerald, Glenn, Greenwood, Millsaps, Newman, Randolph, and Smith, most or all of whom were accused of having ties to Martin D. Hart, a guerrilla who was captain of a Union cavalry unit; the postwar indictment of men for the 1862 hanging and some of the 1863 hangings; the story of wily brush man Frank Chamblee, an unsung Forks watershed folk hero; and surprising allegations that Chamblee was murdered by vigilantes who included prominent Hunt County pioneer William Jernigan, sometimes called "The Father of Commerce, Texas." The book also includes a great deal of new information about the early life of a notorious Texan, John Jack Helms, also known as Jack Helm. A main player in the Hemby-Howard hanging, Helm later earned hatred as a Reconstruction-era State Police captain and gained additional fame in death when he was shot and killed by John Wesley Hardin and one of the gunfighter's cronies.

As should be emphasized, Judy was the person responsible for most of our discoveries, including a number that can be attributed to her unusual research style. While I am the journalist on this team—having served as reporter, art-movie-theater critic, and copy editor during a long career at the *Corpus Christi Caller-Times*—my own style of historical research is traditionally academic. But Judy, an award-winning teacher of English and other subjects at Cooper High School, is aggressively reportorial. Instead of ditch-digging in musty libraries, as I am wont to do, she goes out among the multitudes. On several occasions, this strategy led to immediate breakthroughs. But the real strength of Judy's technique lies in the many contacts she develops along the way, at archives, libraries, genealogical societies, and elsewhere. Some of these have paid off months or years down the road, as when an area genealogy society member she had contacted made an excited call in the night to tell of having unearthed an important record about the postwar trials of the vigilantes we were researching.

Sometime after Judy signed on, the research effort got another boost when we began communicating with relatives of people who were involved in the hangings, including many relatives of the hanged men. Judy and I made contact with many of these people by casting our bread upon the waters via the post office and the Internet. Some queries drifted hither and yon for years before coming to the notice of people with stories to share.

All told, we managed to contact relatives of twelve of the fourteen hanged men who were the primary focus of our research. The relatives are a varied group, running the gamut in age from baby boomers to a woman who first contacted us via letter but who received her first computer from family members for her eightieth birthday so she could communicate with us by e-mail. Every one of the relatives has contributed important information, much of it drawn from family stories. Additionally, some of these family members have actively joined the research effort, making great contributions.

The sum of these efforts is a book that fills in numerous blanks about Texas during the Civil War. *Brush Men and Vigilantes* also adds its mite to an ongoing reevaluation of the Civil War experience in many northern Texas counties, including those of the Sulphur Forks watershed—today's Lamar, Delta, Hopkins, Fannin, and Hunt. Many of these counties have been depicted as enthusiastic supporters of the Confederacy in past histories, especially local histories written by ardent fans of the Confederacy. But this view seems to be eroding as additional evidence surfaces about dissension within the area. Northern Texas—including northwest, northern, and northeast Texas but not far-northeast Texas—may not have been as seriously torn by strife between Unionists and Confederates as eastern Tennessee and some other bitterly disputed areas of the South. It seems clear, however, that a substantial amount of dissent existed in the area. The question is: how substantial was it? The answer is an issue that remains to be weighed by future historians.

While many people made contributions to this book's research, I should emphasize that the writing is entirely my own, as are all interpretations of the evidence and conclusions that are drawn from it. Almost all the original documents we used in our research contained errors, statements of fact that conflicted with others, or statements that just did not ring true. Much of the evidence took the form of statements by elderly men about events of their youth—in some cases, men in their eighties who testified about events of their teens—and errors commonly abound in these accounts. Additionally, much of the evidence was from partisan sources, Confederate or Union, and some of it seemed biased for that reason. The attempt to extract an accurate account from these materials presented me with hundreds of difficult choices along the way. I have chosen as best I could, although some of those who assisted with the book's research may not agree with all my conclusions.

—*David Pickering*
September, 1998

ACKNOWLEDGMENTS

First and foremost, David Pickering wishes to thank his wife, Joan McInerney, for her loving support, advice, and patience during the long course of this project. Judy Falls wishes to acknowledge the understanding and patience of her husband Sam and children Matthew and Callie, who have assisted with much of the research and allowed her to visit so many libraries, courthouses, genealogical centers, historical centers, museums, archives, and private homes over the years in the quest to piece together the tales of the hanged men and others who were part of their stories.

Special thanks to students of Cooper High School who participated in an award-winning stage and video history project about the hanging of the Hembys and Howards: Amanda Seigler, Dana Pickering, Julie Malone, Dustin Hoskison, Josh Steward, Matt Falls, Cody Bettes, Blake Randle, Brett Stowers, and Crystal O'Connor. The project, which helped publicize research about the hangings and opened doors for additional information, benefited from assistance by Cooper High teacher Karen Long, a project sponsor along with Judy Falls; Cooper schools superintendent Fred Wilkerson and Cooper High principals Jerry Stout and Larry Stowers; Texas A&M University-Commerce history professors Ty Cashion and Joe Fred Cox, who provided guidance for the students; and state legislator Pete Patterson, who donated copies of photographs from the state archives.

The authors received invaluable advice during the course of the research from numerous professionals with Texas history expertise. Richard B. McCaslin of High Point University in North Carolina contributed advice drawn from his extensive research for the award-winning book *Tainted Breeze: The Great Hanging at Gainesville, Texas, 1862;* he also gave generously of his time to provide detailed editing of the manuscript. James Conrad, archivist at Texas A&M University-Commerce, has provided advice to the authors during several years of their research and also helped edit the manuscript. Donaly E. Brice, archivist at the Texas State Library in Austin, cooperated on research into the life of John Jack Helms/Jack Helm, based on his research for a book about the Texas State

Police, and he also patiently helped with the authors' research at the Texas State Archives. Richard Lowe and Kelly Stotts of the University of North Texas provided access to the James Bates Papers from the Henry Fink Collection. Matt White of Paris Junior College provided invaluable information about area thickets. The authors also have benefited from contacts with Randolph B. Campbell of the University of North Texas, Gregg Cantrell of Hardin-Simmons University, and Cecil Harper of North Harris College.

A large number of people with kinship ties to hanged men mentioned in the book provided assistance. Clay Randolph of Tuttle, Oklahoma, a descendant of the hanged Thomas Randolph and kin of the hanged Pleasant R. Fitzgerald, contributed a wealth of documents that he had collected over the years. Randolph, a professor of English at Oklahoma City Community College, also put in much hard work editing the manuscript.

Also deserving mention in a special category is Julie Clayton, an electronic-components saleswoman in Santa Cruz, California, who was drawn into our project by a story within her family that her great-great-grandfather James Howard, father of Julie's great-grandmother Mary Elizabeth Howard, was hanged along with a couple of brothers. Julie subsequently spent years investigating the genealogy of the Sulphur Forks watershed's hanged Howards in an attempt to make connection with her family line. Eventually, she was able to establish that the James K. Howard who was hanged in Hopkins County in 1862 did indeed have a daughter named Mary Elizabeth—but that she was not the same Mary Elizabeth who was Julie's ancestor. While Julie's work represented one of those genealogical dead ends that so often confront ancestor searchers, it amounted to a victory for history. In the course of her efforts, she uncovered much valuable information about the hanged Howards and was directly responsible for the discovery of pastor Benjamin Ober's eyewitness account of the Hemby-Howard hanging. For this, she deserves special thanks.

Contributions from relatives of hanged men have been too numerous to enumerate in their entirety, but they included valuable help from retired army colonel Fredwin Mitchell Odom of Pensacola, Florida, great-great-grandson of Austin H. Glenn; Fitzgerald descendant and researcher Beth Gunn of Arlington, Texas; indefatigable octogenarian and retired schoolteacher Browne Elizabeth Millsap Myers of Austin, a member of the Millsaps and Campbell families; chemical engineer Richard W. Hunter of West Dundee, Illinois, James W. Hemby family; Tom and Kathy Hembey of Garland, Texas, James E. Hemby family; Nellie Olsen of Austin, Jonathan Hemby family; Edna Evans LaFour of Edna, Texas, Howard family; Lance Hall of Fort Worth, Howard family; Patricia DEArman Fite of Houston, DeArman family; Jackie Houston Conces of Pasadena, Texas, Campbell family; Ashley Wysong of Cape Coral, Florida, Campbell family; navy retiree Norman Wayne Calk of Stoutland, Missouri, Fitzgerald descendant; Edward H. Brown of Palestine, Texas, Glenn descendant; Dorman Glenn of Philadelphia, Pennsylvania, Glenn family; Wynema Blankenship of Krebs, Oklahoma, descendant of Henry T. Howard; and Dr. Wayne Capooth of Germantown, Tennessee, who generously shared information about his research into Millsaps family genealogy.

In addition to relatives of hanged men, numerous individuals who are kin to various persons mentioned in the book provided valuable assistance. Delma Ober Brown of Austin and her husband Joe spotted Julie Clayton's message about the Howards on the Lamar County website and subsequently made available to us the memoir of Delma's great-grandfather, Benjamin Ober, with its vivid description of the Hemby-Howard hanging and other matters of great interest. Desktop publishing consultant Sharon Jernigan Tingley of Macon, Georgia, who is related to both the Jernigans and the Harts, provided key information about those families' tangled genealogy; she also was among those who went the extra mile in providing editing assistance. James Terry of Arlington, Texas, and J. Dale Terry of Wichita Falls, who are cousins, contributed important information about their Terry ancestors in what is now Delta County. Venita Maddox of Charleston, Texas, contributed information on the history of the Helms and McGuire/McGuyer/Oats families. Lawrence and Sue Dale of Blossom, Texas, contributed information about the Condict/Condit family; and Milton Babb of Denton, Texas, contributed information about the Harts of Hunt County's Wieland community. Thanks also to Jerry Green of Cumby, Texas, Hart family; Ruby G. Campbell of Baton Rouge, Louisiana, genealogist and librarian of the Clan Campbell Society of North America; Glenda Wilson of Jasper, Georgia, Millsaps family; Melba Goff Allen of Trussville, Alabama, Goff family; Nita Zellars of Odessa, Texas, Greenwood family; and Honey Lanham Dodge of Dallas, Early family.

Local historians provided invaluable help. John Sellers of Hopkins County scored an important breakthrough in the research when he discovered Reconstruction-era letters of complaint from area residents about court proceedings involving suspected vigilantes; Sellers also provided valuable information and advice about Hopkins County history. The late Douglas A. Albright of Cooper, Texas, generously shared his research into area hangings. (Many thanks also to his daughter Susan Albright Hyde of Irving, who allowed access to Doug's papers after his death.) Skipper Steely of Lamar County allowed the authors access to manuscripts and historical documents and provided advice on Red River Valley history. Quentin Miller of Cooper, Texas, provided valuable documents from his personal local-history collection and also helped the authors secure information about Masonic history in the area. Tom Scott of the Fannin County Historical Museum provided assistance on Fannin County history.

Other important contributions came from Thomas E. Jordon of Independence, Oregon, who supplied the authors with the manuscript of his article on Martin D. Hart, some of which was published in *Civil War History;* A. Z. Oats, Annell Oats Patterson, and Pud Oats of Delta County for their information about Charleston, Texas, families; Shirley Smith, Katie Malone, and Nell Oliver of Delta County for their information about the history of Charleston and the Helm/Helms family; B. J. "Knob" Chapman of Klondike, Texas; Tom Scott, Bonham, Texas; Murphy Givens of Corpus Christi, Texas; Larry Hogue of Norfolk, Virginia; Cris Pickering Poteet of Fort Worth; Virginia Darden of Eugene, Oregon; Mark Pittman of Austin, Texas; Mary Claunch Lane of Paris, Texas; Scotty Pickering of Atlanta, Georgia; Ron Brothers of Paris, Texas; and Bobby Wadsworth of Carrollton, Texas.

Thanks also to the staff members at numerous libraries and other research facilities. They include Doris Alley, Shirley Walker, and Sylvia Wood at the Delta County Public Library; Daisy Harvill of the Aikin Regional Archives at Paris Junior College; Jean Leathers, archivist at the Church of God General Conference Office in Findlay, Ohio; Betsy Mills of the Lamar County Genealogical Society; Peggy Fox of the Harold B. Simpson Confederate Research Center in Hillsboro, Texas; and staff members of the Center for American History in Austin, Perry-Castañeda Library at the University of Texas at Austin, Evans Library at Texas A&M University in College Station, Bell Library at Texas A&M University–Corpus Christi, Corpus Christi Public Library, White Library at

Del Mar College in Corpus Christi, Rayburn Library at Bonham, Bertha Voyer Public Library at Honey Grove, the Masonic Grand Lodge Library and Museum of Texas at Waco, and Texas A&M University-Commerce.

The authors appreciate the guidance of Dr. James A. Grimshaw, Jr., general editor, for his work and encouragement. The authors acknowledge the great honor of the selection of this book as the first publication in the Sam Rayburn Series on Rural Life.

Brush Men & Vigilantes

CHAPTER I

Where North Met South

THE SULPHUR FORKS WATERSHED COUNTIES
OF NORTHEAST TEXAS

Travelers who entered Texas at its northeast corner during the Civil War and journeyed westward to the Fort Worth area would have noticed great changes in terrain along the way. For a hundred miles or more they would have encountered long stretches of forest, broken by small patches of prairie, while the ratio would have been reversed toward the end of this journey, with much more prairie than forest. But about midway through the trip, the travelers would have had some of their roughest going in a region featuring wide stretches of both forest and prairie but also many formidable thickets.

Because shade from the dense tree canopy suppressed undergrowth, the forests were relatively clear of underbrush and commonly offered easy passage for travel. But underbrush was a dominant feature of the thickets, where brambles, briers, saplings, and other plants combined to weave dense tangles of vegetation. The thickets are thought to have begun as small islands of vegetation that somehow managed to survive fires, ignited by humans or natural forces such as lightning, that periodically swept across the prairies. Once the tangles of vines, saplings, and other plants were established, they continued to be resistant to burning and grew ever outward, covering large sections of one-time prairie.[1]

The toughest of the thickets fell within an area roughly sixty miles square, much of which was within the Sulphur Forks watershed. This area encompassed four counties during the time of the Civil War—Fannin, Hunt, Lamar, and Hopkins—and today includes a fifth, Delta, which was created in 1870 from portions of Lamar and Hopkins Counties.

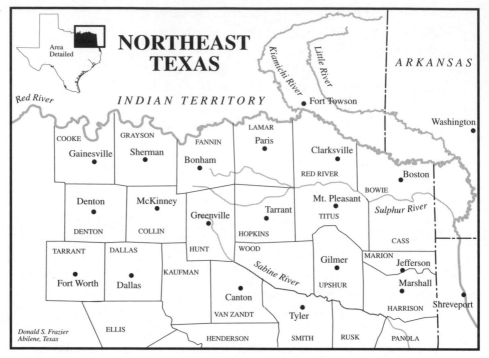

Counties and major cities of Northeast Texas in 1860. Map by Donald S. Frazier.

While parts of the area are drained by the Sabine and Red Rivers as well as other watercourses, the Forks of Sulphur are a central feature, with either the North Sulphur River or South Sulphur River reaching into every county of the region.[2]

Some of this area's thickets were small and nameless or bore names known only to people living near them, such as Hobbs Thicket, in the vicinity of present-day Enloe; Tidwell Thicket, north of Greenville; and Big Creek Thicket, a few miles north of present-day Cooper. But other thickets gained great notoriety throughout the region. They included Wildcat Thicket, which stretched westward out of Fannin County into Grayson County; Mustang Thicket, straddling the boundary between Fannin and Hunt Counties; and Black Cat Thicket, in Hunt County northeast of Greenville.[3] After a visit to Black Cat in 1854, Hunt County pioneer Alfred Howell wrote home to his brother in Virginia saying, "That thicket—you may have read of cane brakes, and heard often of such places, but you cannot conceive of such a place as Black Cat. . . . A person once lost in it, unless by accident, can never get out." He added that Black Cat was "filled with bear, panthers, wolves, catamount, wild cat, deer, etc. etc. There is no end to them."[4]

But the most notorious thicket of all was a larger and wilder place than any of those mentioned. The huge Jernigan's Thicket extended into all counties of the Sulphur Forks watershed, and the very first Europeans to enter the area may have run afoul of it. Luis de Moscoso Alvarado and others came to the New World with the De Soto expedition and then wandered into the Southwest in 1542 following De Soto's death. Chasing rumors about Indian sightings of "Christians," the Moscoso party may have crossed Red River near the site of present-day Clarksville, then traveled westward to near present-day Paris before turning southwest again on the advice of an Indian guide. But the guide led the intruders into a great tangle of trees and brush where they lost their way, wandering in circles for days before breaking into the clear—whereupon the explorers threw the guide to their dogs. Those woods, in an area the explorers called Socatino, may have been what came to be known as Jernigan's Thicket.[5]

Nineteenth-century pioneer William Banta described the great thicket in his 1893 memoirs as "a dense forest of wild locust, bois d'arc, red haw rattan and briars covering a territory of ten or fifteen square miles."[6] Judge L. L. Bowman of Hunt County, a leading regional historian during the 1920s and 1930s, was told by old-timers that Jernigan's Thicket contained patches of briers in which "you could scarcely stick a butcher knife."[7]

Much of the thicket fell within the 4,500 acres that the Republic of Texas granted to Curtis Jernigan, an immigrant from Arkansas. But it was not land ownership that attached Jernigan's name so firmly to the place. William Banta, retelling a popular story, writes that Jernigan wounded a deer around 1843 and followed its trail into the thicket, where he soon lost his way, wandering "for twelve days and nights, during which time he had nothing to eat except one skunk and five rabbits which he had shot," before emerging sick, exhausted and "covered with ticks."[8]

The Jernigan story soon spread and was embroidered by others. According to one version, Jernigan had been lost several days when he heard a gunshot, walked in its direction, and broke free of the thicket. Alas, he saw that the man who had fired the shot was his worst enemy. With a sigh of resignation, he tottered back into the brush and wandered for some days longer.[9]

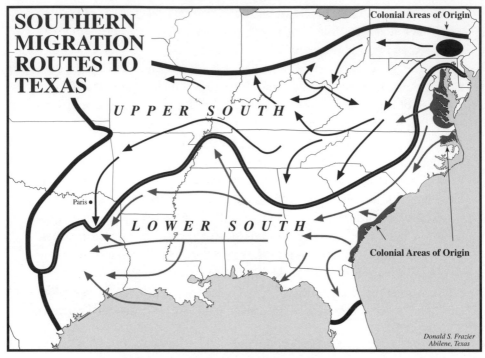

Adapted by Donald S. Frazier from Terry G. Jordan's map "The Upper South and Lower South, 1860" from Terry G. Jordan, "The Imprint of the Upper and Lower South on Mid-Nineteenth-Century Texas."

The earliest pioneers in the thicket-studded Forks watershed, as in other parts of Texas, were the people described by Delta County historian Ikie Gray Patteson in the 1930s as "a mixture of people from both the South and the North."[10] Although she went on to maintain that the latter people were called "Yankees," they were in fact Upper Southerners, who often came from "Southern" border states—mostly Tennessee, Kentucky, Missouri, and Arkansas—as well as such locales as southern Ohio, Illinois, and Indiana. Many of them were the famous "Scots-Irish," also known as "Borderers"—English-speaking Protestants of northern England, the Scottish lowlands, or northeastern Ireland. When the first of their lot had immigrated to America in the 1700s, they landed in Pennsylvania, where their aggressive ways led to conflicts with William Penn's pacifist colonials. Urged to move on, the Borderers headed inland and eventually settled back country all along the Appalachian chain. Then they moved west—

6

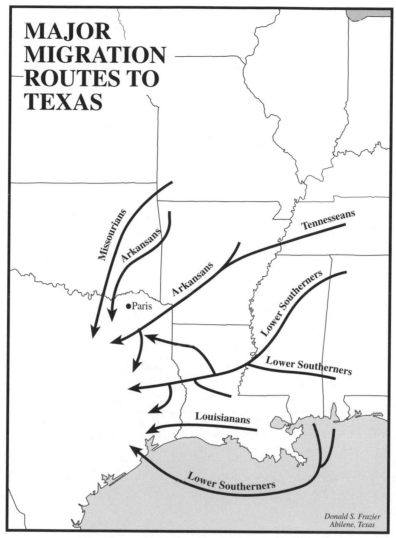

MAJOR MIGRATION ROUTES TO TEXAS

Adapted by Donald S. Frazier from Terry G. Jordan's map "Major Migration Routes of Southerners to Texas" from Terry G. Jordan, "Population Origins in Texas, 1850."

Kentucky, Tennessee, Missouri, Arkansas, sometimes into Illinois, Indiana, Ohio—and finally into Texas. Large numbers of Borderers began coming into the Sulphur Forks watershed in the 1830s and 1840s.[11]

Later, a change in immigration patterns dramatically reshaped the Forks watershed—as well as the rest of Texas and the border states—when immigrants from the Lower South began to pour in. Many of the newcomers were people who traced their ancestry back to the Chesapeake area, including Virginia and environs. These affluent immigrants from southwestern England, including some from noble families, transplanted their culture to the New World when they established estates in the Chesapeake colonies in the seventeenth century. The cotton and slave economy they created soon spread to the southern mid-Atlantic region and into Georgia, Florida, Alabama, Mississippi, Louisiana, and finally into Texas, which, after its break with Mexico in 1836, had no laws against slavery. Some of the largest slaveholders in the Sulphur Forks watershed arrived there in the 1850s.[12]

By the time of the Civil War, Lower Southerners had become the dominant population group in Texas, overall, but Upper Southerners remained numerous in the Sulphur Forks watershed. Some 50 to 65 percent of Fannin County residents came from the Upper South. Upper Southerners also made up the largest population group in Hunt County, Lamar County, and the area that is now Delta County (then part of Lamar and Hopkins), totaling 40 to 50 percent of the population in all these areas. Upper Southerners were substantially outnumbered by Lower Southerners only in the area that is within today's Hopkins County. Even so, about 30 to 40 percent of the Hopkins population came from the Upper South.[13]

Much more was involved here than differences in geographical origin. One important cultural difference between the two geographic groupings was that Lower Southerners were trained in the Virginia manner to bend the knee to their betters, and they expected like deference from their own social inferiors. The Upper Southerners, on the other hand, commonly were rough folk who believed in dealing with one another "more or less as social equals," regardless of wealth or status. The historical record is filled with resentful comments by Lower South "aristocrats" about Upper Southerners, whom they found "insolent" and "impudent" and who displayed "undue 'familiarity' and a lack of deference to age, wealth, birth, and breeding."[14]

So the grounds for conflict between the two peoples were there, even without other differences. Even without, in short, the issue of slavery.[15]

❦

Much has been written about the varied issues that divided supporters of the Union and Confederacy. But slavery, clearly, was the central and fundamental issue. Early on, as W. J. Cash noted in *The Mind of the South*, criticism of slavery became a taboo, which then "spread in ever-widening circles, poisonously. From the taboo on criticism of slavery, it was but an easy step to interpreting every criticism of the South on whatever score as disloyalty—to making such criticism so dangerous that none but a madman would risk it. And from that it was but another and just as easy—an almost inevitable—step to a state of affairs in which criticism of any sort at all was not impossible, surely, but an enterprise for bold and excitement-loving spirits alone."[16]

As in the rest of the South, slavery was the fundamental issue leading to disunion in Texas. As historian Randolph Campbell has noted, "Determination to defend slavery motivated secession, and the secession convention itself said so very directly in its 'Declaration of the Causes which Impel the State of Texas to Secede.'"[17]

It is also clear that slavery was the main dividing issue in the state's Sulphur Forks watershed—despite there having been relatively little slavery in this area. Of all the counties in the watershed, Lamar County had the best river access to markets in the area, was the biggest cotton producer in the region, and had the greatest number of slaves, since cotton growing and slaveholding went hand in hand. By 1860, Lamar had 2,833 slaves, comprising 27.9 percent of the population. There were about 1,682 slaves, or 18.2 percent of the population, in Fannin; 990 slaves, or 12.8 percent of the population, in Hopkins; and 577 slaves, or 9 percent of the population, in Hunt (where only twenty-two bales of cotton were produced in 1860).[18]

None of these counties had a slave presence to compare with that in the domain of Texas' great cotton plantations, located east of a line drawn between Texarkana and San Antonio. Thirteen counties in that region had black majorities, and slaves made up four-fifths of the population of deep-southeastern Wharton County.[19] But the fact that slavery was *not* well established in the Sulphur Forks watershed may have put its defenders—greatly outnumbered by nonslaveholders—on edge.

Alarm among slaveholders grew particularly intense in 1856, when rumors of a coming slave insurrection sprang up in Tennessee and spread to other states. Blacks were killed by whites in some parts of Texas, and the seeds of fear were planted in the Forks watershed and many other locales, where "vigilance committees" were organized to keep watch on slaves and suspicious strangers.[20]

Even earlier, religious divisions centering on slavery appeared in the Forks watershed, with Northern Methodists often being targets of complaint from the pro-slavery camp. In May, 1854, Alfred Howell wrote his brother from the Hunt County seat of Greenville, saying, "I understand

9

preaching is going on in town tonight, by a *missionary* from the Methodist church *North,* an abolitionist, he keeps dark however on the last subject." There had been talk of silencing him, although nothing was done, Howell said.[21] Religious divisions had intensified by 1857, when the Presbyterian church followed in the wake of Methodists and Baptists by splitting into northern, anti-slave, and southern, pro-slave groups. That same year, another denomination, the Church of God, became the focus of pro-slavery anger in Lamar County.

Benjamin Ober, a Pennsylvania native who would figure prominently in the Hemby-Howard hanging of 1862, organized the first Church of God congregation in Texas at the Liberty community, seven miles southwest of Paris, in June, 1856. The parent church, based in Pennsylvania, was strongly against slavery. But Ober and assistant pastor E. Marple were missionaries in an area where abolitionists were unwelcome and where at least two men who joined the church early on, J. M. Brackeen and A. Hamblin, were slaveholders. The missionaries adapted to the situation by breaking with the parent church on the slavery issue, deciding that slavery "is a political question, and much excited at the present period of time by both political and religious men North and South, [and] we think it inexpedient for the Church of God to interfere with it, either directly or indirectly, believing that ecclesiastical authority has no right to interfere with political questions which are matters of law." When the Texas missionaries' stance was reported back in the North, the Church of God's *Church Advocate* newspaper made light of the matter, noting with tongue in cheek that the Texas group had failed to endorse the church's stance against slavery "as is highly probable, through press of business or other causes." This article came to the attention of pro-slavery men in Lamar County who failed to detect the humor in the comments. According to a history of the Church of God, a subsequent editorial in the pro-slavery *Lamar Enquirer* addressed *The Church Advocate*'s articles. The author of the editorial declared that Ober and Marple were members in the North of an abolition church and were sent south "to propagate abolition religion." But finding "anti-abolition sentiment of this latitude too strong for the safe advocacy of their doctrines," these missionaries were constrained to denounce the views set forth in *The Church Advocate* and to change their attitude toward slavery. And so, "if one could have believed a tenth part of the vociferous and wrathful declarations of Elder O. since his sojourn amongst us, the 'Church of God' was as conservative on the subject of Slavery as the most ultra Southerner could desire."[22]

This newspaper attack put Ober's life in danger. He subsequently defended himself against "misrepresentations" of his group's doctrine at a public meeting in Paris, which apparently satisfied his critics, for agitation against the minister soon subsided.[23]

In 1859, Northern Methodists drew complaints from the pro-slavery camp after church members held a large conference at Timber Creek in Fannin County. A citizens' committee was formed, and it attempted to pressure the church members to leave Fannin but failed. Later, a citizen claimed that "a member of the Timber Creek church . . . had sought to influence a local Negro by reading to him after which the slave became useless to his owner. The Negro had changed hands and the new owner claimed that the slave had been told that he could run off to Illinois and make enough money preaching to buy his freedom."[24]

Despite such incidents, tensions in the Forks watershed remained relatively relaxed for several years through 1859. But then, in 1860, a panic resembling that of 1856 erupted in the South. "From the Rio Grande to the Atlantic plot after plot by secret abolitionists and unionists for the raising-up of slaves in bloody rebellion [was] exposed," Richard Maxwell Brown has written. "At this distance it seems that the fears of slave uprisings were groundless, but parts of the South were in the grips of a hysteria that was real enough. Vigilante groups and self-styled committees of safety [sprang] up."[25]

In northern Texas, where the South's "Great Fear" was referred to as the "Texas Troubles," events contributing to hysteria occurred as early as June, 1860. One of these events was the disappearance of the six-year-old son of Alfred E. Pace of Bonham, a member of the group that had attempted to force the Northern Methodists out of Timber Creek. The boy's body subsequently was found in a water hole, and a female slave of Pace's was accused of strangling the child. On June 21, 1860, a commentary in the *Texas Advocate* reported that "After the murder of the child the citizens of Bonham took a vote as to the disposition of the woman. For burning, 54; for hanging, 63. Mr. Pace was one of the committee which waited on the abolition conference near Bonham, of which our readers have heard something occasionally heretofore. It is believed that abolition emissaries linger in that region; and it is supposed to be not altogether improbable that some friends of the said conference are seeking vengeance by stirring up the slaves to commit such deeds as that we have just chronicled."[26]

The Texas Troubles intensified in July, when mysterious fires began breaking out in northern Texas, beginning with a conflagration that ravaged the Dallas town square on July 8, 1860. This fire was followed by blazes at Denton, Waxahachie, Jefferson, Pilot Point, and many other towns. Among them were fires at numerous locations within the Forks watershed, including Black Jack Grove (today's Cumby) in Hopkins County, Ladonia and Honey Grove in Fannin County, and Paris in Lamar County. On July 23, the *Paris Press* reported that Dr. W. W. Stell's home was set on fire "by one of his Negro women, who confessed to the deed."[27]

Confessions by slaves elsewhere, including some admissions extracted by force, helped fuel fears of a black-abolitionist conspiracy. Never mind the contention of many observers that the fires were due to record heat and the spontaneous combustion of new-fangled phosphorous matches (popularly known as "prairie matches") that had just been released onto the market. Editor Charles DeMorse of the *Clarksville Northern Standard*, in Red River County, pointed to the matches as the true culprit.[28]

A. W. Sparks, who grew up just across the Hopkins County line in Titus County, recalled that "the thermometer reached 114 degrees Fahrenheit in the shade at my father's house where I was staying, and sulphur matches caught fire and burned their heads off in the little wooden boxes in which they were kept. . . . So hot was politics that it was generally agreed that the burning was the work of incendiaries sent from the North to burn us out so that we could not resist invasion in the then expected war. Such were the conclusions of a mad people." Adding to the sense of impending calamity was an appearance by the great comet Charles V, which "some of those eminent in science" feared "would strike the earth and destroy it," Sparks said. "We could almost see to read by its light. . . . For three months it was always to be seen in its glory . . . This comet was the theme of learned conversation; old men and women said it was a sign of war, and comets always came to foretell fearful wars."[29]

As hysteria rose, vigilante groups were organized in many areas, including Lamar, Hunt, Fannin, and Hopkins Counties.[30] Whites were among those who came under suspicion and were subjected to vigilante "examination" in the euphemism of the time. Among the suspect citizens was cabinetmaker J. M. Peers of Marshall, who was in the Hopkins County town of Sulphur Springs when the panic broke out. Peers, who held strong proslavery views, initially assisted local vigilantes in "routing out an abolitionist." But for some reason Peers himself soon fell under suspicion of being an abolitionist who had played a part in arson at the

Rusk County town of Henderson on August 5. "After receiving rough treatment in Sulphur Springs," historian Donald E. Reynolds wrote, "[Peers] was taken to Paris, where he was finally released, possibly because the Henderson committee had already found an 'abolitionist' to blame for the city's destruction. Peers then started out on foot for Marshall, only to be overtaken by two of the men who had previously 'examined' him. His tormentors brandished a rope and threatened to hang him; instead, they settled for his money ($67.50) and left him free to continue his walk to Marshall."[31] According to Reynolds, "At least thirty men, both black and white, died at the hands of vigilantes [during the Texas Troubles], and there are indications that the number of 'executions' was much greater. Many others were expelled from the state by vigilante courts. Still others chose to leave the state voluntarily, rather than risk the wrath of the vigilantes. At the peak of the panic, newspapers reported that no fewer than three hundred wagons carrying people out of the state had been seen in the vicinity of the Red River." Reynolds then relates that "probably all the victims of 'vigilante justice' were innocent of the crimes for which they were executed." Most of the reported incidents ("arson, caches of arms and strychnine and confessions") did not occur or occur in the reported form. "Most of the newspaper reports of fires later proved to be false, and those fires that had occurred could be explained by natural causes; reported caches of arms were never produced; and vials of supposed strychnine, in the few cases in which they were tested, turned out to be harmless substances. Moreover, the 'confessions' of blacks, upon which virtually all convictions rested, were the direct result of brutal whippings and/or threats from white interrogators."[32]

Nevertheless, stories of black/abolitionist plots that had spread during the Texas Troubles continued to be believed by many Texans. The impact on the debate over slavery proved to be momentous, both in the Forks watershed and in many other northern-tier counties. As historian Walter Buenger has noted, "North Texans in 1859 were Unionists of varying hues, but they were almost universally Unionists." However: "As a consequence of the publicity given to . . . suspected cases of arson and assassination [during the summer of 1860], the hitherto solid facade of support for the Union in North Texas began to evaporate."[33] The campaign for secession gained momentum throughout this time. Then, in November, Lincoln was elected to the presidency and the pressure to secede became intense, finally resulting in the state's break from the Union in March, 1861.

⊰≫⋅⋅≪⊱

Considerable Unionist sentiment remained in the Forks watershed, even after secession. But the dominance of the area's Upper Southerners now waned as they split over secession while Lower Southerners generally united on behalf of it—a situation that mirrored conditions in border states. Terry G. Jordan has spoken of "two different Souths: the strongly secessionist Lower South and the politically divided Upper South" and noted "there was never any notable degree of opposition to secession" in parts of Texas dominated by Lower Southerners, "in keeping with the mood of the Lower South as a whole," while "the upper southern counties were racked by dissension."[34]

While cultural divisions and disagreements about slavery loomed large in these prewar conflicts, numerous other dividing issues would emerge during the war. Some men resented Confederate conscription laws that allowed wealthy men to pay a substitute conscript or exempted one person (owner or overseer) for every twenty slaves in that person's control (the so-called "twenty nigger law," later revised to allow one exemption for every fifteen slaves). Farmers also disliked impressment laws that permitted the military to commandeer their livestock, provisions, and other goods while the stock in trade of store owners, bankers, and other town people was exempt from impressment. Small farmers also despised an in-kind tax that took a tenth of the farmer's produce for the Confederacy while the chief assets of the wealthy planter class—land and slaves—were not directly taxed. Some critics, pointing to the fortunes being made in the cotton trade and elsewhere while poor soldiers and their families suffered, called the situation proof that the conflict was "a rich man's war and a poor man's fight." Others, steeped in American principles of liberty, decried the Confederacy's suspension of the writ of habeas corpus, which was "used to suppress opposition to official policies."[35]

⟨⟩⟩⟨⟨⟩

Because of prewar divisions and those that later developed, many communities within the Forks watershed were deeply split. In the Fannin County town of Honey Grove, the citizenry was divided for a while over whether to fly the flag of the United States or the Confederacy at the town square. Before the matter was peacefully resolved, Union men had burned the Confederate flag.[36]

In numerous individual cases, only a fine line separated the Confederate from the Unionist. As historian Robert S. Weddle noted, commonly "there was no simple choice" and the question of military service was resolved "on the basis of expediency rather than true loyalty."[37]

One group of Union-leaning men from Lamar County decided early in the war that they would ride a train of cotton wagons to Mexico and "keep out of sight" there until the war ended. But during the course of the trip it became clear to them that the war was going to drag on for years and they decided to take their chances back in their hometown of Paris. They returned home after delivering their cotton to Mexico.[38]

Another group of men, in Hunt County, joined the military on the side of the Confederacy but while home on furlough decided they would escape the war by going to Mexico. The men, led by one John Honeycutt, left the county heading south, then vanished, with no word of what happened to them ever making its way back to their families. The only survivor of the expedition was a little pony one of the men had taken along, which eventually made its way back to Greenville.[39]

In another case the Terry brothers, of the area that is now eastern Delta County, joined separate Confederate cavalry units toward the beginning of the war. Later, illness and death in their family motivated both to desert and return home. Joseph Terry never went back to his Ninth Texas Cavalry Regiment. Instead, he made his way to the North and served out the remainder of the war on the Union side—an option exercised by more than two thousand Texans during the war. His younger brother, Thomas Henderson Terry, eventually did return to his Twenty-third Texas Cavalry Regiment but served out his enlistment reluctantly. For many years after the war, family members recalled, Thomas "would get very agitated when talking about the war, saying that the slaveholders stayed at home and let the poor whites fight their war for them."[40]

But many area men looked neither to Mexico nor to the North as a place of refuge. Instead, they took to "the brush"—thickets, bottomlands, or other wooded areas within the Forks watershed—from which sprang the term "brush men."[41] Here, too, however, the heart sometimes decreed one course at the outset, only to urge a reversal on some other day. In *Plow-horse Cavalry*, Weddle tells of two young men from the Caney Creek area of Fannin County who "decided to take to the woods to escape enlistment but, finding the woods full of riffraff, promptly returned home and enlisted in [a Confederate regiment] along with their neighbors and kinsmen."[42]

But many of those who went grudgingly into the Confederate army never were easy in their hearts, as shown in a February, 1864, letter from J. N. Carr of Fannin County, then serving with the Confederate army in Louisiana, to his wife, Helen: "I wood like [to] Stay at home if [I] cood stay in peace but I no I cant stay thir with out killing some boddy or tha wood kill me. I advise the boys to go into survis on this side of the [Mississippi] river if they wil let them and if they wont let them go into survis on this side I wood lay in the brush til the moss grows to mi back."[43]

The most notable instance of a man who took to the brush involves a remarkable character who achieved both fame and admiration as the Forks watershed's wiliest brush man.

Nothing much is known of where Frank Chamblee came from, although family legend has it that he was well educated and grew rich before the war "smuggling horses across the Rio Grande"—which is to say, stealing horses in Mexico and bringing them to Texas.[44] If the story is true, it is possible Chamblee was a member of the band that was said to use Jernigan's Thicket as a way station for stolen horses. The group would steal animals down south and hide them in the thicket for a while before transporting them on to Missouri, where they would steal other horses, hide them for a while in the thicket, then move them along for sale in South Texas.[45]

In September, 1859, Chamblee married Mary Ellen Terry in Fannin County, to which her family had emigrated from Greene County, Illinois, but the couple may have been living in Hunt County by the time war broke out.[46] Chamblee managed to stay out of the conflict for about a year, but in April, 1862, he became a private in Company C of Stevens Regiment of Texas Dismounted Cavalry, a Confederate unit serving at Fort Gibson in the Indian Territory. However, he soon deserted upon receiving news that his wife was sick.[47] After being recaptured and returned to the fort, he was sentenced to be ridden on a rail, according to the recollection of his friend Ben Briscoe, a Hunt County rancher who had grown up with Chamblee's wife.

"They put him on the rail, two men shouldered it, and two men held him on," Briscoe recalled. "They paraded around until dinner time and let him off." The men then began feeding their horses, whereupon Chamblee told the officer in charge, "Captain I want my horse fed, too"—a reference to the rail. When the captain laughed and shook his head, Chamblee said, "If you don't feed him, I won't ride him again."

Sure enough, when the men finished dinner and prepared to put Chamblee on the rail again, he was found to be gone from the camp. According to Briscoe:

From then on he was kept pretty busy. The scouts caught him once or twice, but he was a shrewd fellow and always managed to get away before they got him to headquarters.

Finally the chase got too warm for him on the Sulphur and he moved down to Kaufman County. The scouts caught him there. Two men guarding him in a one room house. The room had one door and a fireplace. There was a bed in one corner. About dark they told [Chamblee] he could sleep on that bed. He pulled off his shoes and warmed his feet by the fire. When it was good and dark he said, "I believe I will lie down."

He picked up his shoes, darted through the door, pulled it to behind him, and was two or three hundred yards away before they got the dogs on his trail. He heard them coming. When they came close to him, he clapped his hands together and hollered, "Sic 'em, boy! Sic 'em!" and the dogs passed him like a whirlwind.

He hid in some high weeds, put on his shoes, located the North Star, and followed it twenty-five miles that night through high grass.

When Chamblee made it back to Hunt County, he came by Briscoe's home and Briscoe lent him a horse, one of several occasions when the rancher did so. Always, on some morning days or weeks later, Briscoe would discover that the horse had been returned to his herd.[48]

Judge Bowman heard about Chamblee from Hicks Nowell of Hunt County in the 1930s. Nowell, who was a teenager at the time of the Civil War, told Bowman, "The home militia was constantly after [Chamblee], chasing him, trying to catch him, and he was continually evading them and daring them in a most audacious manner."[49]

Some of the men whom Chamblee eluded felt he had made them look like fools and took it personally, according to his widow, Mary Ellen, whose story has been handed down in the family. "They were determined to get him," Mary Ellen's grandson, Sterling Rodney Scroggins, said in 1964. "There was a funeral that he was determined to be at, knowing full well that these men would be there watching for him. He sees them there but he dresses like a woman mourner and again slips by them."[50]

Frank Chamblee was just one of many brush men in the area. In September, 1863, soon after Brig. Gen. Henry E. McCulloch arrived at Bonham to take over command of the Northern Sub-District of Texas, he reported, "I have received most pressing letters already from different portions of the District, urging me to take steps to arrest Deserters and conscripts that have gone into the brush in large numbers in some portions of the District. These men live off of the property and produce of the people near their camps and are a terror to the country about them, and in many instances the lives of our best friends are in danger from them."[51]

Jernigan's Thicket apparently had a reputation of particular notoriety among Confederate authorities. When General McCulloch assumed command of the Northern Sub-District, according to O. M. Roberts, "The object of his going there was by either forcible or pacific efforts to get men out of what was called 'Jernigan's thicket,' which had been made a place of refuge by deserters and others that avoided conscription."[52] But Roberts exaggerated. It is clear that McCulloch's brush man problem went far beyond Jernigan's Thicket. In a letter from Bonham in October, 1863, McCulloch told Maj. Gen. J. B. Magruder that, "I am now perfectly satisfied that there are not less than 1,000 deserters, from the army, conscription, and the militia, in the woods . . . in this sub-district." Roberts estimated that the largest concentration of deserters was within thirty miles of Bonham in three camps of which "200 to 400" deserters were "within 10 miles, all of whom can concentrate within two hours. They keep every road picketed that goes into their vicinity so perfectly that not a man, woman, or child goes near them that [they] don't know it; they have sympathizers all through this country, and, if they can't be induced to come out peaceably, we will have trouble and bloodshed enough in this section to make our very hearts sick, and a war of the most wretched and savage character will be inaugurated."[53]

McCulloch may have been referring to concentrations of brush men in Jernigan's, Black Cat, Mustang, and/or Wildcat Thickets, which were all within thirty miles of Bonham. The distance was ten miles or less from Jernigan's to Black Cat, Black Cat to Mustang, and Mustang to Wildcat.

Some stories have survived about individual bands in the area. Rancher Ben Briscoe said one group of about forty men, under a Mexican War veteran named Capt. Jim Henry, had its hideout in the Caddo Creek bottomlands of northwestern Hunt County.[54] The longtime dean of engineering at the University of Texas, T. U. Taylor, recounted a story about brush men who hid out in Mustang Thicket. In this story the brush men or Mustang Thicket gang accepted an invitation of a "Confederate offi-

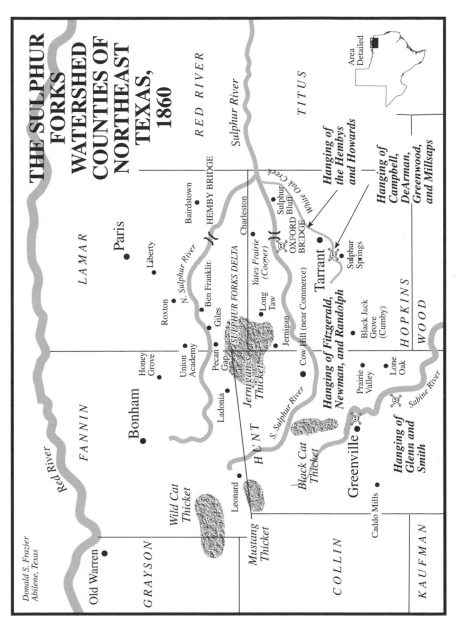

Sulphur Forks Watershed counties of Northeast Texas and the locations of hangings and boundaries of thickets, ca. 1860–63. Map by Donald S. Frazier.

cer" for an interview. "An appointment was made; he was blindfolded on the prairie near the thicket and led into the camp of the gang; there unblindfolded he made a speech; urged them to come to the defense of the South. At the close of his impassioned address he asked all that would volunteer for the Southern cause to raise their hats. A few of them raised their hats half way. When asked what that meant, they replied that they would raise their hats high enough to fight Indians but not white people. The Confederate officer got no results [with] the Mustang Thicket gang."[55]

The group in question may have been one led by Henry Boren. Early in the fall of 1863, General McCulloch sent two Confederate officers who had opposed secession, Col. Robert H. Taylor of Fannin County and Maj. James W. Throckmorton of Collin County, into the brush to talk to Boren. Taylor subsequently reported to McCulloch that Boren and his men demanded they be sent "into service on the frontier"—which is to say, sent to fight Indians in western Texas—as a condition of their surrender.[56] According to historian David Paul Smith, "It appears that Boren first wanted his men to be given arms, ammunition, provisions, and time to put their affairs in order before the reporting date. This leeway McCulloch absolutely refused to give; weapons would not be provided in advance. He made a fortunate decision, for a month later he learned from an informant that Boren's real intention was not to enter the service but to have his men seize Bonham and 'wipe out secession in this part of Texas.'"[57]

Around the time that McCulloch was negotiating with Boren, he also was campaigning to bring other groups of brush men into the Confederate fold. In a broadside printed at Paris and distributed across the subdistrict, he proclaimed: "No deserters will be permitted to remain in this Sub District. It may be well to say that the policy of pardoning deserters, has worked badly, has injured the service, and must be stopped; and that those so lost to honor as to desert, need expect to find no shelter in this Sub District, all will be hunted down and brought to justice."[58] Despite these qualms about pardons, the general went on to make an offer of amnesty. It appeared to meet with some success as hundreds of men—perhaps more than seven hundred—emerged from the brush during the fall of 1863. Many of these were installed in a newly created unit called the "Brush Battalion," with the idea that the unit could be sent to the frontier to root out other deserters and fight Indians. As David Paul Smith has noted, "A Hollywood scenario might envision that these men 'gone bad' would be transformed into paragons of frontier service, but such was not to be. Problems abounded from [the first], and with few exceptions the men were more hindrance than help to the beleaguered frontier. Afterwards, McCulloch reflected that the men of the Brush Battalion behaved abominably everywhere they went, 'committing petty depredations on the property of the people about all their camps.'"[59] When members of the battalion began deserting again, adding to an estimated one thousand or more brush men already loose in the sub-district, McCulloch cursed the Brush Battalion troops aloud, saying, "I have never been in a country where the people were so perfectly worthless and cowardly as here." He disbanded the battalion in March, 1864.[60]

As the South's fortunes worsened, more and more men took to thickets throughout the Sulphur Forks watershed and points west. The brush population became particularly high after the summer months, when it was bolstered by deserters from the Confederate army who were poorly clothed—sometimes barefoot—and sought to avoid the rigors of winter war. "Deserters, absentees, and skulkers must be kept out of the country, or it will be ruined this winter," McCulloch wrote to a subordinate in October, 1864.[61] Around the same time, Gen. Edmund Kirby Smith, who commanded the Confederate Trans-Mississippi Department, wrote that "The frontier counties . . . are . . . a grand city of refuge where thousands of able-bodied men have flocked to escape service in the Confederate Army."[62]

⟨◈⟩

According to Ben Briscoe, Frank Chamblee "had certain meeting places where he would meet with his wife and she would carry food to him. He kept her advised of his movements by a signal code made up of placing sticks in a certain manner. She knew and could read the signs."[63] Mary Ellen Chamblee was far from alone in providing such aid to Forks watershed brush men, as military accounts make clear. General McCulloch wrote in frustration from Bonham that, "In addition to the deserters, absentees, and skulkers almost one-fourth of this population ought to be taken up for aiding and assisting deserters . . . and disloyal expressions and acts."[64]

Standing in opposition to the brush men and their friends were varied enemies. These included regular Confederate troops, sometimes bolstered by irregular forces. At one point, Confederate authorities became so frustrated in their ineffective efforts to root out brush men that they enlisted the help of irregulars whom many of them despised—the notorious Quantrill's Raiders. The experiment proved to be a failure, however.

It ended after William C. Quantrill's men shot up Sherman and committed other crimes. Regular Confederate troops eventually chased Quantrill and his men across the state line, sending them on their way back to their main stomping grounds in Missouri.[65]

Others opposed to the brush men included members of the local home guard, organized under state authority in each county. As described by the Forks watershed's John Warren Hunter, a fugitive from conscription:

> This Home Guard was usually made up of boys under or about 16 years of age, and old men whose age and decrepitude rendered them unfit for the regular service in the army. . . . It may be said that the old men who belonged to these companies were nearly always laid up with rheumatism, or other ailments, real or feigned, and were seldom on duty, thus leaving the burden of service to rest on [the] embryo heroes of rustic chivalry. . . .
>
> These rawhide soldiers soon became a terror to the people among whom they were thrown. They respected no age, nor sex, nor conditions. If they purchased an article and the vendor refused the worthless Confederate money, he was denounced as a traitor, a Unionist, the article appropriated and the owner threatened with arrest. Returning soldiers, on furlough because of disabling wounds, received in battle, were held up by these arrogant striplings on the highway, their papers demanded and examined, and if they chanced to be well mounted and carried valuable arms, a flaw was found in their papers; these had to be sent to Houston or Austin for further scrutiny, while the unfortunate soldiers . . . had to remain in the guard house until their papers came back—unless willing to part with horse, arms, or a moiety of cash, in the event of which he was allowed to escape. . . .
>
> Such was the high-handed, outrageous conduct of the Home Guards, not only in a few sections but throughout the state generally, that they obtained the sobriquet of "Heel-Flies" on account of the similarity of their course to the tortuous proclivities of a pestiferous insect so well known to cattlemen all over Texas. No class of men, or rather striplings, in our great state has ever been the recipient of more righteous contempt heaped upon them by patriotic men and women of Texas than these Home Guards. [66]

The greatest threat to the brush men was not from the military, however—whether regulars, irregulars such as Quantrill, or home militia—

but from civilians. Some of these were individuals who pursued personal vendettas, such as the small group of men who dogged the trail of Frank Chamblee (even beyond war's end, as remains to be described). Others organized into vigilante groups, such as the Sons of Washington, a secret society in what is now Delta County, and the Ten Stitchers, a group based in Hunt County. Still other, nameless, groups came together on brief occasions for concentrated mob action, such as occurred in Hunt and Hopkins Counties.

Although the vigilante actions were wartime events, they had much in common with vigilante operations during times of peace. Historian Richard Maxwell Brown cites religious, class, and ethnic factors that played a part in such vigilante operations as the San Francisco movement of 1856 that, "to a considerable extent . . . represented a struggle for power between two religious, class, and ethnic blocs. Thus the vigilante leadership of upper- and middle-class, old American, Protestant merchants was aligned against a political faction supported by Irish-Catholic lower-class laborers."[67] In the Sulphur Forks watershed, the ethnic split was between Lower Southerners, who made up many of the vigilante bands, and Upper Southerners, who were most of the victims. The religious divisions were between adherents of pro- and anti-slavery branches of mainstream Protestant denominations. And many of the vigilantes were wealthy men or their middle-class followers while records for the victims show that most of them had little wealth. Census records of 1860 for those later indicted in five 1862 hanging deaths show average worth (both real and personal property combined) of $8,605, with the comparable figure for the victims being $807. The 1860 census records for those indicted in four 1863 hanging deaths show average worth of $19,100, with a comparable figure for the victims of $1,269.[68] The difference is such that the vigilantes were wealthier and their victims poorer than the average Texan of that time, whose worth was about $6,000.[69]

It also seems likely that some of the vigilantes considered themselves "upper-level men" based on their association with the planter "aristocracy" while thinking of their victims as "lower-level men" as a result of their back country, Upper South way of life. Either because of status differences such as these or actual economic differences, the "loathing of the upper-level men for the lower element" has often played a part in American vigilantism, as was expressed by nineteenth-century Montana vigilante Thomas Dimsdale, who said, "for the low, brutal, cruel, lazy, ignorant, insolent, sensual and blasphemous miscreants that infest the frontier we entertain but one sentiment—aversion—deep, strong, and unchangeable."[70]

The feelings of Southern "aristocrats" toward members of the lower class in the Sulphur Forks watershed were nowhere better expressed than in the famous diary of Kate Stone, whose Louisiana family took refuge in the area, along with some 130 slaves, in 1863. "Tarrant is the hottest looking, new little town right out in the prairie—not a tree," Kate wrote after a visit to the town that was then the county seat of Hopkins County. "We tried to eat dinner at the roughest house and with the dirtiest people we have met yet. The table was set on a low, sunny gallery and half a dozen dirty, unshaven men took their seats in their shirt sleeves at the dirtiest tablecloth and coarsest ware. We saw the Negro girl wash the dishes at the *duck pond* right out in the yard. That was too much for me." On another occasion: "We went to church this morning at a tumbledown schoolhouse called Liberty expecting to hear the funeral sermon of Mrs. Alexander, who was a near neighbor. . . . It is the oddest looking crowd you could imagine, and the very funniest dressing we ever saw. My pen is powerless to describe it: one girl airy in pink [tarlatan] and another sweltering in red woolen; high horn combs with long ribbon streamers waving from the top; immense hoops; and strand after strand of beads, all colors, wound around their necks. Many of the men were barefooted, and nearly all of their slouched wool hats were decorated with ribbons or an artificial flower. There were few coats but many vests and a display of homemade knit galluses." A few weeks later: "We lost our way and traveled until 8 o'clock when we asked to stay at a pretty, large, white house, white only on the outside. I despair of giving any idea of the dirt. We tried to eat without seeing or tasting and to sleep without touching the bed. They gave us coffee, a horrid decoction of burnt wheat and milk without sugar, in saucers and water in the halves of broken bottles. The table was set in the dirtiest of kitchens with a dirt floor and half a dozen half-naked little Negroes and numberless cats and dogs scampering through the room and under the table. The rafters were festooned with old hoop skirts and worn-out, rough boots. It surpassed any place we have been in yet. We certainly had found the dark corner of the Confederacy."[71]

⟨⟩⟨⟩

Community attitudes toward vigilantism were very different then from now. According to Richard Maxwell Brown, "Today, among educated men of standing, vigilantism is viewed with disapproval, but it was not always so in the nineteenth century. In those days, the leaders of the community were often prominent members of vigilante movements and proud of it."[72] Nevertheless, as Donald E. Reynolds has noted, "Because they deviated from, and in many ways subverted, the established order and because they clearly violated the constitutional rights of the accused, vigilance committees apparently never attained full respectability."[73] Both sides of the coin were present in the Sulphur Forks watershed during the Civil War, where vigilantes included prominent planters, doctors, and others but where some newspaper editors and other professional men deplored vigilante activities.[74]

Scholars have singled out the South as a particular hotbed of vigilantism, with Dickson D. Bruce linking Southern vigilantism to a general propensity for violence in the region. Bruce wrote that, according to existing evidence, "fairly early in America's history, and certainly by the end of the first third of the nineteenth century, the South had acquired such a reputation for violence that few people acquainted with the region failed to comment on it. . . . Not a few Southerners argued that violence itself was natural to society and, if properly employed, actually improved social health. Southern intellectuals from George Tucker to George Fitzhugh asserted an appreciation of this 'fact' of life and contrasted their 'realistic' assessment of the nature of society with the 'baby ethics,' as one writer put it, of Northern intellectuals."[75]

Bertram Wyatt-Brown views Southern violence, and vigilantism in particular, in terms of Southerners' special sensitivity to matters of honor, which were bound up with notions of preserving the existing social order. "When dissenters or deviants called into question the premises of the social order, they had to be rendered powerless. Either by extermination or public humiliation, they were used to cleanse the community of the dangers they allegedly posed," he wrote.[76] Vigilantism exerted a primal appeal for Southerners, Wyatt-Brown asserts in *Southern Honor: Ethics and Behavior in the Old South*. Elaborating on this idea, Wyatt-Brown stated that "the malefactor not only suffered for his crime . . . he also served as an offering to the primal, sacred values of common folk. . . . The humiliation and death of perceived miscreants served as a 'suppurating device,' as one scholar has called it. It was a means of purifying the ailing social body. . . . Life itself was untidy, unclean; to smear tar, blood, and feathers or to employ flame or scaffold purified those who belonged. They rested easier for having eliminated fellow men who had been transformed in their eyes into beasts."[77]

Both Wyatt-Brown, in *Southern Honor*, and Cash, in *The Mind of the*

South, have pointed to a seeming paradox within the South: that Southerners, growing out of a frontier tradition, were strongly individualistic, yet their individualism existed within the context of a rigidly conformist society. As Wyatt-Brown notes, "When Southerners spoke of liberty, they generally meant the birthright to self-determination of one's place in society, not the freedom to defy sacred conventions, challenge long-held assumptions, or propose another scheme of moral or political order. If someone . . . spoke or acted in a way that invaded that territory or challenged that right, the . . . man so confronted had the inalienable right to meet the lie and punish the opponent."[78]

Cash's assessment is this:

> that the individualism of the plantation world . . . would be far too much concerned with bald, immediate, unsupported assertion of the ego, which placed too great stress on the inviolability of personal whim, and which was full of the chip-on-shoulder swagger and brag of a boy—one, in brief, of which the essence was the boast, voiced or not, on the part of every Southerner, that he would knock hell out of whoever dared to cross him. . . . Nor was it only private violence that was thus perpetuated. The Southerner's fundamental approach carried over into the realm of public offenses as well. What the direct willfulness of his individualism demanded, when confronted by a crime that aroused his anger, was immediate satisfaction for itself—catharsis for personal passion in the spectacle of a body dancing at the end of a rope or writhing in the fire . . . and not some ponderous abstract justice in the problematical tomorrow. And so, in this world of ineffective social control, the tradition of vigilante action . . . grew so steadily that already long before the Civil War and long before hatred for the black man had begun to play any direct part in the pattern (of more than three hundred persons said to have been hanged or burned by mobs between 1840 and 1860, less than ten percent were Negroes) the South had become peculiarly the home of lynching.[79]

The violence and vigilantism that were distinctive features of the South as a whole were even more common in the region's westernmost state. Texas was the most violent of all the Southern states.[80] Texas also had "more vigilante movements than any other state."[81] As noted by Reynolds, Texas experienced the same paranoia about slavery as the other Southern states, which accounted for some of the Lone Star state's violence and vigilantism. But, unlike the other Southern states, it also was "a raw, open, frontier land" that "drew more than its share of ne'er-do-wells and out-right criminals who, early on, gave Texas a reputation for violence that it at least partially deserved. Add to these unsettling elements the presence in much of the state of large numbers of Indians, who frequently raided settlements and attacked bands of immigrants, and it is easy to see why Texans may have been quicker than most Americans to resort to extralegal action to protect their vulnerable communities from all possible enemies, both real and imagined."[82] The residents along the Forks during the Civil War did not battle Indians, but the frontier was close by, and many ingre-dients of a volatile social mixture were present.

CHAPTER 2

The Hanging of the Hembys and Howards, 1862

The delta of land between the North Sulphur and South Sulphur Rivers was a notoriously inhospitable place in the early nineteenth century when most of the area, now Delta County, was part of Lamar and Hopkins Counties. In the east, toward the point of the triangle, was a narrow wedge of rugged, heavily wooded ground lying between the frequently flooding Sulphurs and their dense, wild bottomlands. To the west, the terrain was even tougher in places, including the giant Jernigan's Thicket that sprawled across the delta's broad end. However, none of this terrain presented any great deterrent to the area's first Anglo-Americans, many of whom arrived prior to the Texas Revolution. The regions these Upper Southerners had left behind in other states were rough back country very much like their new home, which was known variously as the Sulphur Forks of Red River, Sulphur Forks, Forks of Sulphur, or often just the Forks. In the following text, it is referred to as the Forks delta, to distinguish it from the larger Forks watershed.

Cotton growing, which thrived on the less-rugged lands of the Lower South, had seldom been practiced by the Upper Southerners in their home states, and few of them turned to it upon arrival in northeastern Texas. Many were stockraisers, following a tradition that had originated during colonial times in South Carolina and been passed on westward through the back country of Tennessee and Kentucky. These stockraisers, like those who practiced Mexican-style stockraising in South Texas, marked many of their animals with brands or crops and then allowed them to graze free in the wild between roundups.[1] But the "cattleman" moniker worn by so many South Texans was not a good fit with the stockraiser of the Forks delta. One of the latter, James M. Millsaps, described his varied livestock holdings in an 1860 deed to his wife and children. Millsaps owned "one stallion bay coler about six years old, one sorrell mare about five years old and her colt about five months old. About four hundred and fifty head of sheep marked in each ear with a crop and under half crop. Also thirty head of Goats unmarked. Also one hundred head of hogs in several different marks. Twenty head of cattle more or less marked in each ear with a crop and under half crop."[2]

When people of the area took up the plow, which many did in association with stockraising, most followed the pattern of their native states and grew both corn and wheat. These crops they commonly produced in a single field: after the autumn corn harvest, they would fell the cornstalks, broadcast the wheat seed, then plow or harrow it in. When the wheat was harvested in the spring, corn would be planted there once again.[3]

As noted by Ikie Patteson, many of these people gravitated to the southwestern section of the Forks delta, where the community of Jernigan grew up during Republic of Texas times at the site of the community now called Needmore.[4] Others put down roots in what has long been referred to as "the East End." There, toward the point of the delta, the town of Charleston began in the 1840s, becoming the only town of any size in that area during Civil War times. Charleston owed its growth to its location on one of the few major thoroughfares in the East End, a road connecting the county seats of the two counties that then extended into the delta: Paris, county seat of Lamar County, and Tarrant, then the county seat of Hopkins County. (Tarrant quickly would became a ghost town and then disappear after it was succeeded as county seat by Sulphur Springs in 1871.)[5]

⋖⋗

Members of the Howard clan were among the East End's earliest pioneers, coming to the area following a decades-long family odyssey. Arington (or Arrington) Howard, said by some descendants to have had Cherokee blood, was born in the early 1800s in Georgia and later moved to Tennessee, where Arington married Elizabeth McMahand. They soon moved on to what became Morgan County, Alabama, where most or all of the couple's eleven children were born (years of birth approximate): A. G. W. (1818), John (1823), Eliza (1825), Elizabeth (1827), James K. (1828), Thomas (1830), Henry T. (1832), Sarah (1834), Joseph (1836), and Cornelius and Martha J. (birth years unknown). By 1839, the family was in the East End of the Forks delta, where Arington died around 1844. A

29

number of the children settled in the area, including James K., Thomas, and Henry T.[6]

In the spring of 1846, James K. Howard served in the war against Mexico, later marrying Lydia Crabtree, a Missouri native, in Collin County in 1853. The couple had four children, most or all of whom were born in Lamar County.[7] Thomas Howard is known to have had at least one son, but no details about his wife and other children, if any, are known.[8] Considerably more is known about Henry T. Howard. He married Harriet Young in Lamar County in January, 1853. By 1860, they were living in the Charleston area of Hopkins County with two children, and Henry was preaching as a minister of the Cumberland Presbyterian Church. The denomination was one of the first to establish a presence in the Forks watershed, setting up a congregation in Lamar County as early as 1843 and constructing in the late 1840s what is thought to have been Paris's first church building. In his history of Lamar County, A. W. Neville attributed the Cumberland church's early presence in the area to the fact that "so many of the early comers here were from Kentucky and Tennessee where that church had its origin."[9]

One of the area's early Cumberland Presbyterian pastors, Anthony Travelstead, lived in Paris but was said to have "served over a wide area, going where he wanted, taking as pay whatever was offered, many times taking nothing."[10] Henry Howard may have operated in similar fashion. Also like Travelstead, and like another early Cumberland Presbyterian minister, C. J. Bradley, Howard supported himself with other work when not preaching. Travelstead was a carpenter, and Bradley was principal of the Paris Female Seminary, while Howard was a stockraiser-farmer in the Upper South style.[11] He grew corn and wheat on 25 improved acres, making use of 115 unimproved acres of his property, and most likely adjacent unfenced lands as well, for running livestock that included five horses, nine milk cows, two working oxen, thirty other cattle, and thirty hogs.[12] As was the case with most East End families, including other Howards and members of the Hemby clan, the Henry T. Howard family had no slaves.[13]

A glowing testimonial has survived concerning one of the Howard brothers, although which of the three was being referred to has never been determined. John Warren Hunter, an East Ender boy who was fifteen when the Civil War erupted, had this to say in "Heel-Fly Time in Texas," an early twentieth-century recollection of his Civil War adventures:

"Howard was a perfect gentleman and . . . was loved by every boy for miles around."[14]

⋖⋗⋍⋖⋗

Hemby family records point to North Carolina as that family's earliest known place of settlement in the United States. It is thought that they went from there to Tennessee, which figures in the histories of so many Upper Southern families, and then on to Missouri. Jonathan Hemby was born there around 1822 and came to the Forks delta in the early 1840s when he was about twenty. Other family members who came to Texas at that time included James Wesley Hemby, who was born around 1825 in Missouri and is thought to have been Jonathan's brother, and an older man named James Hemby, who was born in North Carolina around 1800 and may have been Jonathan and James Wesley's father.[15]

The elder Hemby, demonstrating a talent for construction and an entrepreneurial flair, built the earliest known bridge at the North Sulphur crossing of the Paris-Tarrant Road—a location still known as Hemby Crossing. The Hembys augmented their income for a while by charging tolls there, which may have been similar to those recorded for another early toll bridge in the area: five cents walking persons; ten cents for one person on horseback; fifteen cents for a two-animal team of horses or oxen, either buggy, carriage, or wagon; fifty cents for four horses or oxen; and seventy-five cents for a team of six.[16]

When the Mexican War erupted, Jonathan Hemby, then about twenty-four, and James W. Hemby, about twenty-one, enlisted along with another young man from the area, eighteen-year-old James K. Howard, in the first known association of Hembys and Howards. The three volunteered for service under Capt. William B. Dagley in Company G of the Third Regiment of Texas Mounted Volunteers, the so-called "North Texas Regiment." But they were unlucky in their wars. The Third Regiment was torn by the machinations of William S. Harney, a regular army colonel who was placed in temporary command of the unit in San Antonio in June, 1846. Harney schemed to avoid relinquishing command to a Texan properly elected by the troops, which fostered dissension within the regiment. He also acted without orders in leading the Texans and some regular army dragoons on an unauthorized invasion of Mexico. A hard, eighteen-day march southward from San Antonio to the Presidio crossing of the Rio Grande was followed by retreat back across the river under fire, with loss of life, after which Harney was placed under arrest

*James Wesley Hemby, 1824–83, who is said to have
witnessed the hangings of the Hembys and the Howards.
Courtesy Richard Hunter.*

by his superiors. The regiment was disbanded in San Antonio in September, but the Hembys, Howard, and other troopers were not paid until much later; many men had to pawn their watches or guns to finance their trip home.[17]

Back in the Forks, Jonathan and James Wesley soon married and settled in as farmers, with Jonathan also teaching for a while in a school at Biardstown in Lamar County. Jonathan and Indiana-born Anna M. Pair, who wed in January, 1847, had four children by 1860.[18]

Entering the stage relatively late was yet *another* James Hemby—this one with the middle initial E.—whom evidence suggests was also a brother of Jonathan and James Wesley Hemby.[19] (Two brothers of the

same first name was so far from being uncommon in the area that at least
one other Forks delta man who was hanged during the war, James Monroe Millsaps, also had a brother of the same first name, James Thomas
Millsaps.)[20] James E. Hemby, who was born in Missouri around 1831, was
in his twenties when he immigrated to the Forks delta in the 1850s with
his wife, the former Jane Oldham, and a large number of children.[21]

Despite the difference of about nine years in their ages, the elder Jonathan Hemby and younger James E. Hemby apparently were close. They
settled near each other in the vicinity of the Hemby Crossing of North
Sulphur, and both joined the Antioch Church of Christ at nearby Biardstown, whose early records show them listed alongside each other. Later,
they would also appear together as the first and second names on another
record kept by the church—a list of the congregation's dead.[22]

A joint characterization of the three Howards and two Hembys exists.
Paris attorney E. L. Dohoney, who said he met them all, described them
as "uneducated" but added that "every one of them was a good man."[23]

⋘⋙

When slave owners began immigrating to the Forks delta, some "brought
their families through . . . in carriages hitched to high-stepping horses,
an elevated seat in front for the Negro driver, the family sitting back in
the carriage in grand style," according to a local historian.[24] Others came
by wagon, with slaves and livestock walking alongside. Family members
and slaves "camped near streams when possible, washed their clothes and
spread them on grass to dry. When in a hurry to move on, and clothes
were not dry, the slaves spread the garments on their arms to dry as they
walked."[25]

The newcomers carved out an enclave of their own that encompassed
the northwest corner of the Forks delta and adjacent land on the north
side of North Sulphur River. Principal settlements included several communities on the south side of the river: Ben Franklin (named for early
pioneer Ben Franklin Simmons), Pecan Gap (located in a pecan grove
between Jernigan's Thicket and the brakes of North Sulphur River), and
in particular Giles, named after Giles County, Tennessee, a Lower South
area within predominantly Upper South Tennessee from which many of
the newcomers hailed. The Giles community soon boasted substantial
slave-built mansions and such points of pride as the Giles Academy, operated by classics scholar Thomas Hart Benton Hockaday (father of the
woman who would later found Dallas's exclusive Hockaday School for

girls). While much of the Forks watershed was steeped in illiteracy, T. H. B. Hockaday is said to have enjoyed sitting around reading the New Testament in Greek.[26]

Major roadways were among features that drew cotton planters to the northwest Forks delta. One was the Central National Road of the Republic of Texas, constructed in the 1840s. It ran from Dallas—then a village—northeastward, skirted Jernigan's Thicket, passed near the edge of the Forks delta, then ran on northeastward to Paris and Red River. Six to eight months of the year, planters were able to haul their cotton bales up this road to Red River and float them down to New Orleans by light boat.[27] Often they were able to ship the cotton on steamboats. However, that only occurred when the steamers managed to pass upriver through the notorious Red River Raft, an ancient web of tree trunks and other driftwood that extended more than a hundred miles north of Shreveport. Only skillful boat captains were able to pick their way through the tricky network of bayous and other channels within the raft, and only then when the river was up.[28]

During times of low water, the plantation owners could send their cotton to market via the area's other main roadway, the Bonham-Jefferson Road. It led southeastward from the Fannin County seat of Bonham, through Honey Grove, Pecan Gap, and the Forks delta community of Long Taw—so-called by the wagoners because it was a long "taw," or tow, from that watering place to the next at the DeSpain Bridge crossing of South Sulphur River. The road then passed on through Tarrant, Mount Pleasant, and Daingerfield before reaching the steamboat port of Jefferson. Oxen were the draft animals of preference on the two-hundred-mile trip, with two yoke common for hauling the usual four five-hundred-pound bales of cotton and up to ten yoke for larger loads. The ten-mile-a-day trips to Jefferson and back consumed two to four weeks and added greatly to planters' costs, the standard freight rate just prior to the Civil War being twenty cents per ton mile.[29]

Some of the plantations that grew up in the northwest section of the Forks were substantial. Hendley Stone Bennett, the wealthiest man in the area, owned sixty-eight slaves, according to the 1860 census. The McGlasson, Patteson, and Lane families each owned several dozen slaves while other planters, including Greenville Smith, owned a dozen or more.[30]

⬦⋆⬦

Divisions within the Forks delta deepened with the coming of the secession crisis in the winter of 1860–61, as shown by records from the two
counties that extended into the area.

The first clear demonstration of the contrasting political climates in
Hopkins and Lamar Counties occurred when the state's counties elected
delegates to the Secession Convention that met January 28, 1861, in Austin. Hopkins elected William T. Blythe, Richard L. Askew, and Wilson
M. Payne, all of whom subsequently cast their votes *for* secession. Lamar
elected George W. Wright, William H. Johnson, and Lemuel H. Williams, who all voted *against* secession, making the Lamar delegation the
only one in the state to do so in its entirety. (The convention tally was 166
for secession and eight against, with the Lamar countians, famously, being among the "Immortal Eight.")[31]

If Texas had followed the course of many other states, it would have
left the Union and entered the Confederacy at that point. But Gov. Sam
Houston, who strongly opposed secession, insisted that the people be allowed to vote directly on the issue, and a statewide secession referendum
was scheduled for February 23, 1861. The bitterness that would lead to the
hangings of the Hembys and Howards had its origins in the campaign
preceding this referendum.

Among those who argued the Union side in secession debates was
twenty-eight-year-old Eben Lafayette Dohoney, a Kentucky-born lawyer
who had set up practice in Paris in 1859. A nighttime debate scheduled
against W. J. Bonner at Denton's schoolhouse, fifteen miles southwest of
Paris in the Roxton area, made a strong impression on Dohoney, and he
later recalled the event in his 1907 memoir, *An Average American*. Dohoney talked for an hour and a half, after which Bonner rose to speak and
"every man and boy left the house." Dohoney tried to persuade the group
to hear Bonner out but was told "no damned Secessionist could speak
there, or if he did he would speak to an empty house." Dohoney noted:
"Few people in the North [would have believed] that as late as February
1861, there was a neighborhood in Texas without a secessionist in it, and
where a secessionist was not allowed to speak. But such is the fact, and
Denton's school-house in Roxton precinct, Lamar County, Texas, is the
place."[32]

The following day, Dohoney spoke against W. B. Wright at Union
Academy (which was in present-day Harmon) in western Lamar County.
Writing in the third person and referring to himself as Lafayette, as was

E. L. Dohoney. Courtesy Ed Dohoney.

his custom, Dohoney recalled: "Wright was usually a very aggressive speaker, but as there were not exceeding five secessionists among the one-hundred and fifty voters present, he was a very mild-mannered man that day. . . . At this point the Secession leaders quit the field, and Lafayette had the remainder of the canvass all to himself. They evidently concluded that the Sulphur fork of Red River and the adjacent country was solid for the Union."[33]

Paris attorney M. L. Armstrong, a member of the state House of Representatives and a noted member of the anti-secession camp, subsequently joined Dohoney for campaign appearances at Biardstown and Charleston. Those in the audience at the Charleston session, fatefully, included Henry T. Howard. Dohoney says Howard was sufficiently impressed by his and Armstrong's speeches that the farmer-preacher took notes during the talks. Later, Howard drew on these notes to compose an anti-secession speech of his own. This speech, which Howard must have

*Micajah Lewis Armstrong. From Wm. DeRyee, Texas
Album . . . Eighth Legislature, 1860. Courtesy Texas
State Library and Archives Commission, Austin.*

delivered in the Charleston area after Dohoney and Armstrong returned
to Paris, spawned anger among local secessionists.[34]

No record of what Howard said in his speech exists, but it seems likely
that his arguments followed closely on those of Dohoney and Armstrong.
In his third-person memoir, Dohoney summed up the gist of his anti-
secession comments, some of which ranged into the supernatural: "He
[Dohoney] told the people . . . that God had made the country for one
people and one government. That the Mississippi River and its tributaries
were like the great aorta of the human system, the channels for the flow
of the lifeblood of commerce for a single nation."[35] But many of his arguments centered on slavery as an albatross borne by the neck of the South.
Dohoney elaborated that "even if the South should succeed in the first
struggle, no independent nation based on human slavery could be maintained . . . That slaves would continually escape . . . But that back of all

of this, the South would never be able to establish its Independence. That its population was exceeded by that of the North, and that by reason of the condemnation of slavery by the civilized world, the United States would be able to recruit its armies from all nations. That the defeat of the Confederate states was a foregone conclusion."[36]

Armstrong's views are reflected in an "Address to the People of the State," which circulated within a few weeks of his Charleston speech. Armstrong was among two dozen signers of the "Address," and they included many other men from northern Texas and the Forks watershed— notably, state senator Martin D. Hart of Hunt County, whose activities as a Union guerrilla cavalry captain would play a part in a series of vigilante hangings in 1863.

Secessionists immediately denounced the "Address" as a creation of "Black Republicans" and "submissionists" and as a tool of the hated abolitionist author Hinton Rowan Helper. One such attack was printed in the *Texas Republican* published in Marshall, located to the east of the Forks watershed, presumably by editor R. W. Loughery. As described by the *Republican,* some points in the "Address" mirror Dohoney's views, namely, "that all the slave States if united could only maintain slavery 'for a time'; that the border States would soon abolish slavery and join the North; that the greater part of the civilized world is opposed to slavery, and that war would lead to its destruction." But the *Republican* most particularly detested the assertion in the "Address" that "a confederacy of the cotton States alone" would be a "confederacy of slaveholders," in which the survival of "liberty and free institutions" would be endangered. The newspaper denounced that line of reasoning as "an insidious attempt to prejudice the nonslaveholder, not only against slaveholders but slavery itself" and as "freesoilism . . . of the blackest kind."[37]

The anti-secession sentiments of Dohoney and Armstrong stopped short of outright abolitionism. Nevertheless, as Henry Howard would discover after drawing on them for his own speech, these views were sufficient to set pro-slavery hearts aboil.

❦

Bolstered by huge majorities in slave-cotton counties of southeastern Texas, secessionists carried the day on February 23, 1861, by 46,129 to 14,697, a 76 percent majority. The election figures do not reflect how the voting fell out within the Forks delta, but it seems clear from the tally that the delta was a borderland between opposing camps. The two upper counties in the Forks watershed opposed secession, with 58.2 percent of those in Fannin and 54.5 percent of those in Lamar voting to stay in the Union (471 for secession and 656 against in Fannin, 553 for and 663 against in Lamar). These counties were two of only eighteen in the state to vote against seceding. Some of the others were Central Texas counties, located around San Antonio and Austin, with heavy populations of anti-slavery Germans and other Europeans. Almost all others, however, were counties in North Texas with heavy Upper South populations—Lamar, Fannin, Grayson, Collin, Cooke, Montague, Wise, and Jack.[38]

The two lower counties of the Sulphur Forks watershed, by contrast, voted in favor of secession. The outcome was fairly close in Hunt, with 55.1 percent voting for secession (416 to 339). In Hopkins, however, 69 percent of the voters (697 to 315) opted for a break with the Union. The large majority for secession in Hopkins was unusual for this section of the state. From Red River County on the east of the Forks watershed to Jack County in the far west, virtually all counties in the top two tiers along Red River cast at least 40 percent of their votes against secession, with a majority voting against secession in seven of those fourteen counties. Only Hopkins and, far to the west, Clay County, voted by large majorities for a break from the Union. Anger over federal authorities' failure to provide protection against Indian raids may have played a part in the vote in Clay County, but it seems probable that a strong anti-Union element led by members of the Knights of the Golden Circle contributed to the secessionist landslide in Hopkins. Hopkins was the only county within the Sulphur Forks watershed to have a chapter of the KGC, and its Sulphur Springs chapter was one of only thirty-one in the entire state.[39]

The Knights of the Golden Circle, organized in 1854, was a secret society that originally sought to establish a slave empire within a circle 2,400 miles in diameter around Havana, Cuba. In 1860, in furtherance of the group's aims, members made a couple of abortive attempts to invade Mexico, which they hoped to transform into a slaveholding nation, but these efforts petered out before the invaders ever crossed the Rio Grande. By 1861, members had shifted their aim, with many becoming strong supporters of slave-state secession. Most of the society's activities were carried out under a cloak of secrecy, and historians are uncertain about how much influence the organization had on the course of secession. Whatever else may have been the case, however, the KGC enjoyed considerable prominence for a while, particularly in Texas, where they established their headquarters and enlisted many prominent men as members. It seems likely that many of the leading citizens of Hopkins County were KGC members and that the organization helped secessionists hold sway over public opinion there.[40]

⋖⋗⋖⋗

The day the Secession Convention reconvened following the election and officially removed Texas from the Union—March 2, 1861—was a day anti-secessionists had been dreading. State representative Robert Taylor of Fannin County, a signer of the "Address to the People of Texas," had expressed his fears on the floor of the House, asking, "In this new Cotton Confederacy what will become of my section, the wheat growers and stock raisers? . . . I fear [secessionists] will hang, burn, confiscate property and exile any one who may be in the way of their designs."[41] Now, many northern Texas families acted on such fears, joining wagon trains bound for Kansas via the Indian Territory, while others headed west for California. Wagon trains on both routes contained more than a hundred wagons in some cases, and some outbound roads were clogged with fleeing refugees.[42]

Secessionists, for their part, began coming together in vigilance committees of the sort that had flourished during the Texas Troubles and at other times of crisis. One group organized in the northwestern section of the Forks delta and would at some point—although perhaps not this early—call itself the Sons of Washington. At the outset, the organization was under the leadership of H. S. Bennett of the Ben Franklin area, who not only owned more slaves than any other person in the Forks delta but was one of the three richest men in all of Lamar County. Other leading members are thought to have included James McGlasson, member of a prominent slaveholding family from the Roxton area, and Greenville Smith, a wealthy slaveholder of the Ben Franklin area. Smith owned a sawmill and a furniture factory. Located near the furniture factory was a two-story house; its bottom floor was used as a residence by the factory workers, and its upper floor was used as a meeting hall by members of the Masons' Lake Lodge 255. Smith was among charter members of the lodge, and other vigilance committee members most likely were Masons as well. The vigilantes probably used the hall as a gathering place.[43]

The "relationship between Freemasonry and vigilantism was frequently an intimate one," Richard Maxwell Brown has commented. "In Montana, Texas, and elsewhere, Freemasonry was often the shadowy background for the organization of a local vigilante movement."[44] Nothing in the group's creed made Masons more prone to vigilantism or other forms of violence than non-Masons. During much of United States history, how-

40

ever, Masonry was the premier civic group, the one that attracted most leading members of the community, and according to historian Richard McCaslin, they often "provided leadership and a framework for organization during vigilante movements."[45] Significantly, a vigilance group that organized at the Hopkins County town of Sulphur Bluff in 1861 met in the local Masonic Hall, where the group resolved, "That [a] committee of six be appointed to act as Vigilance Committee whose duty it shall be, to organize a patrol to keep a vigilant eye on all strangers, or any one passing through our precinct, and tampering with our negroes, or in any other way exciting discord among us. . . . That said committee shall order such suspected person or persons before them, who shall investigate the charges against them, and act in accordance with their deliberate convictions of duty to their country, and the safety of their fellow citizens."[46] It also should be noted that the vigilante movement which led to the late-1862 "Great Hanging at Gainesville," to the west of the Forks watershed, started when James Bourland "called several of his fellow Masons together as a vigilance committee to investigate matters."[47]

❖

While many of the men thought to have been members of the Forks delta vigilance committee were from the northwest delta and environs, some had settled outside the slaveholder enclave. The most prominent of these was George W. Helms of the Charleston area, a slaveholder who proudly traced his family roots back to Virginia, where the Helmses were said to have been among the early planters. He must have felt much more at home among the prosperous planters of the northwest delta than among the poor Upper Southerners who predominated in the East End, for Helms was among the founders of the first Methodist Church at Ben Franklin. Getting to and from there on Sundays, instead of attending services at Charleston, would have meant a laborious weekly ride for George W., his second wife, Charlotte, and perhaps other members of a large family group that included adult children who lived in the vicinity of the parents. Among them was the Helmses' eldest son.

John Jack Helms was born in Missouri around 1837, during the Helms family's extended odyssey from Virginia, to Tennessee, to Missouri, and finally to Texas, where they arrived about 1839. Around 1858, when John Jack was twenty-one, he married sixteen-year-old Minerva McCown, and a son was born to them whom they named after John Jack's father. The 1860 census describes John Jack, age twenty-three, as a "farm laborer" who possessed very little in the way of land or other assets, but that de-

41

scription was far from the whole story. He must have been viewed by many in terms of family ties, as the scion of his prosperous father, whose household was but a stone's throw from John Jack's own. Some other details about him are known: That his marriage would not last and may already have been an unhappy one, and that he had a technical bent, which would lead him to mechanical tinkering in later years. As for his temperament, we have the testimony of those who knew him during the Reconstruction period, when John Jack Helms would earn notoriety through much of Texas as a hated "regulator," captain of the State Police, and sheriff known as "Jack Helm," as he then called himself. If controversy over Helm's actions as a law officer had not guaranteed him a place in Texas history, the manner of his death surely would have done so: "The notorious" Jack Helm, as a newspaper of the time referred to him, met his end at the hands of "the more notorious" John Wesley Hardin and one of the gunfighter's friends.[48]

A description of Helm from these postwar times mentions "a braggadocio style."[49] Author Victor Rose is more precise when he described Jack Helm as "about five feet nine inches high, rather heavy, but altogether well made, with black hair and eyes, and dark complexion. His appearance was agreeable, but his conversation was directed too much upon himself and his exploits to be entertaining. His education was extremely limited, but his vanity was immense, while his discrimination was always muddled."[50]

It is easy to imagine a person of such temperament, who grew up in a slaveholding family, being angered by the views of men like Dohoney, Armstrong, and Henry T. Howard. But Dohoney and Armstrong were outsiders and of limited concern. Toleration of Howard's views would have been much less easy: he was John Jack's near neighbor.[51]

⋯

Next to nothing is known about another local man, R. M. Cox; possibly, the immigrant from Arkansas was a relative of George W. Cox, an East End pioneer who would figure prominently in the Hemby-Howard hanging. But this much at least is known of R. M.: he, along with John Jack Helms, ran afoul of Henry T. Howard early on, over Howard's speech opposing secession. Henry's brothers James K. and Thomas soon were drawn into the affair, as were, most likely, the kith and kin of Cox and Helms.

An item printed in the *Paris Advocate* around the end of May or beginning of June, 1861, is thought to refer to a milestone event in the development of the feud, a Charleston meeting at which it is thought the

Helms-Cox crowd attempted to organize against the Howard "clan" and perhaps other Unionists of the East End as well. The "reliable source" who reported on the affair to the *Advocate* may have been R. M. Cox or John Jack Helms. The *Advocate* article reported that "there is no doubt of Abolitionists and outlaws in the forks of Sulphur in this county." According to the unnamed source, there was an attempt by people near Charleston to hold a meeting in order to form a "vigilance committee." The "Abolitionists collected and broke up the meeting, declaring that no vigilance committee or patrol should be appointed. There are now one of the clan that there is four writs out for his arrest, for an attempt to murder, and he cannot, it seems, be arrested. Another publicly avows that he is opposed to slavery, and will resist all efforts to foster that institution." Other information in the article includes that "the good people of that locality are calling for aid to rid their neighborhood of such demons. Shall they not have aid!"[52]

While the article fosters the impression that "abolitionists and outlaws" rode down on the Charleston session in a hell-for-leather action, the wording is sufficiently ambiguous to leave it open to other interpretations. As one possibility, the Howards and other East Enders opposed to vigilante action against Unionists simply may have showed up at the meeting in majority numbers and forbade the Helms-Cox group to go ahead with plans for vigilante action. The reference to "one of the clan" being sought for attempted murder may indicate that one of the Howards had already had a run-in with a member of the Helms-Cox group. If so, then the Howard in question apparently was Thomas or James, since it seems likely that Henry was the person referred to as "another" member of the clan who "publicly avows that he is opposed to slavery, and will resist all efforts to foster that institution."

This allegation soon bore bitter fruit for Henry T. Howard. Slaveholders of the northwest Forks, perhaps responding to the *Advocate* article and/or the urgings of Cox and Helms, soon hauled Henry before their group's tribunal to answer charges of treason on account of his slavery views. Sitting in judgment on Howard at this proceeding was Hendley Stone Bennett.

Although Howard's trial was altogether illegal, the judge, at least, was a qualified judge. Bennett, a native of Tennessee, was admitted to the practice of law in Columbus, Mississippi, in 1830 and served as a judge of the circuit court there from 1846 to 1854. Before moving to Ben Franklin in 1859, Bennett also served a term in the U.S. House of Representatives.[53]

In Congress, Bennett took part in debates about the national crisis centering on the future of slavery. Texts of his speeches show him to have been a fiercely articulate speaker in defense of slave ownership, as in an address to the House in 1855. "We would scorn, sir, as southern people, to present ourselves as supplicants at the feet of Abolitionists, and claiming mercy at their hands," Bennett said, "but, sir, we come as equals in this Union—equal in rights and privileges—and claiming nothing more, and determined to accept nothing less than that protection which the Constitution accords to us." He went on to say, "I come in the name of my people, not with threats, but with warnings. If you love the Union, by the high obligation which that sentiment imposes on you, we warn you to preserve it. You can if you will; but if, in defiance of our warnings, and in violation of both law and justice, you are still resolved to encroach upon our rights, see that you are not overwhelmed in its mighty ruins."[54]

Given such views, Bennett was not going to be predisposed toward acquitting an opponent of slavery, and Howard may have considered that as one strike against him at the outset of his trial. One factor he might have regarded as being in his favor, during ordinary times, was the reluctance of many men to commit acts of violence against ministers, but that was not the case in these bitter times. Many Texans had long since lost feelings of reverence for the "Northern" churches, with their anti-slavery creeds, and had come to put their faith in Southern, pro-slavery versions of the major denominations. Texas ministers who refused to embrace slavery as a God-given institution had been fair game for mobs for years. In one of the most notorious instances, the Rev. Anthony Bewley of the Northern Methodist Episcopal Church was accused of instigating slaves to rebel, and he was hanged in Fort Worth on September 13, 1860. Historian Richard McCaslin described the gruesome outcome: "Bewley's body was cut down and dumped in a shallow grave. Because the burial was done in haste, the hole was not large or deep enough, and his knees protruded from the ground. A local physician had him exhumed after about three weeks, stripped the remaining flesh from the bones, and laid the skeleton out to dry on the roof of a nearby storehouse. While it lay there, local ruffians made sport of Bewley's remains."[55]

Clearly, then, Henry Howard stood at considerable risk when taken for trial by the vigilantes. But, in what may have come as a surprise to some of his antagonists, he was not subjected to punishment. Bennett's sensitivity to legal niceties, due to his work as an attorney and judge, surely played a part in the outcome. As Dohoney later reported, "Judge

Bennett presided over the mob, heard all the testimony given against Howard and discharged him saying that the evidence did not show that he had violated any law of Texas or the Confederate States." The minister was released, although Bennett went on to proclaim that Howard, while innocent under the law, was "a Union man, and a damned Abolitionist."[56]

Bennett's accusation notwithstanding, Henry Howard almost certainly was not an outright abolitionist. Abolitionism was a stance that was considered so radical in Texas at the time, it was simply beyond the pale. Even the hanged Reverend Bewley, notorious in northern Texas for his "abolitionist" views, was said by a friend to have been "no abolitionist, though an antislavery man of the Washington and Jefferson school."[57] And the New York *Christian Advocate and Journal* "thought that it was inconceivable that [Bewley] could have been involved in a murderous abolitionist plot, not only because he was a 'devoutly pious and inoffensive' man but also because he was not an abolitionist."[58] Nevertheless, "abolitionist" was one of the great demonizing words of the day and came easily to the lips of secessionists in disputes with Unionists. Earlier in 1861, during the Lamar County secession debates, Bennett had gone so far as to condemn an entire meeting house full of people in the Roxton area as "a set of damned Abolitionists" when they refused to allow secessionists to speak during a meeting.[59]

As for how Henry Howard *did* stand on slavery, it seems certain he disliked the South's "peculiar institution." But his views may have been much like those of a fellow Hopkins County man named S. Landreth. In July of 1861, some months after Howard's own vigilante court ordeal, a vigilance committee hauled Landreth to trial, where "it was proven that he had said he did not make the war now existing between the North and South, and that he would not fight the battles—he admitted he looked upon slavery . . . as wrong, said as it was here he was willing for it to remain, but that if it were not, he would be opposed to its ever being brought—that he believed the country would be better off without it." That stance stopped well short of abolitionism. Nevertheless, it was still too much for the vigilantes to swallow. They ordered Landreth banished from the county.[60]

⋖≋⋗⋗

While accounts of the Henry Howard trial do not mention it, Howard, like Landreth, may have been ordered to leave the area. Or perhaps he simply felt a lingering threat and departed on his own. But leave he did, journeying to a locale described as "the west"—an area that could have referred to almost any area west of the Forks watershed. (An article titled "A Trip to the West," which appeared in the *Marshall Texas Republican* on May 25, 1861, was not about the Texas frontier at all, as might be expected, but rather about the Waxahachie area, south of Dallas.) Possibly Henry went to stay with other members of the Arington Howard clan who had immigrated to various parts of the state.

After Henry's departure, R. M. Cox placed a newspaper ad of a sort referred to as a "card," levying accusations against him. No copies have been found, but the ad's existence may be presumed because it elicited a rebuttal from Thomas Howard, who placed a card of his own in the *Paris Press* on June 24, 1861. "Mr. R. M. Cox, a new comer from Rocky Comfort, Arkansas, is the author of a report charging my brother, Henry Howard, with abolitionism. My brother and Mr. Cox had some dealings during which they had a difficulty. Cox waited until my brother left for the west and then had him published. My impression is that Cox and John Helms tried to raise a mob to get my brother out of the way. R. M. Cox or any other man who had my brother published is a low down thieving liar."[61]

These were fighting words, and somebody's blood surely would have been spilled in short order if the Howards had been in the Forks delta when Thomas Howard's card assailed the eyes of Cox and Helms. However, the absence of Thomas, Henry, and James's names from local records in the summer of 1861 seems to indicate that all were absent from the area at that time. This might have come as no surprise to their contemporaries. The publication of insulting cards by authors who took the precaution of removing themselves to other parts apparently was not an uncommon practice in the area, judging by another *Paris Press* card from around the same time. A man who signed himself Prof. Stephen S. Hayden wrote, "During last spring I sojourned one month in Paris at Travelers' Inn, kept by Turner B. Edmundson," and he goes on to say that he developed a friendship with Edmundson's daughter. But one day Edmundson had called him out of the house, and Hayden went, "believing I was going to be with a gentleman and not anticipating in the least that I was to be the subject of a cowardly and brutal attack." After ordering Hayden to stay away from his daughter, Edmundson "accused me of being a Yankee." When Hayden denied it, Edmundson, "with a blow of his fist to my face, said I was, . . . treating me in so cowardly and dastardly a manner that none but the basest of men resort to and that class I take him to be out and out." Hayden's long declaration concluded:

I have never yet violated the law to get "satisfaction" or a reputation for courage among horse thieves, gamblers and plug uglies, having generally chosen my associates from the ranks of those who have some claim to the title of "gentleman" though I may sometimes have been mistaken as I was in this particular case. I intended to seek redress through the law—that source to which good citizens only resort—but finding such a course would detain me from my business too long I leave Mr. Edmundson to his own reflections—and thanking heaven that his treatment, though so shamefully done, has opened my eyes. I consider that I have made a fortunate escape from an alliance that would have made me miserable. If he or his desire to know my previous history they will find I am not a Yankee but born in North Carolina, which state I am ashamed to say gave him birth (as I am informed) and I have never left that place I was afraid or ashamed to revisit. And were he or his to visit my father's house in Polk county, Mo., they would find among them (and many friends) my statements true.

I have resorted to the press as the only just and honorable means of exonerating myself from the charges of Yankee and sustaining my character as a law-abiding or peaceful citizen would do under like circumstances.

Prof. Stephen S. Hayden,
Paris, July 8th, 1861

Printer's fee eleven dollars and 80 cents.[62]

With Henry and the other Howards out "west," the summer of 1861 passed peacefully in the Forks delta. Unionists other than the Howards not only remained in the area but rubbed shoulders with the Howards' antagonists during meetings held to organize local militia units. An August 5 militia muster for Lamar County Beat 2, which included the northern part of the East End, was attended by not only R. M. Cox, but also by such Unionists as James E. and Jonathan Hemby and members of the Condit family. And on August 24, John Jack Helms and a future fellow vigilante, Charles H. Southerland, were present at a muster session for Hopkins County Beat 3 that also was attended by James E. and Jonathan Hemby's kinsman, James W. Hemby.[63]

While both Unionists and Confederates attended these home guard musters, many of the pro-Confederates did not long remain in the local units. R. M. Cox, who disappears from the record after August, may have been among those who soon enlisted in regular Confederate outfits and went off to war. In October, John Jack Helms did the same.

While men from in and around the Forks delta served in dozens of different units, three organizations attracted the most volunteers: the Ninth Texas Infantry Regiment, organized by attorney Sam Bell Maxey of Paris; the Twenty-third Texas Cavalry Regiment, also known as Gould's Regiment; and the Ninth Texas Cavalry Regiment, also called Sims's Regiment.

Maxey—who would play a role in postwar trials of men indicted for wartime hangings—was a West Point graduate who had served in the Mexican War. He formed a group in the summer of 1861 who called themselves the Lamar Rifles before the unit evolved into the Ninth Texas Infantry Regiment. The group drilled at various locations in Fannin and Lamar Counties, including a site near Giles Academy in the Forks delta. Greenville Smith, whose son J. K. P. Smith served as a sergeant with the unit, donated the land for the camp, which was called Camp Rusk. In early 1862, the Ninth Texas Infantry crossed over the Mississippi and endured hard service at Shiloh and elsewhere during the course of the war. Maxey, who was detached from the unit early on, never served in a major battle, but he nevertheless succeeded in rising to the rank of general. He spent the closing years of the war ferreting out Unionists, deserters, and others in the Indian Territory and northern Texas through a network of spies.[64]

Col. Nicholas C. Gould drew most of the men for his Twenty-third Texas Cavalry from outside the Forks watershed, but the regiment's Company G was organized in Charleston and attracted a large number of men from the East End. They included James Wesley Hemby, the relative of Jonathan and James E. Hemby who had served with Jonathan in the Mexican War. Gould's Regiment was sent to patrol parts of Texas and Indian Territory during 1862 and 1863 before being shifted to Arkansas and Louisiana in 1864 during the Red River Campaign.[65]

The military unit that attracted the most volunteers from the Forks delta and surrounding area was the Ninth Texas Cavalry Regiment, which would serve at Pea Ridge, Corinth, Nashville, and in many other major battles. Companies from the Forks watershed were Fannin's Company B, Hopkins's Company G, Lamar's Company H, and Hopkins-Hunt's Company K.[66] Despite his opposition to secession, Paris lawyer E. L. Dohoney joined Lamar County's Company H as a lieutenant. John Jack Helms enlisted in Hopkins County's Company G as a private.[67]

In early October, 1861, twenty-four-year-old John Jack Helms joined Alonzo L. Leech, who had married John Jack's sister Sarah, and other volunteers under Capt. L. D. King on the ride to a regimental rendezvous at Brogdan Springs, north of Sherman. The troops were an unruly lot, as recalled by A. W. Sparks of Titus County, whose own volunteer unit rode to the rendezvous under the command of Capt. Charles S. Stuart (or Stewart). When the Titus men approached Sherman, Stuart ordered them to maintain close order and not break ranks under any circumstances, but only about 40 of 140 men remained in file when the company emerged on the other side of town. "Captain Stuart was sad," Sparks later recalled, "and I do not believe he ever got over his sadness, on account of the behavior of his company."[68]

The undisciplined troops' actions also could take a deadly turn, as occurred after the companies were mustered into Confederate service at Brogdan Springs. George L. Griscom, the regiment's adjutant, noted in his diary for October 31, 1861, that an officer named J. H. Bell "was accused of Abolitionism & of Bigamy [and] the latter being pretty strongly proven upon him, the boys *en masse* took him out & hung him & gave his outfit to a poor boy a member of the same Co." Then on November 13, "One W. L. Essy who had attached himself to Co 'D' (a worthless character) was detected in the act of committing a rape upon a married woman in the vicinity of Camp—a guard was sent for him, he was brought to Camp & whilst the officers were consulting as to what to do with him the boys *en masse* took him from the guards & hung him, buried him & distributed his outfit among the most needy of the company."[69] Pvt. John Jack Helms, who may have taken part in these hangings or at least witnessed them, surely must have been impressed by the contrast between the previous spring's acquittal of Henry Howard and these deadly proceedings, which may have helped shape his attitude toward vigilante justice.

The news that John Jack Helms—and presumably R. M. Cox—were gone from the Forks delta may have reached the Howards by late October or early November. The brothers may have returned to the area soon afterward—possibly to harvest their corn, since a story about them mentions that fall's corn crop.[70] But any hopes the Howards might have had that the feud would fade away were doomed to be short-lived.

⟨≋⟩·⟨≋⟩

During the mustering in at Brogdan Springs, Alonzo Leech was elected third lieutenant of the Ninth Texas Cavalry's Company G while his

brother-in-law John Jack Helms remained a private. The regiment engaged in a couple of battles in Indian Territory in December, 1861, then
went into winter quarters near Fort Smith, Arkansas, on January 15, 1862.
But Private Helms was either gone from the regiment by then or he left
soon after. According to a family story, he deserted the army and rushed
back to the Forks delta after hearing that his young wife, Minerva, was
having an affair with one Jim Elmore. Elmore was a near neighbor of the
Helms clan and also was a fellow private of John Jack's in Company G. If
Elmore was romancing John Jack's wife, he may have gone home on leave,
or for other reasons, before John Jack's desertion.[71]

Tensions within the East End must have soared immediately upon
Helms's return. But the presence of the Howards and Helms all together
in the East End does not of itself provide an adequate explanation for
everything that subsequently occurred. Somewhere along the way, the
dispute had broadened. What apparently had begun as a small feud had
grown into something much larger, on the order of a broad political purge.
In addition to the Howards, the objects of enmity for those siding with
the Helms camp now included Jonathan and James E. Hemby and a
number of other men from in or around the Forks delta: William S. Condit, T. R. H. "Tommy" Poteet, Wesley Neathery, and a number of others
whose names are not recalled. All or most all of these men may have been
outspoken about their support for the Union, or perhaps just their dislike
for the Confederacy, which would have been enough to earn the enmity
of secessionists. But the witch's brew that led to the vigilante campaign
of February, 1862, had other ingredients as well. One of these ingredients
was celebratory explosions, real or imagined.

Sometime around the 1920s, Confederate veteran Aden Posey of Hopkins County told Judge L. L. Bowman that the Hembys and Howards
had "made a big display by boring holes in trees and filling them with
powder and shooting it off." (Posey added, with what must have passed
for him as wit, "they quit after they hung them."[72]) Another Hopkins
County old-timer, Erastus "Ras" Hopper, gave Bowman a similar but
slightly different account, saying, "when the Yankees had won some important victory . . . these men [the Hembys and Howards] put on a big
celebration by boring holes in trees and logs and stopping up the holes
and attaching a fuse. A kind of an old fashion method of making a big
noise in celebration."[73] But the most detailed statement about the matter,
and probably the most accurate, is from E. L. Dohoney. He said, "some-

body had found where a log had been split by an explosion of powder, and [one of the Hembys] was accused of it on the charge that he was rejoicing over Zollicoffer's defeat at Fishing Creek, Kentucky. Hemby denied it, but the [accuser] said he could see it in his eye that he was guilty."[74]

Many Civil War histories include little or no mention of the Union victory at Fishing Creek on January 19–20, 1862, and the death there of Confederate general Felix Kirk Zollicoffer. The general wandered into Union lines during a dense fog and was shot by a Federal sentry, but the battle and the general's death were regarded with anguish at the time by Confederates in northern Texas. Many of these Texans hailed from Tennessee and Kentucky, and since the previous summer they had been following reports of General Zollicoffer's campaign in those areas (as chronicled in such newspaper stories as one headlined "Porkopolis is Frightened"—about the fear of Zollicoffer's army that supposedly existed in the meat-packing metropolis of Cincinnati). When news of Zolli-coffer's death hit northern Texas around the first of February, 1862, the press held nothing back from praise for "Zollicoffer—the brave, the true soldier, the gifted and the true minded gentleman—[who] is now among the martyrs to the holy cause of Southern Independence." Papers also deluged their readers with sundry other Zollicoffer stories, many of them steeped in celebrity worship. According to one article, "Appearance of Zollicoffer's Corpse," the author described his viewing of the body with Colonel Cornell. Zollicoffer was "wrapped in an army blanket, his chest and left arm and side exposed. A tall, rather slender man, with thin brown hair, high forehead, somewhat bald, Roman nose, firm, wide mouth, and clean shaved face. A pistol ball had struck him in the breast, a little above the heart, killing him instantly." The article then relates that "his face bore no expression such as is usually found on those who fall in battle—no malice, no reckless hate, not even a shadow of physical pain. It was calm, placid, noble. But I have never looked on a countenance so marked with sadness. A deep dejection had settled on it. 'The low cares of the mouth' were distinct in the droop at its corners, and the thin cheeks showed the wasting which comes through disappointment and trouble."[75]

It should also be mentioned that Fishing Creek was not viewed in the South as a solitary setback but as part of a fearful train of developments. Such was noted by diarist Kate Stone, who would become a war refugee in the Forks delta in 1863 but was still at home on the family's Louisiana plantation at the time of Fishing Creek. On January 30, 1862, she wrote,

"The papers confirm our defeat at Fishing Creek and the death of Gen. Zollicoffer. Two lamentable events. . . . The whole Northern Army is now on the move preparing to attack us at all points."[76]

Confederates in North Texas shared Kate's fear of an invasion at this time. But the main source of their concern was not so much the Union army as an old bugaboo, the hated "abolitionists of Kansas." Fearful rumors centering on Kansas—which was nearer to northern Texas than the state capital at Austin—were particularly intense during early February, 1862. On the eighth of the month, page one of the *Marshall Texas Republican* carried an account of the defeat at Fishing Creek and Zollicoffer's death along with an article warning, "There is no doubt that [abolitionist leader Jim] Lane is organizing an expedition from Kansas into Texas, for the purpose of general robbery, confiscation and emancipation of slaves."[77]

Slaveholders' beliefs that Unionists in the Forks delta were celebrating these Confederate setbacks with country-style fireworks apparently was one of at least three developments which played a major part in events that followed. Another was the renewed presence in the area of John Jack Helms, who no doubt was still smarting over Thomas Howard's stinging words in the *Paris Press* and looking for an opportunity to exact vengeance. Finally, H. S. Bennett was now absent from the area. The former judge and congressman, who had exercised such sound judgment the previous year while ruling on the charges against Henry Howard, had organized a company of Confederate cavalry a few months after Howard's trial. H. S. Bennett's Lamar Cavalry, which eventually became Company G of the Thirty-second Texas Cavalry Regiment, was on active service with the Confederacy in February, 1862, and gone from the Forks, its captain along with it. Dohoney commented that, "The original Secession leaders were generally men who said 'one Southern man can whip ten Yankees,' but who never got to the front to try it; being on the inside ring they generally went to the Confederate congress, or got some other bomb-proof position, civil or military. But there were honorable exceptions, and one of these was Judge H. S. Bennett."[78]

The leadership vacuum created by the fifty-two-year-old Bennett's absence was filled by one of his slightly younger neighbors, forty-seven-year-old slaveholder and furniture-factory operator Greenville Smith. Smith had no experience at law, as either attorney or judge, but he fit the typical pattern of the nineteenth-century American vigilante leader. Most of these leaders were ambitious men from settled areas of the East who had moved to the West and "who wished to establish themselves in the upper level of the new community."[79] The Tennessee native's wealth, while substantial, was much less than that of Bennett and many other members of the Forks delta slaveholding community, such as the Lanes and Pattesons.[80] Smith may well have regarded the opportunity to lead angry compatriots in a vigilance campaign as his main chance to make his mark as a community leader.

It may also have been around this same time, early February, 1862, that the vigilantes formally christened themselves the Sons of Washington—a name drawn from the time of the American Revolution. As Richard Maxwell Brown has noted, "Long after 1776 the symbols of the Revolution continued to be used with frequency and sincerity by violent movements to enfold themselves in its sanctifying mantle." Members of the Whiskey Rebellion of 1794 erected liberty poles, and anti-rent protesters in New York state during the 1840s disguised themselves as "Mohawks" in emulating "Indians" of the Boston Tea Party while denouncing opponents as "Tories." And Southerners in particular looked upon the American Revolution as "the great prototype of their own war for independence."[81] "Sons of" was a popular ingredient in the names of pro-South groups, whose members envisioned themselves as latter-day embodiments of the Revolutionary era's Sons of Liberty. Southern sympathizers (sometimes referred to as "Copperheads") in the midwestern states took the Sons of Liberty name for themselves, while a vigilante group in Parker County, Texas, called itself Sons of the South, a name that also appears in a popular song of the Confederacy, "The Southern Marseillaise." Its lyrics include:

> *Sons of the South, awake to glory!*
> *Hark! hark! what myriads bid you rise.*
> *Your children, wives, and grandsires hoary,*
> *Behold their tears and hear their cries.*
>
> . . . .
>
> *To arms! to arms! ye brave,*
> *Th' avenging sword unsheath!*[82]

The remainder of the Forks vigilante group's name clearly paid homage to George Washington. Not only an icon to Southerners at large, Washington would have been particularly esteemed by those among the vigilantes who were Masons. (As was well known, Washington took the oath of office as president on a Masonic Bible and laid the Capitol's corner-stone with a Masonic trowel.) And the great Virginian was very much in the minds of Confederates at this time, since Washington's upcoming birthday had been chosen as one of the Confederacy's special occasions. Washington's forthcoming birthday was the subject of a *Marshall Texas Republican* article on February 1, 1862. The writer believed this day needed to be celebrated because it is "the anniversary of the birthday of him who dared all and risked all to free the American people from the tyranny of British rule, and who, were he living now, would have been as zealous and disinterested in liberating his fellow countrymen from a tyranny still more disgraceful and oppressive, but the day is to be still more memorably sig-nalized, as in effect, the birthday of our new Republic." The writer then observed that this is the day when "its highest Executive officers, for the first time elected by the people; on that day our new Constitution is to go into effect, and the Congress upon whose wisdom our future welfare is to depend assumes its powers."[83]

⊰⊱⊱⊰

One target of the vigilantes was William Spangler Condit, who had im-migrated to the Lamar County section of the Forks delta's East End from Jefferson County, Kentucky, in 1851, along with his wife, Jane. Condit, whose large family included some ten children, became a substantial stockraiser, accumulating several hundred sheep, horses, and cattle. A member of the Methodist church, he apparently subscribed to the North-ern church's anti-slavery views. A Condit family history states, "He was charged with disloyalty to the South because he clung with the spirit of a freeman to his principles."

The family history says Condit was "roused at night from a sick bed by a squad of armed and masked men, some of whom were his neighbors, who ordered him to quit the soil of Texas. Hastily gathering his house-hold, he read a portion of Scripture, and they knelt for the last time around that sacred family altar, where he committed the dear ones to the care of a covenant-keeping God. Mounting his best horse, he began the tedious journey to his native State. But little is known of this trip, except that he reached Kentucky in safety. Here he remained until his death, which took place near the close of the war, at the home of his aged mother."[84]

Dohoney, who attributed the raid on Condit to the Sons of Washing-ton, said it occurred at "about the same time" as vigilante action against the Hembys and Howards. Greater precision about dates is lacking, but

it is possible that the raid on Condit was the opening action in the vigilantes' campaign and that the Hembys and Howards heard about it, which
would have given them time to flee. For whatever reason, they did flee,
their place of refuge being Jernigan's Thicket.[85]

The thicket would become a major haven for fugitives later in the war.
However, many of those who hid there later were hiding to avoid conscription. There were none such present in February, 1862, since at that
time the Confederacy's first conscription law still lay a couple of months
in the future. Nevertheless, James E. Hemby, Jonathan Hemby, Henry T.
Howard, Thomas Howard, and James K. Howard may not have been the
sole "brush men" of Jernigan's Thicket when they took refuge there. By
this time, Confederates were exerting pressure on many local Union men,
or men with ambivalent feelings about the war, to join the Confederate
army, and some of those who refused to do so may have taken to the
brush. At least two other men targeted by the vigilantes, but whose names
are not recalled, may have been the Hembys and Howards' fellow thicket
denizens, and perhaps other men were in Jernigan's Thicket as well.[86]

Almost certainly, the vigilantes greatly outnumbered this small group.
Nevertheless, an attempt to root the fugitives out by force would have
been no easy task. Invaders entering the maze of animal trails that provided the only access to the great woods would have been easy targets for
riflemen hiding in the dense brush. It is also possible that the fugitives
employed a warning system that made it easy for them to tell friend from
foe. Brush men in one of the state's other thickets made use of cowbells
for this purpose: a friend hung one on his horse's neck when he rode into
the thicket, and any person who neglected to do so was riddled with
bullets.[87]

Beginning in January, 1862, and continuing through February, a series
of cold and wet northers swept down through northeast Texas, which may
have created a hardship for the thicket fugitives, but brush men had their
ways of protecting themselves from the elements. It is recalled that a
brush man in one of the region's other thickets kept warm and dry within
a shelter made of "black oilcloth boiled in linseed oil to make it water
repellent and also indistinguishable" from the surrounding brush.[88] The
fugitives did have one great weakness, however, in that their food stores
were limited. The vigilantes took advantage of it. Hopkins County old-
timer Ras Hopper told Judge Bowman that the "Southern men" who
posted themselves outside the thicket "kept their friends from conveying
food to them."[89]

Clearly, the "Southern men" included civilian members of the Sons of Washington. Some accounts also indicate that members of the local militia were a party to the vigilante action. The most likely explanation seems to be that there was some overlap between the two organizations. Notably, M. G. Settle, who held the militia rank of lieutenant colonel and commanded militiamen headquartered at Charleston, may also have been a member of the Sons of Washington. Settle, who was about age forty-four in 1862, lived in the Ben Franklin area. Elected to serve a term as Lamar County commissioner in 1856, he also operated a school west of Ben Franklin for a while and was a trustee of the Methodist Episcopal Church South for the Sulphur Mission along with another man associated with the Sons of Washington, George W. Helms. Settle also was a slaveholder.[90]

Others in the party outside the thicket apparently included militiamen who considered themselves to be acting under orders from superior officers such as Settle. These may have included John Yates from the Atlas community in the Biardstown area of Lamar County.[91]

⊰≈⊱

Eventually, the group barring deliveries of food to the fugitives "starved them out."[92] Then, according to family stories, the fugitives agreed to negotiate, and the vigilantes sent one of their number into the thicket to discuss terms of surrender. The vigilantes' negotiator supposedly was none other than John Jack Helms. According to family stories heard by Delta County historian Douglas Albright, "John Jack wanted to get amnesty for his desertion" and was able to get assurance from militia Lieutenant Colonel Settle that amnesty could be arranged in exchange for John Jack's cooperation in capturing the men in the thicket. John Jack thereupon went into the thicket and "persuaded the [brush men] to emerge at an agreed-upon time and date."[93]

It seems unlikely that the Howards in particular would have placed faith in the word of John Jack Helms, whom Thomas Howard had so bitterly denounced in his *Paris Press* advertisement. But it is impossible to dismiss the remarkable similarity between this alleged situation and situations that would occur a half-dozen years afterward, during Helms's Reconstruction-era days of notoriety. Repeatedly, men who surely hated the regulator chieftain and Texas State Police captain no less than did the Howards would surrender to him. Then, soon after surrender, the men would be killed—"while attempting to escape" according to Helms's ex-

planation of the deaths, which became a standing joke in skeptical newspaper accounts of his deeds.[94]

Whether the go-between for the vigilantes was Helms or some other
person, the starved men finally agreed to surrender after being given
"some kind of assurance of fair treatment."[95] At the appointed time, on
Thursday, February 13, they emerged from the thicket. Perhaps they
expected the militia to take them under its protection at this time. If
so, they were cruelly disappointed, for the militiamen proceeded to clap
shackles onto them. The captives were then loaded onto a wagon.[96]

Where the vigilantes opted to take the prisoners represented an interesting choice: they hauled them eastward, into the East End of the Forks
delta, then cut south on the Charleston-Tarrant Road, crossing South
Sulphur River at Oxford's Bridge. Here, near the south side of the bridge,
they made camp.[97] No accounts state why the vigilantes chose this site,
but it clearly had several advantages from their point of view. It was out of
the Forks delta, where Upper Southerners, many of them with Unionist
sympathies, predominated; it was in the area of present-day Hopkins
County, the part of the Forks watershed where Lower Southerners were
most numerous and pro-Confederate sentiment ran highest; and the
bridgehead site was eminently defensible, in case any Forks delta men
attempted to break up the proceedings and rescue the prisoners.

⋰⊱⊰⋱

Dohoney described the proceedings that followed as a "pretended trial."[98]
Pretended or otherwise, however, some sort of trial was held. In conducting it, the Sons of Washington were following in a long tradition among
American vigilantes, dating back at least to the 1780s in Tennessee, when
Col. Charles Lynch presided over a court of leading citizens who organized to combat stock thieves. Those proceedings were the source of the
term "lynch law," although "lynching" at that time was not synonymous
with hanging. Instead, a man convicted in Lynch's court usually "was sentenced to receive thirty-nine lashes on the bare back, and if he did not
then shout 'Liberty forever'" he was "hanged up by the thumbs until he
did so."[99] It was not until around the 1850s that execution, usually by
hanging, became vigilantes' customary sentence. But the tradition of
holding court continued through the years.[100]

As the first step in putting together a trial, the vigilantes went out into
the community to gather jurors, and one vigilante showed up at the home
of Charleston-area resident Cornelius B. McGuire. But the thirty-nine-

year-old veteran of the Mexican War refused to have anything to do with the mob proceedings. The vigilante was angered and threatened to fight, whereupon McGuire said he was willing to meet the man in a duel if necessary. But McGuire's wife, twenty-four-year-old Salina, emerged from the house with a rifle and ran the vigilante off the premises, putting an end to the matter. The former Salina Duke, whom Cornelius had recently married after the death of his first wife, was a native of Illinois and was said to be sympathetic to the Union cause.[101]

Others soon were found for the jury, however, including some who did so from fear of "the mob," according to Dohoney, and the trial went forward. But this time around, with no Judge Bennett to impose restraint, fine points of legality went by the board.[102]

Greenville Smith, "a prominent citizen and rabid secessionist," led the vigilantes and apparently presided at the trial. Other court officers were said to be militia Lt. Col. M. G. Settle and George W. Cox, an East End farmer who also served as postmaster at Charleston in the early 1850s, although it is not clear what roles they played.[103] The jury was made up of Charleston-area residents: Charles H. Southerland, George W. Helms, John Jack Helms, David Simeon "Sim" George, and, as a surprise, Thomas Rufus McGuire. Rufus, as he was called, was the son of adamant nonjuror Cornelius B. McGuire and was just short of his fourteenth birthday at the time of the vigilante proceedings. That he would have been included as a juror seems unlikely, on the face of the matter. But the information that he sat as a juror did not come from some accuser but from vigilante Charles H. Southerland, in conversation with Cooper lawyer James Patteson. There seems no good reason to doubt Southerland's information about the jury service of Rufus McGuire, who would later serve in the local militia under vigilante court officer Settle.

Other men who have been linked to the proceedings on the side of the vigilantes by witnesses or records, but whose roles have never been described, were Rice Warren, James McGlasson, and J. W. Stansbury.[104]

As Richard Maxwell Brown has noted, "vigilante leaders were drawn from the upper level of the community" while "the middle level supplied the rank-and-file."[105] Four of the above-named men clearly belong in the upper-level category, based on combined holdings of land and other property: Smith, $18,200; George W. Helms, $16,720; McGlasson, $10,500; and Cox, $9,180. Determining where Settle ($3,560), George ($3,000), Southerland ($1,630), and John Jack Helms ($450) fit in is more problematic.[106] Settle and George might be considered *lower* middle-level men, in terms of wealth. Despite his low personal wealth, John Jack Helms was an upper-level man in terms of family connections, while Southerland was lower level in terms of wealth. But John Jack Helms and Charles Southerland probably belong in a category apart from all others. Based on what their contemporaries had to say about them, the two fit Brown's description of vigilantes who constituted a "fringe" category of "sadists and naturally violent types" who often "had criminal tendencies and were glad to use the vigilance movement as an occasion to give free reign to their unsavory passions."[107] More information about these two characters will be offered later. No information is available on Stansbury and Warren, while none of the categories, conceived with adults in mind, fits the adolescent Rufus McGuire.

By the time the Hembys and Howards were captured, Benjamin Ober's Church of God mission had spread to several counties of the Forks watershed and Ober had moved from Lamar County to Hopkins, where he organized a Forks of Sulphur church in the Charleston area. He said in his memoir: "I lived in the prairie at the edge of a dense forest, which was a hiding place [from] mobs, and as that place was principally settled by people from the North, the mob frequently came and inquired for them . . . To arrest a man was sure death if the leader wished to take his life."[108]

But Ober was not among the threatened at this time, no doubt owing, in part, to a further evolution of his Texas mission's policy on slavery. Whereas Ober's group had simply taken a hands-off stance on slavery back in 1857, it had since become an actual defender of "involuntary servitude." At a meeting of August 16, 1860, at North Sulphur Academy in Fannin County, a Committee on Resolutions consisting of Ober, J. E. Cunningham, E. Marple, and J. T. Lyday had affirmed that "the members of the Church of God in the North have become ultra upon the present political issues, and have declared the system of servitude, as laid down in the Bible, an evil, and incompatible with the interest of the American people" and that "by so doing they have violated our book of discipline, the New Testament." The group disclaimed "fellowship in the Church with abolition members North, South, East, or West, or wherever they may be found, and have neither voice nor part, either directly or indirectly, in making, forming, or even winking at abolition resolutions, and declare them unscriptural." A Committee on Slavery, composed of the same members plus A. Hamblin, went on to declare that it had "examined the question of servitude spoken of in the Bible, and the system as it now exists" and was satisfied that the difficulties "threatening the dissolution of our once happy Republic have originated from a mistaken notion of the system," and that members of the committee "believe that involuntary servitude is plainly taught in the Bible."[109]

Despite the Texas mission's approval of slavery, it apparently also attracted people with Unionist sympathies, much like the Antioch Church of Christ in the Biardstown area, whose church rolls of the time include many staunch Confederates as well as men targeted by Confederate vigilantes.[110] Indeed, recent newcomers to Ober's Forks of Sulphur church included slavery opponent Henry T. Howard, whom Ober described as a licensed Cumberland Presbyterian church minister who intended to apply for a license to preach with the Church of God. It is unclear whether Henry's brothers also joined, although Ober said Thomas was the father of a church member, one M. Howard.[111]

On Friday, February 14, 1862, Ober was distressed to learn from a neighbor that Henry, Thomas, and James Howard, along with two Hemby men and two other men, were under arrest and were to be tried that day. Ober was under "the impression that it was a legal trial," and the neighbor persuaded the minister to accompany him to the proceeding.

The two soon arrived at the site near Oxford's Bridge where they had been told the trial would take place—and where Ober was disabused of the belief that he was about to witness a legally constituted proceeding: "There was a large excited crowd at the bank of the creek at a secluded spot by a log fire. There were seven men under arrest and the trial had just begun, conducted by a mob. As soon as we reached the place we were placed under guard as [was] everybody and [were] not allowed to leave until evening."[112]

Dohoney, in recounting what he was able to learn of the charges against the Hembys and Howards, said one of the Hembys was being tried because, as aforementioned, he was accused of celebrating the Confederate defeat at Fishing Creek with fireworks consisting of a gunpowder-packed log. The other Hemby was on trial "because he said that he would lay in Sulphur bottom until the moss grew a foot long on his back before he would go into the Confederate army"—a variation on a popular saying of the time.[113] Another charge is mentioned in Hemby family tradition: That one of the Hembys was accused of having named a son Abraham Lincoln.[114]

Dohoney said Henry Howard was accused of treason for the anti-secession speech for "which he had already been tried and acquitted by

Judge Bennett and his mob," while one of his brothers was accused "because he put up corn in two pens when he gathered it in the fall before and, being asked his reason for it, said one pen was for Jeff Davis and the other for Abraham Lincoln." The third Howard was placed on trial "on some similar silly pretense."[115]

The accusations against the other two men who were on trial, and who may have been captured along with the Hembys and Howards at Jernigan's Thicket, are not mentioned in any accounts. The two got off relatively easy by submitting to the vigilantes' demand that they join the Confederate army.[116]

The Hembys and Howards were not allowed to speak in their own defense, but the vigilantes called a series of witnesses to testify. "I was called as the last witness," Ober said. "I tried to be excused but if a man refused to be examined a rope was placed around his neck and he was made to testify under those circumstances. I took the witness stand when the last question was asked, 'Do you consider these men dangerous in our country?'"

All the other witnesses had "answered in the affirmative," but this was something Ober "could not truthfully do. I tried to avoid answering it but was asked for a plain yes or no. I answered in the negative. When the prosecutor attorney used some authority by asking me why I had answered different from all the rest I told him I had heard no testimony to prove them dangerous."[117]

Ober's refusal to go along, as had other witnesses, made him an object of enmity for the vigilantes and put his life in danger. But it had no effect on the outcome of the trial, which Dohoney characterized as a sham, based on postwar grand jury testimony. Even before the Hembys and Howards were captured, he said, the Sons of Washington had already adjudged them guilty and condemned them to death. The verdict and sentence were made official at the end of Friday's proceedings, however, with the five men condemned to be hanged at eleven o'clock the following morning.[118]

"The next day," Ober wrote, "I went back, thinking perhaps the excitement might have calmed down and I could plead for a new trial as some of the men had said they would call on me, but all their courage failed at the appointed time, and to break off to offer [testimony in the men's defense] without being called would mean certain death." He then watched in silence.

Some of the condemned men's wives showed up but "were driven away with threats without a sight of their loved ones," he said. Afterward, a pole was placed in the forks of two trees and five ropes were attached to the pole. A plank about six inches wide was rigged on a wagon bed, upon which the condemned men were made to stand. Then:

> The ropes were put around their necks by a noted horse thief and murderer, who had broken jail to escape justice. When all was ready, twenty minutes were given for them to make any statement they wished. All spoke of their innocence and requested that their small children be told they died innocently defending the cause they deemed right, which was that of the union. After they all talked some time, Henry Howard began praying, and when I supposed him to be about half through his prayer, the men were dropped. The last sentence spoken by that martyr was a prayer for his enemies. That was one of the saddest scenes I ever witnessed. . . . [Later, the bodies] were taken from the gallows by men cursing and swearing. I have never been able to erase the horrible sight from my mind.[119]

According to Hemby family tradition, at least one pair of eyes had watched the hangings from nearby woods. James Wesley Hemby, who served with the condemned Jonathan during the Mexican War, had returned to the area from Confederate cavalry duty. He is said to have slipped near to the hanging site with his rifle in hand. When the proceedings were under way, he raised the weapon and drew a bead on one of the vigilantes. But then he thought of the additional round of killing that would result if he pulled the trigger. He lowered the rifle and turned away.[120]

After the bodies were taken from the gallows, they were given over to family members, who are said to have buried them on family land. The graves have never been found.[121]

The site where the Hembys and Howards were hanged is on Hopkins County land, located on the south bank of South Sulphur River. Now owned by Thomas Peters, it is across the river from Delta County land owned by Robert Templeton. No bridge or road open to the public is at that location today.[122]

⋘·⋙

The Sons of Washington followed up the exiling of Condit, the hangings of the Hembys and Howards, and the forced entry into the Confederate army of the two other men by issuing threats against others in the area.

Memory has survived of threats directed at T. R. H. "Tommy" Poteet and Wesley Neathery, who lived in the vicinity of Lamar County's Biardstown and Marvin communities. Poteet's grandson, Roxton banker Gibbons Poteet, said the vigilantes sent word that "Tommy Poteet and Wesley Neathery's time will come" in a failed attempt to scare them.[123]

Also on the list of vigilante targets was Benjamin Ober, due to his testimony on behalf of the Hembys and Howards, along with a young Church of God member named A. J. Canady, who refused to serve in the Confederate army, and three other men whose names are unknown.[124] These latter three subsequently agreed to join the army, under threat of death,[125] but the lives of Ober and Canady remained at risk. Ober recalled:

> I was compelled to leave or to try some means to disband the mob. If I succeeded in getting away from them, [I] would leave my family in a strange country and with no means of support, [so] I concluded to try to disband them.
>
> On Friday before [the vigilantes] were to meet the following Monday, I went to an appointment I had . . . near Paris where [Church of God member] W. B. Miner lived. He was Justice of the Peace at the time. I stated the case to him and he agreed to go with me on the day mentioned for the mob to meet, if I succeeded in getting a sufficient number of men to go along to arrest the mob should they resist, . . . which I did. Mr. Miner ordered them to disband and not attempt to make any more arrests, which they did, and that stopped any further trouble in the vicinity as far as mobs were concerned.[126]

During the last two weeks of February, 1862, the Ninth Texas Cavalry Regiment packed up, left its winter quarters near Fort Smith, and headed to join other Confederate units in meeting a Union advance into northern Arkansas. The news must have spread rapidly to members of the regiment who were back home with leave or, like John Jack Helms, home without it. When the men on leave returned to the unit, it is thought that Helms rode along with them.[127]

In the opening days of March, 1862, Helms's Company G and other units of the Ninth Texas Cavalry took heavy losses in northern Arkansas during the Battle of Pea Ridge (a losing engagement also known to Confederates as the Battle of Elkhorn Tavern). Company K, from Hopkins and Hunt Counties, earned plaudits during the fighting for a deadly, headlong charge into Union cannon. Afterward, all other companies in the Ninth paid homage to K; the company's banner, bearing a crescent moon and thirteen stars, served as the flag of the entire regiment for the remainder of the war.[128]

The cavalry unit's sister regiment, the Ninth Texas Infantry, took a battering of its own during April 5–6 at the bloody Battle of Shiloh in Tennessee. But the Ninth Texas Cavalry missed that engagement, being delayed en route by mud-bog roads. On April 14, the cavalrymen were still encamped on the western side of the Mississippi, in Des Arcs, Arkansas, when an order came down for the regiment to be dismounted and converted to infantry. Rather than dismount, John Jack Helms chose to desert. When he left the army this time, it was for good.[129]

Sometime after his return to the Forks, John Jack apparently broke up with his wife, the allegedly adulterous Minerva. What became of her is not known, but it is known what became of her alleged lover, Jim Elmore. Contrary to what might have been expected, he was not shot by enraged husband John Jack. Instead, he married John Jack's own sister, Sarah Ann Helms Leech. She had been widowed soon after John Jack's desertion when, Ninth Texas Cavalry muster rolls show, 3rd Lt. A. C. L. Leech "died of disease May 62."[130]

⬦⬦⬦

How John Jack Helms spent the remainder of the war following his April, 1862, desertion is not known. Perhaps Lieutenant Colonel Settle allowed him to serve as one of his home guards. Such arrangements, in which home guard units harbored deserters from the Confederate army, were not uncommon.[131] But it is possible that Helms found a different way of getting through the war without being arrested as a deserter; at least one man who participated in the hanging of the Hembys and Howards— perhaps Helms, perhaps not—fled to Mexico and sat out the war there, according to local teenager John Warren Hunter.

The hanging of the Hembys and Howards had a powerful effect on sixteen-year-old Johnny Hunter, whose family lived in the East End of the Forks delta near the Howards and, in particular, the one Howard of the three whom the boy particularly admired. Years later, Hunter would mention the hangings in a memoir of his wartime experiences that includes praise of this special Howard in its introduction: "Howard was a perfect gentleman and often gave boys of the community good advice, and was loved by every boy for miles around; in fact, he was a real friend to boys. This man Howard was at heart a Union man, although he kept his own counsel and did not talk freely of his sentiments. But be that as it may, he was waited upon by a committee of Southern sympathizers and hung because he did not espouse the Southern cause." Hunter wrote that this incident made him determined to "avoid enlistment or conscription, so he [Hunter] accordingly secured employment with a cotton train hauling cotton to Brownsville, and, as a teamster, he set out for the Mexican border, where he spent the remaining years of the war."[132]

Hunter's cotton wagon pulled out of the Forks in the fall of 1862, finally reaching the border at Brownsville and crossing to Matamoros, Mexico, in January, 1863. But the young émigré later made a surreptitious trip to Lavaca County, Texas, to locate a pair of valuable mules owned by a fellow exile. On this journey, he encountered another train of cotton wagons that was southbound from the Forks.

Hunter was camped at the time in San Patricio (west of Corpus Christi), on a popular cotton route from northern Texas, which was probably the route his own cotton train had taken. The road here was among many that continued southward to converge at the King Ranch, where wagons formed into miles-long trains for the final 125-mile haul down to Mexico. At the Mexican port of Bagdad, cotton was loaded onto ships from England and elsewhere that could not call at ports on the blockaded Texas coast.

In San Patricio, Hunter realized with a shock that two men he saw on a cotton wagon were "Confederates" and that "one had assisted in the hanging of the three Howards and two Hembys—Union men—at Oxford's bridge, near Charleston." Hunter feared the men would recognize him and call for his arrest as a draft evader, but he was wearing Mexican garb at the time and the two failed to penetrate his disguise. He need not have worried, however, because "these two men, with others of their train, abandoned the Confederacy when they reached Brownsville and skipped into Mexico. I met them the following summer and recalled our meeting in San Patricio."[133]

⊰≫⋅≪⊱

Hunter's report of a vigilante who fled to Mexico is among indications that the Sons of Washington, while successful in the extermination of five enemies, did not enjoy a peaceful aftermath. Another indication was that the Masons' Lake Lodge 255, thought to have provided a fraternal bond for many of the vigilantes, ceased meeting around April, 1862, within just a couple of months of the Hemby-Howard hanging. The lodge remained inactive for more than two years before briefly reviving in late 1864 and then being ordered to surrender its charter by high Masonic officials in late 1866.[134]

While unsettled war conditions may have had something to do with the lodge's problems, an investigation by Masonic officials determined that the lodge was torn by "dissensions and divisions among the brethren." The officials did not elaborate on the source of this unrest, but it is possible that some lodge members may have disapproved of their colleagues' vigilante activities, leading to the split. Those who disapproved may have included Capt. H. S. Bennett. His Thirty-second Texas Cavalry Regiment, like the Ninth, had been ordered to give up its horses. In a letter to Confederate president Jefferson Davis in May, 1862, Bennett pleaded his inability to serve on foot due to "my feeble health and age," and he was allowed to return home.[135] He soon would have heard that Henry Howard had been hanged, basically on the same charge that Bennett had considered, then dismissed. It seems unlikely that Bennett's subsequent relationship with Greenville Smith and his fellow vigilantes would have been cordial.

⊰⊱⋅⊰⊱

Soon after Helms's desertion, the Confederacy adopted the Conscription Act of April 16, 1862, which made all white males between the ages of eighteen and thirty-five subject to a draft. One historian summarized the significance of this act thus: "Those already serving were required to remain in the military for three more years or the duration of the war."[136] The act would have kept Helms—a "twelve-month man" whose term of enlistment was about to expire—in the army for years to come.

Another feature of the Conscription Act—intended as a sop to twelve-month-men now being transformed into "no-end-in-sight men"— provided for "reorganization" of existing military units, with elections allowing men of the units to choose new officers and noncommissioned officers. The Ninth Texas Cavalry Regiment staged its elections in early May, 1862, with Maj. Nathan W. Townes—a fellow attorney of Dohoney's from Paris, who also had opposed secession—winning election to the regiment's top post of colonel. Lt. James C. Bates, Dohoney's close friend from Paris, won election to the rank of captain in Company H. Dohoney, who already had risen from lieutenant to captain, initially held back from the balloting. But on the day of the voting he decided to stand for election as lieutenant colonel and lost out to Dudley W. Jones. Bates wrote home saying, "too much caucusing & wire working had been done [by others] before he [Dohoney] announced himself." In another letter, he said Dohoney "would have been elected, I think, if he had announced himself a week sooner."[137]

The Conscription Act provided that officers who failed to win re-election at the time of the reorganization would be free to leave the regiment. Dohoney prepared to return to Paris.[138] But before he did so, word came to him of the hanging of the Hembys and Howards. He was outraged at the deaths of five men he had known and respected and said he "hoped that he would live through this unfortunate war and have the privilege of prosecuting the leaders of this mob for murder."[139]

CHAPTER 3

Hangings in Hunt
and Hopkins Counties, 1863

The hanging of the Hembys and Howards proved a harbinger of more deaths to come in the Forks watershed. During the remainder of 1862, however, the region was on the fringe of vigilante actions, the most notorious of which occurred to the west of the Forks watershed, centered on Gainesville in Cooke County. Early in September, 1862, slaveholders there uncovered the existence of a Peace Party composed of Union-minded men. Many party members subsequently were arrested and tried during kangaroo court proceedings. Historian Richard B. McCaslin thinks that few of the Peace Party members posed any real threat to the Confederacy. Nevertheless, at least forty-three were killed—forty-one by hanging—in October, 1862, during the "Great Hanging at Gainesville," which has been termed "the largest incident of its kind in United States history."[1]

The hue and cry that accompanied the Gainesville proceedings reached beyond Cooke County, and a couple of those hanged may have been residents of the Sulphur Forks watershed. However, even before the Peace Party affair began coming to light, Confederates in the Forks watershed were having their own suspicions about some of the area's residents. A number of these suspect individuals were men associated with Martin D. Hart of Hunt County.[2]

Members of the Hart family have popped up in northeast Texas history since at least 1823, when John F. Hart came to the area from Indiana on a trapping expedition. Hart lost most of his gear to raiding Indians but still managed to turn a profit by carving himself a sixty-foot dugout from a cottonwood tree and using it to float a load of furs down Red River and the Mississippi to New Orleans. Some years later, he settled in Fannin County, where a nephew who also was named John figured in the story that gave Jernigan's Thicket its name; when Curtis Jernigan came stumbling out of the thicket after his long wandering ordeal, he was taken to the home of John Hart, his brother-in-law, to recover.[3]

By the time of the Civil War, Harts were legion in the Sulphur Forks watershed. These included Harts who had come down from Illinois and settled in Hunt County's Wieland community. A number of these Harts sided with the Confederacy, but most other Harts in the area sided with the Union.[4] They included Jonathan "Fox" Hart and James C. "Jim" Hart, sons of Jonathan "Jackie" Hart. Jackie, thought to have been a cousin of John F. Hart, settled in the southwestern Forks delta section of then-Hopkins County (present-day Delta County near the Needmore community).[5] The region's other Unionist Harts included Martin D. Hart, a son of John F. Hart, who grew to adulthood in Fannin County along with his seven-years-older brother Hardin Hart and other siblings.

Martin, who was born around 1821 in Indiana, came to the state around 1833 when his father opened a store in Jonesborough (also spelled Jonesboro), a community in present-day Red River County that drew some of Texas' first Anglo-American settlers. In 1836, after the Texas Revolution erupted, John Hart recruited a company from the area called Hart's Mounted Men and took fifteen-year-old son Martin along on the ride south while elder son Hardin watched the store. The company of Captain Hart—as he was ever after called—arrived at San Jacinto too late to take part in the fighting.[6]

In 1837, not long after Hart's Mounted Men returned home, the Hart family moved to the community of Warren. Now in Grayson County but then in Fannin County, the community on the south side of Red River would serve as the seat of justice for Fannin from 1840 until 1843, when Bonham (formerly called Bois d'Arc), was named the county seat. At the time the Harts arrived in Warren the region suffered from periodic Indian attacks, thought to have been carried out by bands to the west. Area men responded with a series of punitive raids against tribes in the Trinity River area over the course of several years, including a ninety-man raid led by Capt. John F. Hart in April, 1838—during which the captain took several scalps—and a ranging patrol led by Hart toward the end of the same year. While several other family members participated in one or more of these expeditions, it is not known whether Martin went along.[7] Perhaps he was

Martin D. Hart. From Wm. DeRyee, Texas Album . . .
Eighth Legislature, 1860. Courtesy Texas State
Library and Archives Commission, Austin.

already busy with studies; records from 1839, when he was eighteen, show him to have been enrolled at a log-cabin school that furnished education to its nine students using an arithmetic, a grammar, a speller, the New Testament, a biography of Methodist preacher John Nelson, *Pilgrim's Progress,* and *Fox's Book of Martyrs.*[8]

The Harts were not slaveholders—in keeping with the family's Upper South background in Kentucky and the Midwest—but the slaveholder presence was very strong in Warren. The founder of the community, which grew up around an abandoned stockade, was slaveholder Daniel Montague, who "became the first surveyor of the Fannin Land District, and by the customary practice of accepting fees in land accumulated a vast estate." People came from afar to attend Daniel Montague's huge, two-day Fourth of July Ball in 1839 to celebrate the completion of the host's new house, which was the most luxurious in the area. For the huge celebration slaves "busied themselves preparing chickens, turkey, pigs, and all kinds of wild game in every manner known to backwoods culinary practices," and once the guests arrived they drank "liquors of every variety from persimmon beer to 'Ohio' whiskey."[9]

The business dealings of Martin's father not only involved Montague but also two more of the area's wealthiest slaveholders, Holland Coffee and Silas Colville of Coffee, Colville, and Company, traders. Around 1837, Coffee and Colville developed land in the Preston Bend area of present-day Grayson County (then in Fannin). The same year, John F. Hart and a couple of partners laid claim to land in the same vicinity. When a dispute arose, Hart insisted that he and his partners "built three cabins on the land, cleared and cultivated four acres, then leased the place to John F. Moody, who abandoned the property without warning." Upon Moody's departure, Holland Coffee took possession. Also, Hart claimed, he had directed Basil Cason to survey the land, "but Daniel Montague, the county surveyor, would not enter Cason's papers as being official."[10]

Hart sued Coffee for title to the disputed land but lost. He later met Coffee's partner, Silas Colville, at Warren, where a fight ensued and Hart was shot to death on May 1, 1841. In a letter to his brother-in-law in Tennessee, Colville wrote, "I acted on the defensive and Hart fell, a Victim [of] a misguided and overbearing disposition." Additionally, Colville said that many of Hart's relatives have a similar disposition. "They are a lawless Set and have always carried their points by violence. Since the affair between their leader and myself they have watched my path for an opportunity to assassinate me up to the time of my trial, since which time their anger has greatly subsided. Public opinion was so much in my favor that it seems to have cowed them." Colville continued his explanation by stating that on May 1 the trial was held, and the magistrate was Judge Terrell. "The trial was short but created a great deal of excitement. The friends of both parties were on the Court yard Armed and equipt (not according to Law but according to custom). The Verdict of the Jury and the Judge of the Court and the warm congratulations of the Spectators who were anxiously awaiting the Issue proclaimed me Justifiable."[11]

Justifiable, perhaps, but soon dead nonetheless. Colville was killed around 1844 on the road between Preston Bend and Warren. While the evidence pointed to renegade Indians as the killers, "many in the county seemed assured that the Hart brothers had had their final revenge."[12]

Martin D. Hart went on to sue Daniel Montague over his alleged failure to record Cason's survey of the disputed Preston Bend land but lost.

"Although the court upheld Montague, it is hard to suppose that the decision was just," Graham Landrum commented in his history of Grayson County. Landrum theorizes that Martin's bitterness toward this "personal injustice perpetrated . . . by the principal slaveholders of the county" may have played a part in his later actions toward slaveholders in Arkansas during the Civil War.[13]

Despite the setback of their father's murder and the loss of the Montague suit, Martin, Hardin, brother Free Liberty, and sister Rebecca—all children of John F. Hart's first wife—inherited a substantial amount of land after defeating a lawsuit by children of their father's second spouse, Prior Wallace Hart. They successfully claimed that the second wife "was a common law wife and her children not lawful heirs."[14] Much of the inherited land would be in Hunt County after Hunt was created from Fannin and Nacogdoches Counties in 1846.

During the latter part of the 1840s, Martin and Hardin moved to the Hunt County seat of Greenville, "which was then a mere urban possibility or expectation," and set themselves up as lawyers in "a small shanty" near the log-cabin courthouse.[15] Martin in particular prospered, domestically, professionally, and financially. He and Mary Green (sister of Hardin's wife Nancy) married in the early 1840s and had at least five children by 1860. Both Hardin and Martin were elected to terms in the legislature. Hardin served as state senator from 1849 to 1854, while Martin served as state representative in 1857–58 and as state senator during 1859–61. Martin's law practice was particularly successful. Many of his cases involved disputed land titles, and he frequently took a portion of the property involved as payment of his fee. By 1860, his substantial landholdings had made him one of the wealthiest men in Hunt County.[16]

Anecdotal evidence about Martin Hart points to an adventurous spirit and perhaps a tendency toward big talk as well. In the fall of 1853, several months after lawyer Alfred Howell arrived in Greenville from Virginia, he wrote home saying, "The attorney Martin D. Hart, who left here for El Paso a few days after I arrived here, returned yesterday evening. He tells many tales of murders, outrages etc., of every description and has had many narrow escapes from the Indians." By 1854, Howell had taken a dislike to Hart and characterized him as "an unpopular trickster." But the following year, Howell revised his opinion, saying Hart, a lawyer "noted for his trickery and cunning," had had a bad reputation for a while "but for many months he has been laboring to overcome it and has succeeded in gaining considerable popularity." Howell was free with derogatory opinions about many men, including Martin's brother Hardin, whom he termed "an ignoramus."[17] It also should be noted that Howell and the Harts were professional rivals, and Howell's comments about them must be taken with a grain of salt. But it is also worth noting that Howell's characterization of Martin as somebody noted for "trickery and cunning" surely would be regarded by many—then as now—as high praise for a lawyer.

Martin Hart opposed secession in public speeches before the break with the Union and was among signers of the anti-secession "Address to the People of Texas." But it must have appeared to many in Hunt County that he had resigned himself to serve on the side of the Confederacy when he formed a company of cavalry at Greenville in June, 1861. In a written communication, Hart tendered the services of this "Greenville Guard" to the governor "in defense of Texas when ever she is threatened with invasion."[18] Like many volunteer companies in those times, however, this one apparently was short-lived. Many members soon went on to join other Confederate units; none are known to have taken up the Union flag along with Hart.[19]

Martin Hart stayed in Hunt County for more than a year after he formed the Greenville Guard. By the following summer, however, the unit most likely had dissolved, for Hart was by then occupying himself with recruiting men to the cause of the Union. Perhaps he had already conceived the idea of forming a Union cavalry company. Or perhaps he was a member of the Peace Party and, like many Peace Party members in the Gainesville area, simply hoped to associate with like-minded men for protection against abuses by local Confederates. Whatever might have been the case, Hart and his friends may have been goaded into action when Confederates became suspicious of some of those men whom Hart recruited, and possibly Hart himself. News of the Confederates' suspicions leaked to Hart and the others before any arrests could be made, however. Soon afterward, in August, 1862, Hart and his followers—thirty-seven of them by his widow's later count—took to the saddle and rode northeast, with Hart in the lead.[20]

Hart and his men stopped at Fort Smith, Arkansas, then held by Confederates, and obtained commissions to raise a Confederate company to operate in northwest Arkansas. The group then used these commissions to pass through a Confederate outpost to the north, traveling on from there into Union-held territory in Missouri.[21] In Springfield, Hart and some of the men accompanying him applied to the Union commander

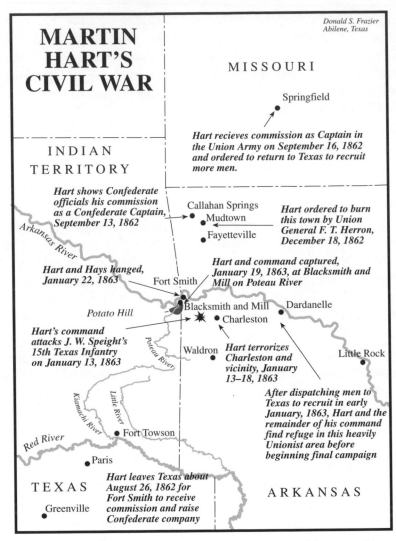

MARTIN HART'S CIVIL WAR

Donald S. Frazier
Abilene, Texas

MISSOURI

Springfield

Hart recieves commission as Captain in the Union Army on September 16, 1862 and ordered to return to Texas to recruit more men.

INDIAN TERRITORY

Hart shows Confederate officials his commission as a Confederate Captain, September 13, 1862

Arkansas River

Callahan Springs
Mudtown
Fayetteville

Hart ordered to burn this town by Union General F. T. Herron, December 18, 1862

Hart and Hays hanged, January 22, 1863

Fort Smith

Hart and command captured, January 19, 1863, at Blacksmith and Mill on Poteau River

Potato Hill

Blacksmith and Mill
Charleston

Dardanelle

Hart's command attacks J. W. Speight's 15th Texas Infantry on January 13, 1863

Poteau River

Waldron

Hart terrorizes Charleston and vicinity, January 13–18, 1863

Little Rock

Kiamachi River

Little River

Fort Towson

After dispatching men to Texas to recruit in early January, 1863, Hart and the remainder of his command find refuge in this heavily Unionist area before beginning final campaign

Red River

Paris

TEXAS

Greenville

Hart leaves Texas about August 26, 1862 for Fort Smith to receive commission and raise Confederate company

ARKANSAS

Martin D. Hart's movements between August, 1862, and January, 1863, conflict in academic articles, personal recollections, and family affidavits. Map by Donald S. Frazier.

and received Union commissions, with Hart as captain. J. W. Hays of Illinois joined the group as Hart's lieutenant.[22]

News of Hart's band was not long in arriving back in the Forks watershed. Residents who had been fearing imminent invasion for a year saw Hart and his men as yet another threat. E. L. Dohoney, who had left the Ninth Texas Cavalry and was back in Paris by this time, wrote a friend in

November expressing fear of "the two Armies of invasion that are to be led in on us very soon. Viz one by Jack Hamilton by way of the East & one by Martin Hart from Kansas. The aforesaid Hart some two months since escaped from Hunt County with 40 or 50 new conscripts & scoundrels from Hunt, Hopkins, Fannin &c & got to the Federal Army—drawing rations as he went from the Confederate Commissaries in the [Indian] Nation. And it is reported that he is proposing to lead an Army into northern Texas. And by the way there is little to prevent their coming if they are [of] a mind to do so."23

On December 6, soon after Dohoney wrote his letter, the *Dallas Herald* published an item that provided additional cause for alarm in northern Texas. "Martin D. Hart, late Senator from Hunt & Fannin, who left Texas some time since, with 35 or 40 tories, has arrived at St. Louis, Mo. & in a speech there stated that all that was needed, was for an abolition army to make its appearance in Texas, to be warmly welcomed by thousands."24

❧❧

Judging by subsequent events, Martin D. Hart operated under two different sets of orders. Under one set, he was to recruit other Union-minded men back in his home territory of Texas. The plan was ambitious. Hart's Company, as the original thirty-man unit was called, was far below the standard company strength of around a hundred men. But Hart and/ or the Union officers who gave him his orders apparently envisioned him recruiting enough additional men to fill some ten companies, making up what was to be known as the First Texas Cavalry Regiment. To carry out this first set of orders, Hart directed part of his unit to return to the Hunt County area and recruit more Texans. According to the only available evidence—a postwar application for a Union pension by the widow of one of Hart's men—this detachment set out for Texas on January 9, 1863, and arrived there around January 25.25

Meanwhile, Captain Hart, Lieutenant Hays, and ten or so remaining members of the company engaged in guerrilla operations in Arkansas while picking up additional recruits among the Arkansans. These guerrilla activities were carried out under orders of Union general Francis Jay Herron, who in December wrote Hart two letters (later found on Hart when he was captured). General Herron ordered Hart to operate against Confederate guerrillas in northwest Arkansas, especially the notorious James Ingraham, or Ingram. According to historian Leo E. Huff, "This cunning and almost illiterate guerrilla harassed the Federals in the Fayetteville area by constantly ambushing their trains and mail carriers. Numerous detachments of loyal Arkansas troops were sent after Ingraham, but he always evaded them."[26]

General Herron ordered Captain Hart to take no prisoners (except the hated Ingraham, if it was possible to catch him), to burn a town where Union mail carriers had been fired upon, and to show no mercy to bushwhackers. Herron's hard-line policy was characteristic of those for both Union and Confederate operations in northwest Arkansas.[27]

In addition to operating against guerrillas, Hart's band also acted against regular Confederate units. In early January, 1863, the company carried off a successful action against the rear guard of a Confederate infantry brigade commanded by Col. Joseph W. Speight, capturing twenty Confederate soldiers (subsequently released on parole), confiscating slaves and mules, and attempting to destroy wagons and corn. Gen. William Steele, commanding Confederate troops in the area, reported that "This lawless band is under the command of one Martin D. Hart . . . who now represents himself as a captain in the First Texas Regiment (Federal). I am satisfied that communication is being kept up between Hart and Abolition sympathizers in Northern Texas, and it is possible that, should he conceive himself strong enough, he may attempt to push his raid into that section."[28]

In addition to targeting Confederate guerrillas and regular military units, Hart's Company directed some attacks at civilians. Accounts of these deeds must be regarded with wariness. The authors all sided with the Confederate cause, and their views may be inferred from one memoirist's characterization of Captain Hart and Lieutenant Hays as "soulless rogues"[29] and another's characterization of Hart as a "blood-thirsty biped."[30] Historian Cecil Harper has taken a skeptical view of reports about outrages against civilians allegedly committed by Hart's Company, saying "there is absolutely no evidence to support the contention that he and his men were engaged on a regular basis in 'a career of rapine and plunder.'"[31] Nevertheless, there seems little doubt that members of the company did commit some crimes against civilians. These occurred in the vicinity of Charleston, Arkansas, some thirty miles southeast of Fort Smith, around January 12 or 14—apparently, several days after the Texas detachment had left for home.[32]

The acts in question occurred on several plantations, with planters Edward Richardson and DeRosey Carroll being called from their homes, shot, and killed. It is said that men whom Hart had recruited in the area, including one named McGoing, had grudges against the planters. McGoing "seemed to have a bitter hatred for all slave holders and two or three days before the death of Col. Carroll had stated that he would rather go into the woods and maul rails at 50 cts. per day than go into the war, but, if he had to take any part, he [would] devote his operations to killing every slave owner in the country."[33] McGoing and Lieutenant Hays may have fired the shots that killed Carroll, while Hays alone may have pulled the trigger on Richardson. According to one man's recollection, Captain Hart would later say he had ordered the shooting of both men.[34]

Some other plantation owners managed to save themselves by fleeing before Hart's Company arrived at their property. In another case, the Union guerrillas found Judge Thomas Aldridge at home on his plantation, but Hart told Aldridge he would allow him to live because he had been told by men on both sides of the war that Aldridge was "a mighty good man."[35]

The killings of Richardson and Carroll soon became notorious in Arkansas, and news of them also spread back to Texas. Alexander Cameron of Hunt County, who was serving in Arkansas with the Confederate Thirty-first Cavalry Regiment in January, 1863, mentioned the killings and Martin Hart in a letter home, saying, "he [Hart] had two citizens killed in the Country because they had been Strong Secessionists."[36]

Varied theories have emerged about the killings. Historian Thomas E. Jordon believes the Arkansans who joined Hart steered him into banditry and that he "lost control of his men."[37] Historian William F. Sawyer has expressed a slightly different view, saying, "Hart ordered such men as Richardson and Carroll murdered" to please the Arkansans, in the belief that doing so would cause them "to serve him better."[38]

There may be truth in both of these views. But it is also possible that Hart himself was possessed by the same hatred for slaveholders that filled his Arkansas men. Possibly he developed such feelings of enmity back in Texas as a result of conflicts between his family and leading slaveholders in the Fannin-Grayson area. Also, Hart's exposure to the vicious guerrilla war in northwest Arkansas may have had a brutalizing effect on him. As Huff has described, the area was the site of guerrilla operations where "no quarter was asked and none was given," a war "characterized by murder, arson, robbery, pillage and ambush."[39] Numerous guerrilla bands, both Union and Confederate, operated there, and acts of atrocity, many of them against civilians, were common. It was a war that eventually drove much of the populace out of the area, leaving desolation behind that was described by a newspaper correspondent in 1866. The correspondent wrote that "wasted farms, deserted cabins, lone chimneys marking the sites where dwellings have been destroyed by fire, and yards, gardens and fields overgrown with weeds and bushes are everywhere within view. The traveler soon ceases to wonder when he sees the charred remains of burnt buildings, and wonders rather when he beholds a house yet standing that it also did not disappear in the general conflagration. Such was the terrible intensity of the recent civil war."[40]

The level of hatred generated by the conflict is nowhere better illustrated than in comments an elderly woman made to Confederates who took to the trail in pursuit of Hart's Company after the Charleston raid. Maj. A. V. Reiff, one of the Confederate officers, said the woman mistook his group for "Kansas Jayhawker" allies of Hart. In response to their greeting, "the old lady replied, 'Yes, God bless you, Captain Hart and his company passed today. He said that they had killed old Carroll and Richardson at Charleston. That's right, boys, just wring their necks wherever you find them.' She emphasized this . . . remark by giving her hands a wringing motion as if she was wringing the neck of a chicken."[41]

The woman also provided an interesting description of Hart, whom she said was not traveling on horseback, as might have been expected, but was in a buggy, with a pretty mulatto woman for a companion—a "nice yaller gal"—and with his feet up on a stove.[42]

⋘⋙

The pursuit of Hart's Company was led by Lt. Col. R. P. Crump of the Texas First Cavalry Regiment, Partisan Rangers, under difficult conditions; when the Confederates set off on January 16, they had to cope with tired horses and snow on the ground.[43] But Crump's advance guard of six men, led by Major Reiff, hit on a piece of luck. They were able to persuade a local Union man that they were Union cavalrymen from Kansas who were trying to join Hart. The Unionist, named Phelps, agreed to lead the troops to Hart.[44]

The Confederates arrived at the Hart's Company camp, an old mill and blacksmith shop on the Poteau River, around two o'clock in the morning on January 17 and laid plans to surround the property, then attack. Confederates who met each other in the dark were to ask, "Who are you?" and to reply to that question with "Carroll"—after the planter of that name slain near Charleston.[45] In the assault that followed, said A. B. Lewis, who was with the attackers, the Confederates killed one man and captured "Hart and seven Texans," along with "nine renegade Arkansas men."[46] Hart's female traveling companion, Milly Burnside of Fayette-ville, also was captured, while two men escaped barefoot in the snow.[47]

News of the capture provided an occasion for rejoicing among Confederates back in Texas. Under a headline that announced "Capture of the Traitor Martin D. Hart, with Twenty Three Men," the *Marshall Texas Republican* proclaimed: "Hart, it will be remembered, was a unionist of the stripe of which we have a few unblushing specimens yet left in our State, who venture to the very borders of open treason, and with whom, when lately a citizen, he affiliated. . . . He and his twenty-three followers have fallen into hands that will make short work of them."[48]

Captain Hart and Lieutenant Hays were taken to Fort Smith, tried, and sentenced to be hanged on January 22. The day of the execution, they were allowed final comments. "Lieutenant Hays was first to speak. He was unnerved, shed copious tears, and could scarcely talk. With choking sobs, he begged for mercy, pleading his youth and the awfulness of such a doom." However, "Captain Hart exhibited no fears of death. He stated that he alone assumed responsibility for all that he had done. He said that he had nothing to ask for himself. He added that he had taken his chances and was ready to meet his fate. He asked leniency for his men since they merely obeyed his orders."[49]

The hanging of Hart and Hays went ahead following the speeches; other members of Hart's command were sent to Little Rock to prison. The execution of the two officers and imprisonment of other members of the troop was in keeping with standard practice. As Huff has noted, "It was customary for both Federal and Confederate authorities to summarily execute notorious guerrilla leaders when they were captured. . . . Unless caught in the act of committing a crime, the privates of a guerrilla band sometimes were imprisoned rather than executed, as it was considered that these poor, misguided souls had been deceived by their leaders."[50] But some of these poor souls apparently did not live to reach the Little Rock prison. Local historian T. A. Pettigrew of Charleston, Arkansas, told L. L. Bowman in a 1932 letter, "I have been informed by parties who were part of the company that captured Capt. Hart and his men that [the enlisted men] were delivered to a company of Missouri soldiers who were noted for not letting prisoners escape, to escort to Little Rock, and it was reported that some of them attempted to escape and were killed."[51] What happened to Hart's traveling companion, Milly Burnside, is not known.

As for Hart and Hays, they were buried with little ceremony near the place of execution. After the war, their bodies were removed to the National Cemetery at Fort Smith, but the rehabilitation of their names began even earlier, following the Union occupation of Fort Smith in September, 1863. On January 16, 1864, under the title "Honor to Capt. Hart and Lieut. Hays," the *Fort Smith New Era* lauded "these patriotic adventurers in the cause of their country [who] suffered death by the hands of vile traitors then in authority at Fort Smith."[52]

⋖⊶⊷⊷⊶⊷⊷⊶⊷⊷⋗

About twenty men are believed to have been in the detachment that set off for Texas before Hart and the others were captured.[53] Some of these men, too, were fated to die at the end of a rope. Before the spring of 1863 was out, vigilantes in Hunt and Hopkins Counties would capture and execute at least nine men, including six or seven who were alleged to be members of Hart's Company. This deadly campaign may have been incited, in part, by the arrival in Texas of a "young man" whose relatives had been killed by Hart's Company and who was said to have trailed members of the company to Texas seeking revenge.

Hicks Nowell of Hunt County, who was about fifteen years old in 1863, recalled that the Young Man said Hart's band "had tied his father and mother up by their toes to make them tell where their money was hidden and when they had told that the band had murdered them." Witnesses' accounts from Arkansas mention no such crimes. However, such stories of atrocity may have helped spark the hue and cry after Hart's men in the Sulphur Forks watershed.[54]

As for the possible identity of the Young Man, at least two young relatives of men killed by Hart's Company are known to have sought and exacted vengeance in Arkansas. The two were Charlie Carroll, son of the murdered DeRosey Carroll, and Callie (or Carroll) Armstrong, DeRosey Carroll's nephew. On the day Hart and Hays were executed in Fort Smith, the doomed men were forced to stand, each on his own coffin, in a wagon while Charlie Carroll stood facing them with one foot on each coffin. Callie Armstrong, for his part, climbed out onto a tree limb that extended above the coffins. He tied two ropes to the limb, then remained on his perch as the nooses were placed on the necks of the condemned men and the wagon was driven from beneath their feet.[55]

Perhaps it was one of these two men who followed up the hangings with a trip to Texas in search of further vengeance.

Almost certainly, there was no "tracking" involved. The Young Man would have had a well-marked road to follow. He almost certainly traveled on the most direct route linking Arkansas and Texas—a major roadway that ran from Fort Smith to Fort Towson in Indian Territory, then crossed Red River to connect up with the Central National Road of the Republic of Texas, which passed through Paris and on into Hunt County where, the Young Man would have known, Hart's band had been organized. He also might well have known which individuals to seek. Some accounts mention that Confederates in the Forks watershed possessed a muster roll of Hart's Company that was taken from Captain Hart at the time of his capture. It is possible that the Young Man was the person who brought the list to the area.[56]

It is easy to visualize the Young Man going among Hunt County residents showing such a list. In looking it over, the local residents would have spotted the names of men well known to them. Perhaps they also recalled seeing some of these men in or around the property of a Hunt County farmer and minister known as "Parson" Glenn, setting in motion one of the first known events of the vigilante campaign of 1863.

Austin H. Glenn was born in 1802 in Surry County, North Carolina, one of ten children of Thomas and Ann (Speer) Glenn. After growing to manhood, Austin married Rhoda Turner, who was born in 1806 in Surry County, and they soon migrated along with many other members of the Glenn family to Monroe County, Tennessee. There, eleven children were born to Austin and Rhoda between 1829 and 1847, during which time Austin farmed and also was active as a minister—of the Methodist Episcopal Church, it is thought. Monroe County records show he presided at a number of weddings during the 1840s and early 1850s.[57] But many members of the Glenn clan soon felt the need to pull up stakes once again. Some of Austin's kin migrated to southern Illinois, while Austin and Rhoda moved to Hunt County, Texas, arriving there along with several sons and daughters by 1858.

According to one story, three early pioneer families of the Forks watershed did not own a single pair of scissors among them and had to cut cloth with a butcher knife. The Glenns may have lived in similarly rugged conditions, which were common in the area. But the Glenns were set apart from many in the community in at least one respect: education. Austin took the lead in teaching the children to read, and a large number of them would go on to adopt literate professions in adulthood, including one who became a doctor, at least three who taught school, and one who became a minister.[58]

It is said that Austin was opposed to slavery, which suggests that he allied himself with the northern, anti-slavery branch of the Methodist church, and other family members may have held like views. But such unanimity, if it existed, did not translate into agreement about the war, on which the Glenns, like so many families, were divided. On October 12, 1861, son Thomas Tyre Glenn, a physician, enlisted at Sulphur Springs in Company G of Maxey's Ninth Texas Infantry Regiment as a lieutenant and assistant surgeon. Meanwhile, daughter Missouri Ann Glenn had married a Hunt County man named Joseph H. Ball who also served with the Confederacy; she apparently supported his choice. But three of the Glenn sons cast their lot with the Union: Joseph Wilson Glenn, who would join in late 1863; James H. Glenn, said to have joined the Union army around the same time; and Austin H. Glenn, Jr., who signed on with a Federal unit in the summer of 1862.[59]

Austin, Jr., who is of particular interest, was about twenty-two when he enlisted as a private in Company A of the Eighth Missouri Cavalry (USA) and was "detailed as a spy in John Jenkin's Company of Scouts or Spys," according to his postwar pension application. The pension papers show Austin, Jr., in Arkansas in 1862, but Glenn lore places him with the family in Hunt County in the spring of 1863. If both pieces of information are correct, Austin Glenn, Jr., of the Eighth Missouri Cavalry may have met up with Hart's Company—which was organized in Missouri—and returned to Texas with its detached members in January, 1863. It is also possible that some other member of the Glenn family may have been part of Hart's Company; the activities of Austin, Jr.'s slightly older brother Joseph and slightly younger brother Robert are unaccounted for during this time. A link between one or more Glenn sons and Hart's Company is speculative but provides a possible explanation for an otherwise baffling development: that some of Hart's men went to the Austin H. Glenn, Sr., farm upon their return from Arkansas.[60]

According to one account, Hart's men used the farm, located about five miles north of Lone Oak, as a storage place for arms captured in Arkansas, some of which they hid on the premises. According to another account, Austin, Sr., aided an injured member of the Hart's Company detachment, hiding him in his barn and treating his wound. These activities did not go unnoticed by local Confederates. Hunt County men who organized themselves into a vigilante band staged a raid on the farm and, it is said, discovered the hidden weapons.[61]

Most of Hart's detached men who had been on the premises apparently were either gone from the place by that time or somehow managed to escape during the raid. But the elder Glenn, then about sixty-one, was captured by the raiders, whom daughter Rhoda would describe years later as bushwhackers.[62]

Around the same time, the vigilantes arrested a man recalled as "Trace Chain" Smith. Since accounts do not make any mention of the circumstances of his arrest or any special allegations against him, it is possible he was arrested along with Glenn on the Glenn farm.[63] The identity of Smith remains uncertain, although it is possible he was a Thomas Smith who was mustered into the militia company for Hunt County, Precinct 9, on July 19, 1861, along with a couple of the Glenns. Thomas Smith's name appears next to that of J. H. (James) Glenn, and near that of A. H. Glenn (presumably Jr.) on the roll, which is non-alphabetical and where placement of names may point up special relationships between men—for example, that those listed adjacent to each other might have arrived at the mustering session together.[64]

After their capture by the vigilantes, Smith and Glenn were taken to Dagley's Mill on the Cowleech Fork of the Sabine River. They were held there under guard for a while, but a mob overpowered the guard, took the two out, and hanged them. The date of the hanging is not known beyond the likelihood that it was around late February or early March, 1863.[65]

Glenn was buried on the Glenn farm, in the vicinity of the Prairie Valley community, according to family members. Smith was buried along with Glenn, Judge Bowman was told.[66]

Bowman placed the hanging site as "on the right side of the Mineola Branch of Katy at the edge of the bottom on the west side near where the Dagley Lake or slough now is located," a site south of the present-day community of Dixon, which is on U.S. Highway 69 six miles from Greenville in southeastern Hunt County. Jerry Green of the Hunt County community of Campbell, who has extensively researched the 1863 Hunt County hangings, said the site is north of Lone Oak, on the east side of the Cowleech Fork of the Sabine and north of U.S. 69.[67]

⟨⟩

Among the members of Hart's Company who remained on the loose was the man Austin H. Glenn, Sr., had treated at his farm. Thirty-three-year-old Horace DeArman was a member of an Upper Southern family that illustrates about as well as any the restless striving that lifted many of America's pioneers from spot to spot, carrying them ever west to the frontier. DeArman's parents, James and Polly DeArman, were in Rockcastle County, Kentucky, as the eighteenth century gave way to the nineteenth, but by 1823 they had moved their family to McMinn County, Tennessee, where Horace was born around 1828. The family had migrated to Benton County, Alabama, by 1833, but left there after 1840, possibly staying over in Arkansas a while before heading on to Navarro County, Texas, by 1850, and thence to Fannin County, near Garrett's Bluff, by 1860.[68]

It is said that others in Fannin County's DeArman family were supporters of the Confederacy. But in 1854, Horace married into the Hart clan, his wife being the Illinois-born Martha Hart, whose branch of the family resided in the southwestern Forks delta. If Horace was torn between the Union and Confederacy, his ties to the Harts may have been a deciding factor. In joining Martin D. Hart's cavalry troop, Horace became part of a group headed by his wife's cousin and whose members included at least two of her brothers.[69]

DeArman found his niche with the cavalry troop as its blacksmith. No doubt he got plenty of practice at shoeing horses in the job, but he nevertheless slipped up one day and seriously injured himself by driving a horseshoe nail into his knee. This was the injury that the Reverend Glenn is said to have treated while hiding DeArman in the loft of his barn.[70]

Before vigilantes closed in on the Glenn farm, DeArman and other members of Hart's troop slipped away to the northeast. Some fifteen miles distant, they went to ground in Jernigan's Thicket.

⬥⬥⬥

Military reports of hundreds of brush men within thirty miles of Bonham in late 1863 probably indicate that a large number of men already were hiding in Jernigan's Thicket by the spring of that year.[71] But the brush men may have been divided among a number of camps within the thicket. The Hart's Company men, who apparently camped separately from others, numbered about twenty men, according to one account.[72] Who most of them were, and what became of them, is unknown. Accounts mention only seven by name, these being Horace DeArman and six Hopkins County men whose homes lay near the southern edge of the thicket in what is now Delta County. The term "stockraiser" most likely provides the best description of all or most of them. They are thought to have been people who ran hogs, cattle, goats, and sheep in the rough country thereabouts, raising crops on the side.[73]

The men included DeArman's brothers-in-law, twenty-nine-year-old Fox Hart and twenty-four-year-old Jim Hart. These cousins of Martin D. Hart were the sons of the late Jackie Hart and his wife Synthia, who had immigrated to Texas from Tennessee, via Illinois, first settling in Fannin County in the 1840s and then moving to the Forks delta of Hopkins County after 1850.[74] The other men in Jernigan's Thicket were Fox and Jim Hart's near neighbors: Joseph D. Campbell, Thomas Greenwood, James Monroe Millsaps, and, according to some evidence, James's brother, Cicero Franklin Millsaps. Campbell and Greenwood were Upper Southerners, with Campbell hailing from Tennessee and Greenwood from Kentucky. The Millsaps brothers hailed from northern Georgia, which was sharply divided between the Union and Confederacy. Their ties to the Union were perhaps solidified by marriages into Upper Southern families; the family of James's wife had come to Texas from Tennessee, and the family of Cicero's wife came from Tennessee via Missouri.[75]

At least four of the men—Campbell, Greenwood, and the Millsaps brothers—had begun the war together in the summer of 1861 as ostensible Confederates when militia officials included their names on a muster roll for the state militia unit in Hopkins County's Beat No. 8. Unlike some muster rolls from this time, this one was not limited to men who attended a mustering session but was "a correct and true list of all those residing in said beat between the ages of eighteen and forty-five years."[76] However, Campbell, Greenwood, and the Millsaps brothers actually may have attended meetings of this militia unit, just as many other men with Union leanings were attending musters around this same time for state militia units or other local units in their areas—notably, James E. and Jonathan Hemby in the Forks delta's East End, several Glenn sons in Hunt County, and several Fitzgerald brothers in Titus County.[77] Some of these men may only have been responding to community pressure in joining such units, or they may actually have been willing to serve on the side of the Confederacy if their home county was invaded—but not otherwise—or they may still have been uncertain of their true allegiance.

The men who chose Jernigan's Thicket as their hideout in the spring of 1863 clearly did so on account of the thicket's proximity to many of their family members. Fox and Jim Hart's mother, the widowed Synthia Hart, resided nearby. Her daughter Martha—Horace DeArman's wife—may have been living with her, along with Martha and Horace's six-year-old son Jonathan J., since wives of soldiers often chose to wait out the war at their parents' homes.[78] Joseph D. Campbell's widowed mother, Rachel, lived just south of the thicket in a home where bachelor Joseph, thirty-one, had been head of household before the outbreak of war. Various other Campbell relatives also resided under this roof, all part of a clan that had immigrated to the area from Hickman County, Tennessee, in the 1850s.[79] Thomas Greenwood's wife and children also lived nearby. The

Kentucky-born Greenwood, forty-one, and his wife, Mary, thirty-five, apparently married in Illinois and had five children there before coming to the Forks delta in the late 1850s, where at least one other child had been born.[80] James Monroe Millsaps's homeplace also was in the vicinity of the thicket. Millsaps, thirty-one, was born in Jackson County, Georgia, and had come to Hopkins County with his parents in the late 1840s. In 1853, James married Algeretta Milholland, who was four years his junior, and they had two children.[81] Thirty-three-year-old Cicero Franklin Millsaps—thought to have been nicknamed "Tid"—and wife Emeline (Chafin) Millsaps lived near James in a household that sometimes also included an older brother, Jacob, as well as the Millsaps brothers' sixty-six-year-old mother, Minta, known as "Minky." The former Minta Vanderford had been a widow since her husband Jacob died sometime prior to 1850.[82]

Clearly, the Jernigan's Thicket fugitives were attempting to have the best of two worlds by staying out of the hands of the enemy while remaining in touch with their families. They no doubt depended on their families for food, but they may have hoped to watch over and protect them as well. With so many men hiding near their families, however, the fugitives' location may well have been a poorly held secret. Perhaps the brush men did not care. Perhaps they were counting on the size of Jernigan's Thicket to deter action by any vigilante group of ordinary size.

❦

The group that moved on Jernigan's Thicket sometime around the end of February or early March may well have been larger than the fugitives had expected. Hicks Nowell, who witnessed the vigilante operation at age fifteen, would later say he had never before seen so many men together in one place.[83] Almost certainly there still were not enough men to surround the whole huge thicket. But there apparently were enough to surround the southern section in which the Hart's Company men were hiding, with some vigilantes most likely being posted outside the thicket and others positioned along paths cutting through the brush.

Accounts do not mention how long it took for the fugitives to be starved down. Witnesses just say that they were and that the men finally agreed to negotiate. Fox Hart spoke for the brush men, while those chosen to negotiate for the vigilantes were well-known Hunt County men with ties to the fugitives.

One of these negotiators was William Jernigan (or Jernigin), brother of the Curtis Jernigan for whom Jernigan's Thicket was named. Bill, who was born in Giles County, Tennessee, in 1819, moved to Missouri in 1834 and later to Arkansas. He served in the Arkansas House of Representatives during 1854–55 before moving in 1856 to Texas, where his brother had preceded him. Bill Jernigan operated a store at the Hunt County community of Cow Hill. (The city of Commerce would later grow up around this store, after it was moved a short distance from its original site following the war.) Jernigan may have been chosen as a negotiator because he was related to the Harts—his sister Elvira was married to John Hart, a cousin to Fox and Jim Hart.[84] Others mentioned as envoys who negotiated with the fugitives were William Jernigan's business partner and future brother-in-law, Josiah "Cy" Hart Jackson (a partner in Jernigan's store for a while and also a cousin to Fox and Jim Hart), and Martin D. Hart's brother, attorney Hardin Hart of Greenville.[85]

The fugitives were understandably reluctant to surrender, but somebody came up with a proposition that seemed fair to some of them. The vigilantes would pick the names of a large number of men—either thirty-six or a hundred, according to different accounts—and the suspects would be allowed to choose a dozen men from the group to serve as their jury.[86] The agreement even went into detail as to who would serve as the men's guards if they gave themselves up. Hicks Nowell's father, Bernard Gilbert Nowell of Hunt County, was among those so chosen.[87]

The negotiators hammered out the last details of the agreement late one afternoon, and the fugitives put the matter up for debate among themselves that night. Some of the men said they were willing to give themselves up, but Fox and Jim Hart argued against it, saying they "would be signing their own death warrants" if they did. Later that night, the two Harts acted on their fears and succeeded in slipping through the vigilantes' lines. They made their way northwestward into Fannin County, where the Harts had many family members they could turn to for support.[88]

It is also possible that others, whose names are not recalled, fled along with the Harts. That left just four or five men in the thicket. After the sun rose, they gave themselves over to the vigilantes and also surrendered some weapons. One of the captives gave Bernard Gilbert Nowell his pistol and "gun" (probably shotgun), requesting that he pass them on to his sons when they got old enough to use them.[89]

Most accounts give the names of the men who surrendered as Joseph D. Campbell, Horace DeArman, Thomas Greenwood, and James Millsaps. But Hicks Nowell recalls that two Millsaps brothers surrendered, James and "Tid"—thought to have been James's older brother and near neighbor Cicero Franklin Millsaps. Some additional evidence also supports the idea that Cicero was among those who surrendered.[90] But if Cicero was among the prisoners, he may have escaped, disappeared, or been killed early on. Witnesses' accounts and other records agree that only four men were placed on trial by the vigilantes.

Just as the vigilantes who captured the Hembys and Howards made a logical choice in choosing the south side of Oxford's Bridge as a trial site, the vigilantes who captured the Jernigan's Thicket men made a logical choice in choosing a trial site. These vigilantes, too, departed from the Forks delta, with its numerous Upper Southerners and Unionists, hauling the prisoners into a stronghold of pro-Confederate sentiment: Sulphur Springs, home of the area's Knights of the Golden Circle. There, trial proceedings were organized at a house located a couple of blocks west of today's town square, on Main Street.[91]

Judge Bowman was told by Ras Hopper: "At this trial they had the muster roll or list of names from Martin D. Hart's papers taken from off of him when he was captured in Arkansas. They also had witnesses present from Arkansas to testify to the outrages committed there by Hart and his men." The Young Man was among these witnesses.[92]

Despite the agreement between the prisoners and vigilantes about jury selection, the staunch pro-Confederates among the vigilantes managed to "hand pick" the jurors, according to one account. Another account described the proceedings as a "mock trial."[93] After two days of testimony, jurors reached a verdict. O. M. Pate later said he was never able to forget the expression of surprise on the defendants' faces when the men were told of the jurors' decision: guilty.[94]

Bowman, in an account based on statements by Ras Hopper, described what came afterward:

These men were carried out from S.S. [Sulphur Springs] to the place of execution in two wagons. Two in each. They were seated on a board placed across the wagon bed. They were required to stand up on this plank and the noose was affixed and then the wagon driven out from under them. They first hung two of them and the other two sat in their wagon until they were pronounced dead and then the other two were executed. [Hopper] thinks Campbell and Millsaps were first executed. They were given an opportunity to talk. Campbell started to talk but his companion shut him up with the statement that he would haunt him beyond the grave if he did. He says that either DeArmond [sic] or Greenwood told them that his mother lived nine miles N.E. from Little Rock, Ark., and that he had never belonged to or joined Hart, that he had met him in Ark. and Hart had written his name down.[95]

Jeff Mason, another Hopkins County old-timer, gave Bowman a different account of the hanging, which he claimed was on March 18, 1863. Mason said the men were driven to the place of execution in a wagon, with each man seated on a coffin. He also recalled that Millsaps and DeArman, who were "bold and defiant," were hanged together, followed by Greenwood and Campbell. Bowman said Mason told him the executioners "drove the wagon under the limb of a tree, fixed the rope and noose and then drove the wagon out letting the men drop. That Millsaps and DeArmand as the wagon was driven out jumped as high as they could in order to break their own necks and die without strangulation if possible. The other two men died shaking hands and with hands clasped."

Mason said the site of the hanging was "just south of White Oak [Creek] between Old Tarrant and Sulphur Springs." (Hopkins County historian John Sellers places the site within today's Sulphur Springs city limits, on State Highway 19/154—Church Street—on the west side of the road about half a mile south of Loop 301, just south of 2007 Church Street.)[96]

However, a different sequence of events is given by William P. Petty. On April 8, 1863, the *Tri-Weekly Telegraph* of Houston, Texas, published a statement by Petty in which he claimed that the captured men were taken to Tyler and then returned to Sulphur Springs for trial and punishment. Petty wrote that the hangings occurred on March 27 (1863), near Sulphur Springs, and that "four men, members of Martin D. Hart's famous freebooting company, were hanged by the neck till they were 'dead, dead, dead.'" Petty reported that Colonel Earley (Early) of Fannin County led the prosecution and that the charge was "treason and complicity with a company of murderers and robbers."

Joseph D. Campbell's mother is said to have been the one who cut her son's body down. His death was one of four she had to endure during the war. Son Armsted and two sons-in-law, James Marrs and Charles Smoot, also died in the course of the fighting, according to family stories, although which sides they served on is not clear.[97] The hanged men were all buried near their families' homes, at what are now the Shiloh and Horton communities of Delta County.[98]

⊰⊱

Two weeks after the hangings, on Wednesday, the first of April, a doctor from the town of Tarrant journeyed eastward to Harrison County, where he had formerly resided, and stopped by the *Marshall Texas Republican* to visit with editor R. W. Loughery. The doctor gave Loughery a report about wheat prospects "on the prairies" that appeared in the *Republican* the following Saturday. He was probably also the source of an adjacent story in the same edition, an account of the hanging in March of 1863:

> Excitement and Hanging—We learn that considerable excitement exists in several of the Northeastern counties of this State, and particularly those of Hunt and Hopkins, growing out of the appearance in that section of some men belonging to the notorious Martin D. Hart. After the execution of Hart, a portion of his followers brought a lot of stolen property to Texas. It seemed that they found a few sympathizers who aided them in concealing it. Suspicion having been excited, search was made, and some of it was found on the premises of a preacher in Hunt county. Hart's men, having been scented out, took refuge in the Jernigan thicket. Two or three of them were subsequently captured in Hunt and hung. On Wednesday, the 18th ult., four others were hung in Hopkins county. They were all traitors to our cause, one of them having been formerly a resident of Titus county. Our informant states that they were accused of robbery, murder, and treason, were regularly tried before a jury of twelve men, selected from various counties; and before being executed, confirmed their guilt.[99]

The account errs in suggesting that the "two or three" men hanged in Hunt (Glenn and Smith) were captured in Jernigan's Thicket. Also, the article's contention that the doomed men "confirmed their guilt" before being executed is the suspect assertion of an ardently pro-Confederate newspaper that is not mentioned in other accounts. It is reminiscent of secessionists' claims—despite abundant evidence to the contrary—that the Rev. Anthony Bewley confessed to crimes before he was hanged.[100]

One of the discrepancies in this account is the stated date of the hanging. According to Greenwood's will, Thomas signed this document on March 25, 1863.[101] Because of the date of the will, the hanging may well have occurred on March 27, 1863, as the Petty article states, and not on

90

March 18, as the other statements, made after the turn of the century, suggest.

Another notable feature of the account is that it makes no mention of "the fifth man"—Cicero Franklin "Tid" Millsaps—whom Hicks Nowell said was captured in the thicket along with James M. Millsaps, Campbell, DeArman, and Greenwood. Nor did other old-timers whom Judge Bowman interviewed in the 1920s and 1930s make any mention of this man. Still, it seems possible that he was indeed among the captured, based on Nowell's account and civil lawsuits that would be filed following the war. Three suits were lodged against Elbert Early, one of the men indicted in the 1863 Hopkins hangings, by Emeline Millsaps, wife of Cicero; Minta Millsaps, mother of Cicero and James; and Rachel Campbell, mother of Joseph. Details of the suits have not survived. However, it seems likely that these were suits alleging wrongful death by Early.[102]

Some suppositions that fit these assorted facts are that Early was the prosecutor and thus considered by surviving family members to be the leader of the vigilantes and that the survivors held him primarily responsible for the deaths of James M. Millsaps and Joseph D. Campbell, by hanging, as well as the death of Cicero F. Millsaps (however that may have occurred). He was far and away the most prominent of those men later indicted, and he had a record as an Indian fighter and sheriff, which might have inspired others to look to him for leadership in a vigilante operation.

Early, who was born in Kentucky in 1811, spent some of his early years in Mississippi and Tennessee as a business partner of James Bourland, a man who would gain great notoriety after both Bourland and Early moved to Texas.[103] Bourland, who eventually settled in Cooke County, was the leader of the slaveholders who instigated and carried out the Great Hanging at Gainesville in the fall of 1862. He later served as colonel of an unusual Confederate regiment that operated on both sides of Red River, in Texas and Indian Territory, spending much of its time rooting out brush men. David Paul Smith has commented: "Bourland, once referred to as 'the hangman of Texas' for his participation in the Gainesville hangings, was a small, quick-tempered man known as a strict disciplinarian. He remained a controversial leader for as long as he commanded his regiment, known as Bourland's Border Regiment. The qualities that drove him to pursue disloyalists without mercy never left this man, whom one observer called 'a good fighter and a good hater.'"[104]

While Bourland went farther west, Early and his wife, the former

Mary Anne Dent, settled in 1839 just north of the western Forks delta at what was known as Fort Lyday, a stockade that had been built as protection against Indian attacks. Early, Bourland, and others were among area men who took part in the 1841 punitive raid against Indians of the Village Creek area, near the Trinity River, with Bourland serving as a captain of one group and Early as his lieutenant. Early also served a brief stint as sheriff of Lamar County, in 1844–45 (gaining the office in a roundabout way, by running for sheriff, losing, then being appointed to serve out the victor's unexpired term after the man resigned). Early's property was partially in Lamar and partially in Fannin, with his homeplace being in the Fannin section (near the present Dial community). He was carried on the Fannin County census roles, with the 1860 census showing him to have been one of the county's most prosperous farmers, possessing personal property worth $6,500 and land worth $25,000. A slaveholder, he served in 1861 as a Fannin delegate to the state Secession Convention, there casting his vote for secession. At least two of his sons and a son-in-law served with the Confederacy.[105]

⟨≈⟩⟨≈⟩

Among the men in Hunt County during the spring of 1863 were some who were derided by others in the community as "stay-at-homes." But the men, after banding together, did not allow the opinions of others to prevent them from choosing a name for their group that was full of boast: "Ten Stitchers," intended to signify the group's vow to kill ten of the enemy for every one of their own who was felled. These vigilantes went looking in northern Hunt County for other members of Hart's Company.

Some members of the Ten Stitchers, who were led by "old Doc Nicholson," may have borne a grudge against the Fitzgeralds because of an old feud between local families that grew out of a dispute over hay.[106] It is also possible that the vigilante group knew from the muster roll of Hart's Company that some local Fitzgeralds were members. For whatever reason, the Stitchers began to take an interest in the comings and goings of a civilian member of the family, Bradford Fitzgerald, who lived near the southern edge of Mustang Thicket.[107]

"Brad" Fitzgerald was one of about fifteen children of Anderson and Charity (Bailey) Fitzgerald, who had come to Texas in the 1840s following a dramatic departure from Tennessee that lives on in family legend, as recounted by family historian Beth Gunn in *The Fitzgeralds: From Tennessee to Texas*. As the Fitzgeralds prepared to leave Tennessee on a raft Anderson Fitzgerald had constructed, he sought to tie up loose ends by collecting outstanding debts. A skilled millwright, Anderson had constructed liquor stills—legal then—for many local men, including a man who was notoriously stingy and would not pay up. Losing patience, Anderson "cut branches to use for whips" and stationed himself beside a road used by the man: "When the man came along, Anderson proceeded to whip the man . . . until he had cut the man's hat into pieces. He hurried home, knowing the law would be after him, and loaded his entire family in the floating barge he had made and embarked on the Tennessee River—leaving Bradley County, Tennessee—down the Mississippi and [traveling up the] Red River, to East Texas and Cass County—not too far from Jefferson."[108]

Cass County, Texas, was a place not greatly like the Fitzgeralds' Tennessee homeland. Located on the Arkansas-Louisiana border, with good Red River access to cotton markets, it was cotton-slave country in the style of the deepest South, and strongly pro-secessionist. Sometime after 1850, the Fitzgeralds moved on westward, to Titus County, where the Upper South transplants' views must have been more like those they were accustomed to in Tennessee.[109]

Titus County, Hopkins County's neighbor on the east and later split among Franklin, Titus and Morris counties, was far from being solid for the Union. But Titus, unlike Cass, did have a strong Unionist element. Joshua F. Johnson, one of the "Immortal Eight" who voted against secession at the state Secession Convention in 1861, was a Titus County delegate. And when the people of Titus voted on secession on February 23, 1861, the margin of victory for the secession party was far from resounding: 411 to 285.[110] The Fitzgeralds, like the larger community, were deeply divided. Some Fitzgerald sons and some husbands of Fitzgerald daughters took the side of the Confederacy while others served on the side of the Union—and at least one Fitzgerald son gave service with the Union a try before casting his lot with the Confederacy. But the divisions were based less on ideology than expediency, according to one descendant, with varied circumstances putting them either on the side of the Union or the Confederacy.[111]

During the halcyon summer of 1861, however, when hard choices about loyalty lay in the future, the Fitzgerald family enjoyed a brief moment of apparent unity when six of Anderson and Charity's sons joined up with locally organized Confederate companies in Titus County. Eldest son William Fitzgerald became a second lieutenant in the Gray Rock Dragoons while next-oldest-son Pleasant R. "Plez" Fitzgerald joined as a second lieutenant in the local state militia company, called the Bell Rangers after its captain, E. E. Bell. Anderson Lafayette "Fate" Fitzgerald became a private in the Bell Rangers while three other sons—Wesley, James Star, and Bradford—became privates in the Gray Rock Dragoons. Two of the sons, Pleasant and Bradford, apparently were already living in Hunt County by this time but would have been within riding distance of Titus for drills.[112]

❦

Bradford "Brad" Fitzgerald, tenth child of Anderson and Charity, was born in 1837 in Tennessee and came with the family to Texas. On February 14, 1861, he married Sarah E. Stubbs, whose Tennessee-born parents, John and Elizabeth Stubbs, operated a farm in Hunt County just a mile southeast of Mustang Thicket, where the couple took up residence.[113] After the Ten Stitchers set up a watch on the farm, they were rewarded by the sight of Brad Fitzgerald leaving the property. It must have gladdened the vigilantes' hearts to note that he was not only heading toward Mustang Thicket but was carrying food—a near-certain tip-off as to his mission. The vigilantes trailed Brad into the thicket where they surprised him and four relatives, succeeding in capturing all four: brothers "Plez," "Fate," and James Star Fitzgerald, and Thomas Randolph, the Fitzgeralds' brother-in-law.[114]

Around the same time, a man whom witnesses recalled only as Newman was captured in the same vicinity, but across the line in Fannin County, on the Ransom Butler farm west of Leonard. Accounts do not provide a clue as to whether the Butlers might have been attempting to hide Newman or whether his capture on the Butler property was coincidental. At any rate, accounts do not indicate that any members of the Butler family were arrested.[115]

As for Newman, he may have been Martin V. Newman, whose Fannin County hometown of Ladonia was within about twenty miles of the place where he was captured. On February 26, 1863, Martin V. Newman was listed along with several hundred others in a newspaper account as Texans who had deserted in Arkansas after Union troops captured Fort Hindman (also called Arkansas Post). The time of the battles, January 4–12, was around the same time that the detachment of Hart's men headed for Texas. While Newman may have returned to his home area on his own, it seems possible that he threw in with the Hart detachment in Arkansas and rode back with them.[116] But it is possible the captured man may have been one of the many other Newmans in the area, including some who lived in Hunt County and others who lived in the vicinity of the Fitzgerald-Randolph clan in Titus County.[117] Interestingly, accounts do not mention that Brad Fitzgerald was taken prisoner. The vigilantes may have regarded kin helping kin as understandable and forgivable, even when the kin who received aid were among the enemy. However, Newman, Randolph, Plez Fitzgerald, Fate Fitzgerald, and James Fitzgerald were taken to an old barn and kept there under guard.[118]

Pleasant R. "Plez" Fitzgerald, age about thirty-eight, married Emeline Bunyan in Tennessee, and the couple joined the rest of the Fitzgerald family in Texas in 1852, moving on to Hunt County before 1860. By the fall of 1862, when Pleasant was among the group that set off northward with Martin D. Hart, the couple had six children and Emeline was carrying a seventh; their last child was born in January, 1863, about a month before Plez's return to Texas.[119] James Star Fitzgerald, a farmer who was about thirty, made the trip to Texas with his parents, after which he married Lydia D. Bray, another Tennessee native, in 1854 in Cass County; the couple later moved on with the other Fitzgeralds to Titus County, where twins were born to them in 1855.[120]

Anderson Lafayette "Fate" Fitzgerald, who was about twenty-one, made the move with the family to Cass and Titus Counties; in the spring of 1863, he remained a bachelor.[121] Thomas Randolph, age about thirty and a carpenter by trade, married Malinda Jane Fitzgerald in Tennessee, where they had a son, born around 1849, before they moved to Cass County by 1850. Later, they moved on with others in the Fitzgerald clan to Titus County where, by 1860, their family had grown to five children.[122]

Plez Fitzgerald, James Star Fitzgerald, Fate Fitzgerald, Randolph, and Newman, their hands tied, may have been kept in the barn for some days. During this time, James Fitzgerald is said to have had a "vision" that, if the prisoners could get away from the barn, they could escape from the area by passing through an "old fort" on the river. Fate, who had small hands, was able to work himself free of his bonds and untie James as well. Fate and James were unable to loose the bonds of Plez Fitzgerald, Randolph, and Newman but secured their own freedom by overcoming the guard, then rushing out of the barn and away. Their flight soon led them to a river, where an old woman told them that the main ford was being watched but that another, at the site of an old fort, was unguarded. They crossed there, fulfilling James's vision, and made their way to freedom.[123]

Sometime after this escape, Pleasant Fitzgerald, Thomas Randolph, and Newman were taken to Greenville and imprisoned. Frank B. Norris, who was about eighteen at the time and had taken part in the capture of Newman, recalled in 1929 that the three men were held in the log-cabin courthouse, which was about twenty feet square. He said the three captives "were tried right here in Greenville by the Ten Stitchers." Old-timer W. B. Horton told Judge Bowman that "the sentiment of the majority of the people was against hanging them." His statement hints at several possibilities: that substantial opposition to vigilantism existed in Greenville, that Unionist sympathies still remained here, and/or residents who disagreed with vigilantes were not afraid to speak their minds.[124]

Horton, who was about eighteen at the time, said that the men's accusers "could not prove any thing against them," which seems to indicate that questions of guilt or innocence actually may have been debated at Greenville under conditions resembling those of legally constituted courts. These proceedings apparently stood in sharp contrast with the Hemby-Howard trial, where men were compelled to testify with nooses around their necks, and the trial of Campbell, DeArman, Greenwood, and Millsaps, which witnesses characterized as a sham.[125]

As a result of the proceedings, Fitzgerald, Randolph, and Newman were not found guilty of the charges brought against them—presumably treason and other criminal acts, although no charges are specified in any accounts. The local residents apparently decided to regard the captives as military prisoners, for a decision was made to send the men to the Confederate army's prison camp at Tyler.

What some members of the community could not achieve through a trial, however, they achieved by force, with Fitzgerald, Newman, and Randolph meeting the same end as Glenn and Smith. Horton said the three prisoners were being transported to Tyler when "the mob run on" guard Bill Hefner east of Greenville, whereupon "Hefner throw up his job." Taking charge of the three captives, mob members "trid them with out Jury or Judge" and then "pull them [up] a tree and strangled them to death . . . all hung on one limb." Horton gave it as his opinion that "They ought to keep them as prisoners of war [but] at that time things was hot." He recalled that Newman's last words were "Farewell world, I am going home." What Fitzgerald and Randolph said was not recalled.[126]

Pleasant Fitzgerald's widow, Emeline, placed the date of the hanging as April 11, 1863. She said it occurred in timber about a mile from Greenville and that her husband was buried at the foot of the tree from which he was hanged. Judge Bowman was told that all the victims were buried at the same location, which he described as being on the west bank of the Sabine at the "old crossing" of the river. Jerry Green of Hunt County places the hanging site as "close to the Naud-Burnett Slaughter Barn or 'old slaughter barn' as it is known by locals." He said the site is located between Interstate 30 and the old Greenville Compress property.[127]

⟨⟩

Several months after the hangings in Hopkins and Hunt Counties, a family of refugee slaveholders arrived in the Forks delta from Louisiana.[128] The Stones, who had fled the Brokenburn plantation along with 130 slaves during the Union advance on Vicksburg, included the widowed Amanda Stone, twenty-two-year-old daughter Kate, and others, who took up residence at a hardscrabble farm Kate facetiously named "Elysian Fields," which was owned by a local "Mr. Smith" whom the Stones hired as overseer.[129] In her now-famous war diary, Kate wrote about her life in the Sulphur Forks area. "Here we are safely hidden in a dark corner of the far off County of Lamar after a tiresome, monotonous trip of less than three weeks, and I am already as disgusted as I expected to be. This part of the land abounds in white-headed children and buttermilk, my two pet aversions. It is a place where the people are just learning that there is a war going on, where Union feeling is rife, and where the principal amusement of loyal citizens is hanging suspected Jayhawkers."[130]

While the farm was in Lamar County, it apparently was very near the Hopkins County line—probably within just a few miles of the graves of Campbell, DeArman, Greenwood, the one or two Millsaps men, and the homes of the men's grieving families. On July 12, 1863, Kate wrote, "We hear no news now but accounts of murders done and suffered by the natives. Nothing seems more common or less condemned than assassination. There have been four or five men shot or hanged within a few miles of us . . . No one that we have seen seems surprised or shocked, but take it as a matter of course that an obnoxious person should be put to death by some offended neighbor."[131]

Disaffection with the Confederate military of the area also is reflected in her observations. In another diary entry the same month, she wrote: "A few evenings ago a captain in the army had just reached home on a furlough three hours before when he was shot at through his window. He was killed and his wife dangerously wounded. The authorities are trying to find the men who did it. It is supposed to be one of his company who vowed vengeance against him."[132]

Her comments abound with references to the extent of Union sentiment in the area. "Unionism is rampant about here," she says in one diary entry. "There was a company of Jayhawkers for the Federal side raised in this county"—a possible reference to Martin D. Hart's band.[133] Elsewhere, she reported, "We paid a three-day visit to Mrs. Slaughter up in the famous Union neighborhood, Honey Grove, where they say there is only one Confederate family. There, everyone you talk to says of course we will be conquered. In Louisiana one rarely heard such an idea expressed."[134]

⟨⊱⟩⟨⊰⟩

It seems probable that at least one other death had some connection with the 1863 hangings, if only because two of the parties involved were kin of the Fitzgeralds and Harts. The persons in question were Sarah "Sally" Fitzgerald and Cyrus "Cy" Hart. She was the daughter of the hanged Pleasant Fitzgerald, but it is not clear which of the area's many Harts were his relatives. Cy and Sally apparently married around 1861, when she was about fifteen.

On a day in 1863, so the story goes, the two "stopped their horses for water" at McGrew Creek in Hunt County and "a man raised up out of the bushes and shot" Cy. Sally "ran to get him a drink of water and he died in her arms."[135]

Whether this occurred before or after the hangings is not recalled, nor is there mention of the reason for the killing. Was Cy a member of Hart's Company, and was he killed by a vigilante? Or was Cy killed as a result of a feud that grew up between families of men who were hanged and the vigilantes who carried out the hangings? It remains yet another mystery.

⟨⊱⟩⟨⊰⟩

For those who had managed to survive the Hunt-Hopkins hangings of 1863, the scramble for security went on. Among them were Fox and Jim Hart, who apparently had found a good spot for hiding somewhere in Fannin County after escaping from Jernigan's Thicket; nearly a year after the escape, they were still in Fannin, still on the loose.

The heat must have been growing more intense for Unionists in the county by that time, however. In February, 1864, the Hart brothers were among local men who joined Dr. Eli S. Penwell of Bonham in planning an escape to the North. In addition to the Harts, members of the group included James W. Childs and his son, James Lovelace, Martin Lovelace, Will Shanklin, Dan Morrison, William Leachman, and probably Elbert

Drennan and Jack Rutherford, plus about a dozen "brush soldiers"—brush men—who came forth from hiding at the last moment.

Unfortunately, this latter group included one "Cap" Harris. He apparently was a double agent and told Confederate authorities of the group's plan to travel to the nearest Union stronghold of Fort Smith, Arkansas—which the Federals had occupied in August, 1863—and from there make their way to Illinois.[136] Owing to the spy's information, Confederate troops under the command of General Maxey in Indian Territory killed seven members of the party and captured Penwell and eight others. Four of the captured men were deserters from the Indian Territory, Maxey discovered. He ordered them executed by firing squad.[137]

The Harts made it through to Illinois. Jim lived out the remainder of his life in that state while Fox is thought to have spent the last years of his life in Scott County, Arkansas.[138] Others who made it through to Illinois included James and Martin Lovelace, William Shanklin, Elbert Drennan, and James Childs. Dr. Penwell, who was later released from captivity, gave escape from Texas another try the following year, via Mexico, and finally managed to make it to Illinois.[139]

⌖

Family lore has it that most of the Glenns packed up on the same day Austin H. Glenn, Sr., was hanged, departing from Hunt County the following morning. Eldest son Elias Turner Glenn, suddenly the family patriarch at age thirty-three, led the refugee party, which included his wife Lucinda, and children Austin T., John J., and Joseph W. Glenn. Elias had lived apart from his parents, on his own farm, as did his brother Robert Wilson Glenn, age twenty-eight, who also was in the refugee party along with his wife and their children, Mattie and Charles. Others in the group included the widowed Rhoda Turner Glenn; her teenage daughters Rhoda, Margaret, and Mary; and her sons Joseph, James, and Austin, Jr. Her daughter Missouri Ann Glenn Ball, whose husband Joseph Ball was in the Confederate army, elected to stay in Hunt County.[140]

The refugees "did not stop until the wagon broke an axle in Arkansas," according to family lore, but they eventually made their way to southern Illinois, where the Glenns had kin. En route, three members of the clan dropped out to join the Union army. On November 2, 1863, Austin, Jr., signed on as a Union scout and was sent into action in Arkansas, but he was hospitalized at Fort Smith on December 13 with "gunshot wounds to both shoulders." He managed to survive these wounds and a later gunshot wound in his hip as well. According to family lore, Austin's brother James also served with the Union army and survived the war, although no military records have been found for him. As for their brother Joseph Wilson Glenn, according to an undated Glenn family letter, he served as "a scout leading Steele into Little Rock" and "was killed there in 1863." Union general Frederick Steele occupied Little Rock on September 10, 1863; this death presumably occurred around that time.[141]

It is uncertain when the Glenns learned about yet another family death caused by the war, but the news may not have reached them until the family was in Illinois; Confederate lieutenant Thomas Tyre Glenn had been captured by Union forces at Danville, Kentucky, in 1862, was in ill health after being freed in a prisoner exchange, and died on January 20, 1863—several months before his father was hanged as a Union sympathizer.[142]

⋖⋗⋘⋙

Following their escape from the barn in the spring of 1863, James Star and Fate Fitzgerald may have taken refuge with family members or in some thicket for a while. Nothing is recorded about their whereabouts until late in the year, when both seem to have made firm choices about the courses they would follow during the remainder of the war—choices that placed the brothers on opposite sides.

Fate Fitzgerald made his way to Springfield, Missouri, and enlisted in November, 1863, as a private in Company E of the Union army's Fifteenth Missouri Cavalry. But Fate had left a sweetheart in Hunt County and was not a man to let the war stand between them. Some months after his enlistment on the Union side, he returned to Texas and slipped back into Hunt County. There, he and Mary Emma Henson were married on March 21, 1864, after which the two made their way together back to Missouri. Fate served for the remainder of the war on the Union side, being discharged at Springfield, Missouri, in May, 1865.

In the same month that Fate enlisted in the Union army, James Star Fitzgerald showed up in the Confederate army rolls, according to a letter from another Fitzgerald brother, Hiram, who was serving with Chism's Regiment in Louisiana. In a letter of November 13, 1863, to his wife, Emaline, back in Titus County, Hiram wrote that "James is hear with me. He is not stout. I dont no how we will stand the wintor for cold and wet wheather dos not agree with us." Apparently Hiram also was expecting Bradford—the Fitzgerald brother who had carried the food to Mustang

Thicket—to join them as well, for he told Emaline, "I hope that Brad will come by when he comes to the redgment."[143]

The military records on Bradford and James Star Fitzgerald are unclear as to their actual service, but Brad is said to have been wounded in the leg later in the war, which caused him to walk with a cane thereafter. As for James, it was said that he "would not shoot into the enemy line for fear of hitting a brother."[144]

✦ CHAPTER 4 ✦

"Blessed with Peace!"

WAR'S BITTER AFTERMATH

The Frank Chamblee home must have been very near Jernigan's Thicket, because family stories tell of him emerging from hiding there, then returning to the thicket after pulling the wool over his pursuers' eyes yet again. This was a pattern that continued even after war's end.

According to a story told by his widow Mary Ellen and retold by her grandson, Sterling Rodney Scroggins, Frank was enjoying being home with his wife in the spring of 1865, soon after the conclusion of the war. But one afternoon, as he was resting in the house and Mary Ellen was walking to the well, she spotted two of her husband's old enemies riding up the road. The men, whom Frank had humiliated over and over with his tricks, told her that they knew Frank was home and they were determined to stay on the premises until he came out and surrendered to them—war or no war.

As the men took up station on the grounds, Mary Ellen went about her business. They watched as the figure in long dress and bonnet passed with water pails between the well and the house, and the well and the barn, where some of the livestock was located. But finally, after several hours, Mary Ellen put down her pails, went out to the watchers and told them Frank was not there. She said they were welcome to search the premises, which they did, without result. Mary Ellen then invited the men to stay for supper, which they did, and then they thanked her and took their leave.

The men soon must have heard via the grapevine how they had been outwitted once again by Frank Chamblee.

Frank had installed a hidden trapdoor in the floor of the house. Upon learning from Mary Ellen that his pursuers were outside, he dropped through it, then crawled under the house and slipped from there out to the barn, keeping the house between himself and the watchers all the while. Mary Ellen, meanwhile, dressed herself in a double layer of two identical dresses and two identical bonnets. Then she walked to the well, filled the water pails and carried them to the barn, where she slipped out of the top dress and bonnet. Frank put them on, picked up the pails, walked down to the well, then ducked out of sight, slipped into the brush and headed back for Jernigan's Thicket. A short while later, Mary Ellen emerged from the barn, walked to the well, picked up the buckets Frank had left sitting there, and returned with them to the house. The deception—including the fact Mary Ellen had carried no buckets on the last trip to the well but had returned carrying some—passed unnoticed.[1]

In May, 1865, apparently within weeks of this feat, Ben Briscoe began asking around about the whereabouts of his old friend "Shamly," as he spelled the name, but heard nothing. Then one night he had a dream:

> I dreamed . . . that Shamly and I had been hard pressed all day. We went into an old log school house to get some rest. We lay down on the puncheon floor. As we were beginning to doze we heard guns firing and bullets hitting the logs. We got up, poked our pistols through the cracks and fired at the enemy. There seemed to be about twenty of them. I saw two or three of them fall. Then Shamly said, "Let's go outside and clean them up."
>
> When we stepped out he said, "You go around that way and I will go this way."
>
> We were firing all the time. The enemy gradually faded away. When we met at the back of the house, everything was still as death. Neither of us spoke. Shamly stood before me with no flesh on his bones. His thigh bones looked like big rusty iron rods, and the knee and hip joints were like rusty iron. The dream faded away slowly. After these many years it is as vivid to me as it was that night.
>
> I suppose it was six months after I had this dream that I heard they had found Shamly in the Black Cat Thicket. He had been betrayed and murdered. The skeleton looked as he had in my dreams.[2]

Briscoe may have been mistaken about Chamblee dying in Black Cat Thicket, since two other accounts say his death occurred in Jernigan's Thicket. One account came from Hicks Nowell, who told Judge Bowman that "Dave Henslee, Wily Napper, and Hargis" were hunting in Jernigan's Thicket when they came upon Chamblee's body. He was "on his blanket and in a kind of kneeling position face downward" with "his hands tied behind him."[3]

According to his descendants, Frank Chamblee's killers were the two men who had been duped by his disguise and the water pails. In one version of the story, told by Mary Ellen's daughter Lena McFarland, "These men searched the thicket and found him, shooting him. . . . They then returned to his home and told his wife that they were hunting birds and had shot him by mistake, and that they had buried him there." Scroggins identified the thicket in question as "Jurnigan's Thicket."[4]

The description of Chamblee's body being found with bound hands seems to indicate that he was not killed by some passing thief but by somebody who bore him great malice. His old enemies, whom he had made to appear foolish on so many occasions, may well have felt such malice toward him.

Who were these men? Based on his recollection of stories by Mary Ellen, Scroggins identified them as the brothers "Bill and Frank Jurnigan."[5] William Jernigan did not have a brother named Frank. However, he was the brother of Felix, whose name might well have been recalled as Frank with the dimming of memory.

That William Jernigan, the "Father of Commerce, Texas," took part in a brutal murder is not an allegation that is likely to be proven at this late date. But it cannot be dismissed, inasmuch as another account also links Jernigan to Chamblee. Hicks Nowell told Judge Bowman that "Bill Jernigan was in the party that captured" Chamblee in the thicket.[6]

⟨⟩

The killing of Frank Chamblee was just one example among many of violence in Texas' northern counties after the war's end. Military authority had collapsed, civil authority was on uncertain ground, and weaponry was all too available. Many Confederate soldiers had managed to keep their pistols out of the hands of Federals by disassembling them, unsoldering their metal canteens, then hiding the weapons inside the canteens. Men from the Ninth Texas Cavalry, for example, journeyed home from Mississippi, passing through Marshall as other ex-Confederates were preparing to blow up the local arsenal to keep weapons out of Union hands. The troopers loaded up with all the rifles and cartridges they could carry.[7]

Some of the war's leftover weapons would be employed in small private confrontations, as in Lamar County, where the *Paris Press* reported, "On

Monday evening, Mr. Duval was murdered by Harvey Hickes, for having 'been with the Federals.' It is thus our county is blessed with peace!"[8] Before the virulent phase of such hatreds had run its course, the African Americans in Lamar County had to seek refuge in the woods for fear of nightriders; old Unionists and Confederates would square off in the long-running Lee-Peacock feud, centered on the Four Corners conjunction of Fannin, Hunt, Grayson, and Collin Counties; and outlaws such as Cullen "Swamp Fox of the Sulphur" Baker and Ben Bickerstaff would carry out campaigns of murder and looting under the pretense of anti-Federal crusades. Baker had, ironically, deserted from the Confederate army while Bickerstaff had been as much an outlaw within the army as outside it.[9] A correspondent from Cincinnati would write from Sulphur Springs: "Armed bands of banditti, thieves, cut-throats and assassins infest the country; they prowl around houses, they call men out and shoot or hang them, they attack travellers upon the road, they seem almost everywhere present, and are ever intent upon mischief. You cannot pick up a paper without reading of murders, assassinations and robbery. . . . And yet not the fourth part of the truth has been told; not one act in ten is reported. Go where you will, and you will hear of fresh murders and violence."[10]

Much of this violence was yet to come, however, when leading citizens gathered in Paris on July 17, 1865, for the purpose of making known to Reconstruction authorities "our willingness to submit to the constitution and laws of the United States, and to ask the privilege of regulating our state government at an early day, and thereby reestablish order in society." Some of those attending were men who had signed the anti-secession "Address to the People of the State," including Fannin County's Robert H. Taylor and Lamar County's George W. Wright and William H. Johnson.[11]

Although the report of the meeting did not say so, it is clear that one of the session's purposes was to seek official appointments from the new provisional governor, Andrew Jackson Hamilton—the "Jack Hamilton" whom Dohoney once feared would lead a Union invasion of the state. Hamilton had the power to fill numerous offices with men who would pledge loyalty to the government of the reunited nation. Those seeking office were many. Some had opposed secession and had also steered clear of ties to the Confederacy. Others were in the position of a Fannin County man who would write a letter to Union military authorities attempting to explain his wartime cooperation with the Confederacy: "I was under the circumstances oblige[d] to at times make out to howl with the times and at the same time I had never seen any time but what if I had been in possession of power sufficient I would [not] have crushed the Rebellion."[12]

Some of those who attended the July, 1865, meeting in Paris subsequently would be retained in their present positions—including B. W. Gray, a state district judge whose jurisdiction included Hopkins County. Other appointees included Martin D. Hart's brother Hardin, who was named a federal judge. Federal troops subsequently accompanied Judge Hardin Hart when he traveled to hold court in such area cities as Bonham, McKinney, and Greenville. Despite this bodyguard, Hart would be attacked from ambush in Fannin County on September 3, 1869, losing an arm and narrowly escaping with his life. A witness attributed the attack to unreconstructed Confederate followers of Bob Lee, a chief figure in the Lee-Peacock feud.[13]

Around the time of Hart's appointment, Governor Hamilton also filled the post of district attorney for the Eighth Judicial District. His choice was a man bent on seeking justice for wartime crimes.

⟨⟩⟩⟩⟩

In the spring of 1862, around the time of his vow to avenge the deaths of the Hembys and Howards, Capt. E. L. Dohoney left the Ninth Texas Cavalry, then in Tennessee, and returned home to Paris, where he served during the remainder of the war as Confederate commissary.

Dohoney's main job in the post was to obtain supplies for the army, but in 1863 he was ordered to raise a new company of men in Paris, leading to an experience that underscored the extent of local opposition to war service. After Dohoney put together a company-strength list of conscripts, "The men were notified to assemble on a certain day, but on that day the recruiting officer found only the captain and his lieutenants, all the [conscripts] having got themselves detailed to drive cotton wagons to Mexico for the purpose of securing medicine and supplies."[14]

While serving as commissary, Dohoney also was allowed to practice law, which led to his involvement in an important civil liberties case involving one John C. Noble, a Hopkins County resident who was a member of Benjamin Ober's Church of God congregation in the Forks delta. Noble, who was in poor health, sought exemption from military service as a conscientious objector after being drafted in the summer of 1863. The Confederate conscript law "exempted Quakers, Dunkards and other religious denominations on account of their non-combatant principles, upon the payment of $500 annually to the nearest post quartermaster," Dohoney noted, so he instructed Noble to pay this sum to the quartermaster in Bonham, headquarters for the Northern Sub-district of Texas. When Noble attempted to do so, however, Gen. Henry McCulloch ordered him thrown into the guardhouse. Dohoney subsequently had a fiery confrontation with McCulloch, who told him he wished "all the non-combatants would die like sheep with the rot." He refused to release the prisoner.

Getting Noble out of the guardhouse required a trip by Dohoney to the Hopkins County seat of Tarrant to secure a writ of habeas corpus from Judge B. W. Gray. Gray sent a posse to Bonham to bring back the prisoner and then held a three-day court session on the issue of Noble's military status. Dohoney called some twenty-five witnesses to this session, including Church of God pastors Benjamin Ober and E. Marple, and said he "proved conclusively that Noble had been a non-combatant from his infancy; also that it was a fundamental principle of the Church of God not to bear arms even in self-defense or in the defense of the state." Judge Gray, however, ruled that Noble was not exempt, whereupon the man was sent to the front and "in less than sixty days he died," Dohoney said, the "exposure and hardship of camp life" being "too much for his feeble body."

Dohoney summed up his feelings by saying he believed Judge Gray "was convinced that the man was exempt from service, but fear of the military and the mob caused him to quail before his environment and to sacrifice this good Christian man."[15] Despite their differences, however, Judge Gray and Dohoney had maintained an amicable working relationship during the Noble case. That bode well for the future; two years later, Dohoney, newly appointed as district attorney, faced Judge Gray again as he sought indictments for wartime crimes.

⋄⟫⋅⟪⋄

It is not known whether Dohoney was aware of the hangings of Pleasant R. Fitzgerald, Austin H. Glenn, Thomas Randolph, Newman, and "Trace Chain" Smith. Probably he had at least heard rumors about these deaths, but he was in no position to seek indictments in these cases, since his jurisdiction as district attorney did not extend into Hunt County, where the men had been hanged. Nor did any other prosecutor seek indictments in the cases, as far as can be determined.[16]

The Eighth Judicial District, to which Dohoney was appointed as district attorney, included Bowie, Cass, Lamar, Red River, Titus, Marion, and Hopkins Counties. Whether wartime executions of Unionists occurred in any of the first-named six counties or whether Dohoney was aware of any such cases is unknown. If so, he did not involve himself in their prosecution. The only hangings he targeted for prosecution were those that occurred in Hopkins County, of James E. Hemby, Jonathan Hemby, Henry T. Howard, James K. Howard, and Thomas Howard in 1862, and of Joseph D. Campbell, Horace DeArman, Thomas Greenwood, and James M. Millsaps in 1863.

While Dohoney apparently deplored the 1863 hangings, he must have had ambivalent feelings about the victims. These were men who had felt some of the same misgivings about the Confederacy as the Hembys, the Howards, and Dohoney himself. Yet, unlike the Hembys, Howards, and Dohoney, they had taken up arms on the side of the Union. Some or all of these hanging victims no doubt were Hart's Company members, whom Dohoney had referred to as "scoundrels" back in 1863 when he first learned of the group's existence. Yet they had been illegally hanged—an act that was in violation of civil rights, which Dohoney had spent his career protecting. He had little to say about the men in his memoir, giving no details about their lives or the vigilante proceedings that resulted in their deaths.

In sharp contrast, it is clear from Dohoney's detailed account of the hanging of the Hembys and Howards that he felt a personal interest in these cases. As he wrote in his memoir, Dohoney "knew these men and, though uneducated, every one of them was a good man, and not one of them had violated any law of Texas or the Confederate states. They are clearly entitled to be considered martyrs to their principles and patriotic impulses."[17] As one of his first acts in office, he moved to arrest five men he had heard mentioned in connection with this hanging. Their arrests were reported in an article that appeared on September 16, 1865, in the *Dallas Herald* under the headline "Committed to Jail." The article said, "Five of [the] parties charged with having been engaged in mobbing and hanging the three Howards and two Hembys at Charleston, Hopkins County, on the 14th [sic] of February 1862 were arrested by the soldiers under the command of Lt . . . Mackey and committed to the Lamar County Jail on Wednesday last to await the action of civil authorities of Hopkins County. The names of the parties arrested are as follows: G. W. Cox, Sim George, J. W. [sic] Helms, McFarland and Southerland."[18]

David Simeon "Sim" George, G. W. (rather than J. W.) Helms, and Charles H. Southerland have been identified as three of the five men who sat as jurors at the trial of the Hembys and Howards, while George W. Cox was one of the trial's three officers. "McFarland" is thought to have been East End farmer Robert McFarland, who had kinship ties with Sim

George; McFarland had married Nancy McGuire and George had married her sister Lucinda. Both women were sisters of Cornelius B. McGuire[19] and, perhaps significantly, were aunts of McGuire's son Rufus, which may help explain how a boy so young came to be involved in the vigilante proceedings as one of the jurors. Rufus may well have looked on the occasion as a grand opportunity to tag along with adult uncles he admired.

While men from the East End *and* northwest Forks eventually would be indicted, all those initially arrested were residents of the East End—perhaps because the hanging occurred in that area, the victims lived there, and Dohoney first focused his investigation there.

The arrests must have created a stir in the area, for the *Dallas Herald* followed up its September 16 account with an opinion piece on October 2:

The Mob on Sulphur

Since the arrest of some parties engaged in the hanging of the Howards and Hembys on Sulphur some persons who were present and engaged in the trial have become unnecessarily alarmed thinking that wholesale unrest and punishment will be the result. Such will not be the case. Admitting all the alleged facts will be established; it results in simply this, that while justice may require the punishment of those who maliciously instigated the hanging—those who used the mob [as] the instrument of murder—it will equally require the discharge of all persons who were led or dragged into the affair for they could have no criminal intent and the intent becomes necessary to make the crime.

There are some men so constituted that they are liable to lose self-control when excited . . . as were the citizens at Charleston at the time referred to and thus they became passive and helpless instruments in the hands of others. We believe that those who led the affair—those who planned the murder—will be punished and not those who were led by others. Hence we trust that there will be no more excitement or unnecessary discussion of the matter.

The government will aim to secure the really guilty parties if it has to send to Mexico after them. The government is not actuated by a spirit of revenge, and we are glad to learn from reliable sources that the friends of the murdered men express no feeling of revenge toward the parties engaged in the mob. They leave to the law the settlement of the questions.

We trust the suggestions we have made will neither prejudice nor aid the individual cause of any of the parties. Our motive being to correct a false impression and quiet all unnecessary excitement.[20]

The policy espoused in this article—that those who lead are fully culpable, while those who are led or "dragged" into criminality are not—is, interestingly, similar to that adhered to by Confederates in Arkansas who hanged Captain Hart and Lieutenant Hays but who did not seek to execute their band's enlisted men.

⊰⊱·⊰⊱

Dohoney took both the 1862 and 1863 hanging cases to the grand jury in Tarrant during six days at the end of October and beginning of November, 1865.

The court records for that fall include a list of those who served on the grand jury. None of those listed is known to have served on active duty with the Confederate army while at least two are thought to have taken part on the Union side.[21] Of particular interest, the records also include what appear to be lists of witnesses who testified for both the prosecution and the defense.

Those described as prosecution witnesses included Erastus Blackwell, N. G. Bryant, T. C. Carpenter, Josh. Clark, John Condict, C. B. McGuire, A. M. Stein, James W. Stell, Z. R. Terrell, Jas Vancil, and W. H. Webster.

Those described as defense witnesses included Wm. S. Brown, Joshua Clark, J. B. Craig, D. S. George, Henry Little, W. D. Lovelady, Robert McFarland, C. McGuire, Robt. McGlaughlin, Danl. Morgan, M. S. Neely, C. R. Ringo, E. F. Ringo, David Sanders, Joseph Sanders, H. S. or H. W. Woody, and Leander Wright.[22]

Most men on the lists are thought to have been residents of Lamar or Hopkins Counties. Some presumably testified about the 1863 hanging, although none of those listed are mentioned in witnesses' accounts.

A number of the men almost certainly testified about the Hemby-Howard case or related matters. Those on the list of "State's Witnesses" included John Condict, a son of the William S. Condict (or Condit) who was driven out of the Forks delta by the same vigilantes who hanged the Hembys and Howards. C. B. McGuire, another prosecution witness, was undoubtedly the Cornelius B. McGuire whose wife chased a vigilante out of the McGuires' yard after her husband refused to serve as a juror in the Hemby-Howard trial. It seems likely that he testified to the grand jury about that incident. He is also thought to be the "C. McGuire" who appears on the list of "Defts Witnesses," in which case he may have spoken on behalf of his son Rufus, who did serve as a juror. Perhaps Cornelius cited the boy's youth and his susceptibility to pressure from older vigilantes.

Another man on the list of defense witnesses, D. S. George, is the David Simeon "Sim" George of the Charleston area who has been named as one of Rufus's fellow jurors. And the defense list's Robert McFarland is thought to have been the McFarland arrested along with George and others in September. George and McFarland may have been speaking in their own defense before the grand jurors, perhaps arguing that they were among those had been "led or dragged into the affair" by others. They possibly spoke up for their nephew Rufus McGuire as well.

Lawyer James Patteson of Cooper was shown the lists of prosecution and defense witnesses by Judge Bowman, who asked Patteson's help in providing identifications. In a letter to Bowman on February 3, 1933, Patteson indicated that Erastus Blackwell, Z. R. (Dick) Terrell, John Clark, A. M. Steen, C. B. McGuire, T. C. Carpenter, John Condict, W. H. Webster, and James W. Stell were from the Charleston area. Patteson knew nothing about James Vancil or N. G. Bryant. Blackwell was identified as "being the first sheriff of Delta County" and the father of the wife of Howard Templeton, who was with the Southern Pacific railroad as one of its leading lawyers. He added that "Jas. W. Stell was the father of Aubrey Stell . . . of Cooper, Texas."

Patteson's letter continued, relating that E. F. Ringo and C. R. Ringo were part of the family that lived in the northeast part of Franklin and northwest part of Titus Counties, and that they were the family for whom Ringo Lake was named. Other probable Charlestonians included "Joseph and David Sanders, Robert McFarlin, Leander Wright, and D. S. George. Daniel Morgan is the man who was shot at his own supper table just after the war, or rather he was just sitting down when shot," Patteson continued, adding that Henry Tittle lived nearer Mt. Vernon and Robert "McGloflin" lived close to Peerless. Men that Patteson did not know included W. S. Brown and W. H. or H. S. Woody, and W. D. Lovelady. Patteson did not know M. S. Neely, "unless it be that he after this married and moved to near Giles Academy, where he from drinking in one spell was taken off of the earth."[23]

Jas. W. (James Wynne) Stell, age thirty-nine in 1865 and a native of Tennessee, is among the more intriguing prosecution witnesses. The son of Lamar County pioneer George Washington Stell, he was the brother of Dr. Wilson Wynne Stell of Paris, whose home had burned, allegedly torched by a slave, during the Texas Troubles of 1860. James W. Stell, who would serve as mayor of Cooper following the creation of Delta County in 1870, was an early pioneer of the East End of the Forks delta. No Unionist, he was one of the Lamar County Secession Club's leading members and went on to serve as a Confederate cavalry captain. Curiously, after M. G. Settle was indicted and jailed in the Hemby-Howard case, Stell was among those who guaranteed payment of his bail—the only person appearing on court lists who guaranteed bail *and* served as a witness for the prosecution. (All others who guaranteed bail money for jailed men— John B. Craig, Daniel Morgan, and Joseph Sanders—are listed, in full consistency, as witnesses for the defense.) Stell served with Gould's Regiment, in which J. W. Hemby also served. Both Stell and Hemby may have been home on furlough at the time of the Hemby-Howard hanging, which J. W. Hemby is said to have witnessed from hiding.[24]

At least four men on the list of prosecution witnesses served in the Ninth Texas Cavalry's Company G along with John Jack Helms. They are Erastus Blackwell, Alfred M. Stein, James Vancil, and Z. R. Terrell. It is possible they were home on leave at the time of the Hemby-Howard hanging and had knowledge of John Jack's part in the crime.[25]

Joshua Clark, an Illinois native who was about thirty-four in 1865 and who lived west of Charleston, appears on both the prosecution and defense lists. Clark was the man appointed by Judge Gray in 1863 to head the posse that enforced a writ of habeas corpus removing J. C. Noble from the guardhouse at Bonham. After the Civil War Clark operated an unusual mill that extracted seed from Osage oranges (also known as horseapples or bois d'arc apples); before the invention of barbed wire in the 1880s, property owners would plant these seeds to grow hedge fences.[26]

John B. Craig, a defense witness, was among the most prominent men to appear in the lists. A one-time member of the Clarksville law firm Craig & Denton, he gave up the law to become a Methodist minister and settled on what became known as Craig Prairie, a few miles northeast of present-day Cooper, in the early 1850s. He served as pastor of the Craig-Tranquil Methodist Episcopal Church South, which was organized in 1854 and drew its congregation from the Craig and Tranquil communities. At the time of the 1860 census, he was sixty-four years old and was shown to own five slaves, which made him one of the leading slaveholders in the slave-poor East End.[27]

Another minister also appears on the list of defense witnesses: W. D. Lovelady, an Alabama native who was age forty-seven in 1865 and was, like Craig, a Methodist. Lovelady lived in the Sulphur Springs area, and it seems possible that his testimony may have related to the 1863 trial and subsequent hanging there.[28]

⋘≫⋘≫

Perhaps Cornelius B. McGuire, speaking to grand jurors on behalf of his son Rufus, and Sim George and Robert McFarland, speaking for themselves and possibly Rufus as well, were persuasive. On November 3, when indictments were returned for the murders of the Hembys and Howards, Rufus McGuire, Sim George, and Robert McFarland were not among the indicted. Nor was Rice Warren, another man who was linked to the Hemby-Howard hanging in a contemporary account.

The eight men who were indicted, and the roles they played, based on various accounts, were: Greenville Smith, who led the Sons of Washington and was among those presiding at the victims' trial; M. G. Settle, who took part in the men's capture in his capacity as militia officer and who helped run the trial; George W. Cox, East End farmer and early Charleston postmaster, who also helped run the trial; Charles H. Southerland, George W. Helms, and John Jack Helms, who sat on the jury; and James McGlasson and J. W. Stansbury. McGlasson was a member of a prosperous slaveholding family in the Roxton area, across North Sulphur River from Ben Franklin, but what his role might have been in the Hemby-Howard affair is not known. What part Stansbury might have played also is unknown, and the man himself is a bit of a mystery as well. He may have been the "J. W. Stansberry," also referred to as "Captain Stansberry," who testified in the spring of 1862 about some gunpowder that was stolen in Lamar County. Stansberry testified that "he had been a merchant, engaged in selling powder."[29]

Indictments were returned on the same day against five men for the murders of Joseph D. Campbell, Horace DeArman, Thomas Greenwood, and James M. Millsaps. Those indicted were Merritt Brannom, a prosperous Hopkins County farmer; Thomas Searls (or Searles), a Sulphur Springs physician; Council Goff, a member of a family that settled in Hunt and Titus Counties; Elbert Early, prosperous Fannin County farmer; and a G. Smith who has never been identified. No accounts have surfaced about the roles any of these men might have played in the hanging, except for one family story about Searls. During the 1920s or 1930s, Judge Bowman met Searls's son, Bob Searls, who was "in the Shoe Business at Sulphur Springs," and afterward wrote: "He tells me that his father's connection with the hanging of the four men was simply the adjustment of the shirt collar of one of these culprits so that his shirt collar would be between the rope with which he was hung and his bare neck."[30]

While former Indian fighter and sheriff Elbert Early was the man other vigilantes turned to for leadership, at least one other of the indicted men had served in a leadership capacity. According to local tradition, Merritt Brannom served as a lieutenant in a locally organized ranging company during a fight against Indians near Jernigan's Thicket in what is now Delta County (then Hopkins County) around 1839. A dozen Indians were said to have been killed and several of the rangers wounded.[31] In the summer of 1861, Brannom aspired to a captaincy as he and other Hopkins County men each set out to raise a Confederate cavalry company, which each man planned to lead. According to a newspaper biographical sketch from the turn of the century, Brannom's enlistment efforts fell short, and he abandoned his recruitment for a while. The others went ahead, however, recruited men, and rode with them to Camp Reeves, north of Sherman, where other units from the area were rendezvousing for muster into the regiment being formed by Col. William B. Sims. Once there, the Hopkins County men discovered they did not have enough men for even a single company. They then sent word to Brannom "to bring on his men and make the company complete." Brannom did so, and the men he had recruited were thrown together with the other volunteers from Hopkins and Hunt Counties in what would become Company K of the Ninth Texas Cavalry Regiment. But Brannom was passed over when the men elected their officers and even when they elected the company's half-dozen or so sergeants and corporals. He instead entered the ranks as a private and served about nine months, until receiving a medical discharge for "chronic opthalmia" (ophthalmia), an inflammation of the eyes, in June, 1862. He finally fulfilled his desire to head a company of men more than a year later, when he organized a local home guard unit designated Company I of the Second Cavalry Regiment, Texas State Troops, and was elected to serve as its captain in November, 1863. The Hopkins-Lamar unit saw some active service in 1863–64 when it was assigned to duty at Camp Wharton on the Texas coast.[32]

Among the intriguing features of Brannom's militia company is the fact that it included at least two other men indicted for vigilante hangings: George W. Cox and Greenville Smith, both of whom served as privates.[33] Since it seems likely that Brannom drew on his circle of friends when he organized his company, the presence of Cox and Smith in Company I suggests that the two were acquainted with Brannom. And it seems almost certain that Greenville Smith was acquainted with Elbert Early; their homes were within ten miles or so of each other, and, as leading slaveholders, they most likely moved in the same social circles. Some or all of these men—Brannom, Cox, Early, Greenville Smith, along with other indicted men—may well have been fellow Masons and/or members of the Knights of the Golden Circle. It also seems possible that Greenville Smith might have been the G. Smith indicted along with Brannom for the 1863 hanging, although such a possibility is purely speculative.

After the indictments were handed down, George W. Cox, George W. Helms, and Charles H. Southerland, who already had been arrested in September, were ordered to remain jailed on charges in the 1862 hanging case, while Merritt Brannom was ordered jailed in the 1863 hanging case. M. G. Settle was released on bail in the 1862 case, and Thomas Searls was released on bail in the 1863 case.[34]

All the remaining indicted men managed to avoid arrest, with some of them known to have fled the area and the others presumed to have done so. Greenville Smith fled to Tennessee, whence he had come. John Jack Helms fled to southeast Texas, melting into temporary anonymity as one of the cowhands for famed pioneer rancher Abel H. "Shanghai" Pierce.[35] Nothing is known of what happened to J. W. Stansbury and James McGlasson, indicted in the 1862 hanging, or Elbert Early, Council Goff, and G. Smith (if he was not Greenville Smith), indicted in the 1863 hanging.[36]

Out of thirteen men named in the two cases, then, only four were jailed. However, *not one* of these four remained behind bars for long: Cox, Brannom, Southerland, and George W. Helms all escaped. How they managed to break loose is not mentioned in contemporary accounts, but escape probably was not difficult if the Tarrant jail of the 1860s resembled a log structure where Hopkins County prisoners were held several decades later. In the early 1890s, farmer George Elias Chapman was thrown into the log-walled, dirt-floored jail after a rousing drinking bout at the local fair, where he had shown his prize bull. That night, Chapman's Choctaw wife, Genova Ladosky Chapman, rode onto the jail grounds, tied one end of a lasso to the jail, threw the rope over the roof, hitched the free end of the rope to her saddle horn, then pulled the entire jail up and over onto its side, whereupon George walked free.[37]

After Brannom's escape from the jail, his friends arranged for him to eat supper with his mother, then he left the area on "a fast horse."[38] Cox remained in the Forks delta for a while, with the surreptitious help of the Bernard M. Patteson family.

Bernard Patteson, whose plantation was located between Ben Franklin and Giles, was one of three brothers in the area who owned substantial acreage and, until war's end, numerous slaves. An ardent secessionist, Bernard served as one of the officers of the Secession Club that formed in Lamar County before the war; he later served as a local commissary agent for the Confederate army, in which his brother James served as an officer on General Maxey's staff. Bernard was married to Greenville Smith's sister Myranda and clearly was in sympathy with Smith and other indicted vigilantes. Apparently he also was a supporter of all sorts of characters who were at odds with Unionists and/or the Reconstruction government. Bernard's son James, who was about nine years old in 1865, would later recall that the notorious outlaw Ben Bickerstaff, who had a hideout in Hopkins County's White Oak Creek bottom, visited the Patteson house on occasion. The Patteson family also arranged for fugitives with the right sort of politics to be provided with food on the sly; the men would hide in a three-acre grape orchard on the Patteson property, and young James would be sent out to the orchard bearing food for them. One of those who got food in this way was Simp Dixon, an ally of Bob Lee in the Lee-Peacock feud. Another was jail escapee George W. Cox.[39] Sometime later, however, Cox left the area and went to Mexico. Where his fellow jail escapees Brannom, Southerland, and George W. Helms fled is not recorded.[40]

Settle and Searls, who were out on bail and presumably still in the area, might have been tried during the February, 1866, term of court. However, due to delays secured by defense attorneys, none of the hanging cases were tried in February. This pushed the cases on the docket to the fall, 1866, session of court—a rescheduling that would have profound consequences for the prosecution's case.[41]

⬧⬧⬧

Developments similar to those in Hopkins County were occurring elsewhere in northern Texas. On November 11, 1865, a grand jury in Cooke County indicted twelve jurors and two court officers who had participated in the Great Hanging at Gainesville. But no attempt was made to arrest the indicted men until a week after the court adjourned, allowing many of them to escape and providing no opportunity for speedy trials.[42]

Around this same time, the first gusts of what would become powerful winds of change began to be felt, as old Confederates around the state began waging a campaign aimed at preventing them from being prosecuted for wartime crimes. A leader in this campaign was James W. Throckmorton of Collin County, who had opposed secession but served the Confederacy throughout the war. While presiding over a February, 1866, convention in Austin to draw up a new state constitution, he urged the delegates to "bury, upon the altar of our common country, all the recent past, with all its painful associations and recollections."[43] Urged on by Throckmorton, the convention adopted Ordinance No. 11, "which mandated that no one was to be prosecuted or sued for any acts performed under Confederate authority." Governor Hamilton responded by denouncing the delegates on March 31, 1866, for "legislating wholesale robbery and murder throughout the land," adding, "You have an account to settle before the people yet. You have not done with this. You shall confront them, and shall answer to them, and if God spares my life, I pledge myself to go before the people of the state and draw these men up and make them answer. I may not get through, but the same precautions will not be necessary as two years ago. The ready rope and convenient limb will not be used as they were then."[44]

The constitutional convention was followed by a statewide election in June. Offices up for election included those that had been filled by Governor Hamilton's appointments immediately following the war, as well as the governorship itself. The state's Unionists nominated prewar governor Elisha M. Pease, who had opposed secession. But Throckmorton rolled to victory by a margin of more than three to one. Throughout the state, other appointed officeholders also lost out to the returning tide of the Old Guard. In northeast Texas, B. W. Gray went down to defeat, his judgeship going to Hinche P. Mabry, a former Confederate colonel. Dohoney lost his district attorney office to George T. Todd, a former Confederate captain.[45] It may be significant that George Todd was the son of William Smith Todd, who served for several terms as judge of the same Eighth Judicial District to which George won election as district attorney. Just a couple of years before his death in 1864, William Smith Todd lost his judgeship in an election defeat, after which Dohoney wrote his friend James C. Bates, saying, "we beat Todd for Judge most scandalously. Greg of Mt. Pleasant was elected by about 4 votes to 1 in the district. Todd says the Churches the Union men & the Conscripts conspired against him, and formed a secret society throughout the district."[46] It is possible his son George Todd bore a grudge against Unionists on account of this defeat—a possibility that could help explain events during the son's tenure as district attorney.

There followed a rocky time for Texas Unionists and a comparatively smooth one for the Old Guard, because, according to Richard McCaslin, "Throckmorton, having secured election through the creation of a conservative coalition that turned its back on wartime excesses, did nothing to protect Unionists."[47]

Ordinance No. 11 did not apply to either the 1862 or 1863 Hopkins County hangings, since it protected acts "performed under Confederate authority," while the hangings were illegal actions conducted by no duly constituted authority. Nevertheless, the men who had fled following their indictments for the hangings did not need a weather vane to know which way the wind blew. Shortly after the June, 1866, election, which put into office former Confederate officers (or Confederate officeholders), many of them, including George W. Cox, George W. Helms, Greenville Smith, Charles H. Southerland, and Merritt Brannom, returned to the Forks watershed. Clearly, they did not fear what the courts might hold for them under the new regime, since loyal fellow Confederates now occupied many positions in the judicial system.[48]

⟨≋⟩

With old Confederates back in power, the hanging cases finally came up for trial in the Hopkins County seat of Tarrant, with Judge Mabry presiding, District Attorney Todd as prosecutor, and, as the first defendant, Charles H. Southerland.

Southerland, who was about forty-five at the time of the Tarrant proceedings, was the vigilante whom friends of the Hembys and Howards most despised, judging by their comments. While the Tennessee native had served on the jury that condemned the five victims, it was not his role as juror that aroused such animosity toward him. Instead, it was his work as a hangman, although it is uncertain exactly how many necks he noosed.

In his description of the Hemby-Howard hanging, Benjamin Ober wrote, "The ropes were put around their necks by a noted horse thief and murderer, who had broken jail to escape justice." That Southerland was the man referred to is clearly indicated by an 1867 letter to authorities from Hopkins and Lamar men who described him as a man who "after having committed murder in Missouri escaped to this State." A *Paris Press* article from the fall preceding the Hemby-Howard hanging may also have referred to Southerland, inasmuch as it mentions a man who had been jailed and later turned to vigilante activities, although in this case, the man was said to have been a bank robber instead of a murderer and to have paid his way out of jail rather than escaping—possibly just two variations on the same story. The article, presumably written by attorney-editor F. W. Miner, deplored vigilante activities and stated, "the most lawless and worst citizens are foremost to have a hand in such matters. We know of one case in which a man turned a bank robber loose upon the payment of a large sum, and in less than twelve months the same man was splurging around at the head of a vigilance committee formed 'to protect society.'" The article may have been making reference to Southerland's participation in vigilante actions of early 1861 against Henry T. Howard, S. Landreth, or others.[49]

But Ober, who was seventy-eight years old when he wrote his memoir—forty years after the Hemby-Howard hanging, may have erred in recalling that Southerland placed the ropes on all five victims. According to a Hemby kinsman, Southerland was the man who placed the rope on Henry Howard's neck. But men who were prepared to testify to that act were not prepared to testify that Southerland was also the man who placed the rope on James Howard's neck—an important distinction, as it turned out, during the trial proceedings.[50]

Southerland was charged with five counts of murder, one each for Henry T. Howard, James K. Howard, Thomas Howard, James E. Hemby, and Jonathan Hemby but was to be tried separately for each death. Witnesses were called by District Attorney Todd to appear in court at Tarrant on Friday, October 26, 1866, for the first trial.

Officers of the court who gathered that morning included no less than one former Confederate general, two former Confederate colonels, and a former Confederate major. These men were former general and now defense attorney Sam Bell Maxey, former colonels H. P. Mabry (now judge) and defense co-counsel W. H. Johnson, and former major W. B. Wright (defense co-counsel). Had District Attorney Todd been present, that would have added a former Confederate captain to the assemblage, but for some reason he was absent that day. Attorney J. M. Patterson, of whom nothing is known, stood in as "district attorney pro tem," according to court records.[51]

Also on hand, as a witness for the prosecution, was former Confederate private James W. Hemby. The brother of the hanged Hembys, who is said to have watched the hanging from hiding, had served with the Twenty-third Texas Cavalry Regiment until December 7, 1864, when the battered South's energies were waning. Hemby had then crossed over Union lines at Red River Landing in Louisiana and taken the oath of allegiance to the United States, later returning to his home in the Charleston area.[52]

Hemby's appearance at Tarrant, seeking justice for his kin and the Howards on October 26, 1866, did not come off well. Soon afterward, he took out an advertisement in the *Paris Press* to describe what happened on that day:

> In the first place, one Mr. Charles Sutherland was called to trial on the indictment for the hanging of one Henry Howard, but in reality was carried through what I call a mocked trial for the hanging of one James Howard. No convicting evidence being produced, Sutherland was consequently cleared without a bobble. Court adjourned.
>
> I then went to [District Attorney Todd], in company with other state witnesses, and asked him when he was going to have Mr. Sutherland tried for the hanging of Henry Howard (the man whom he, Sutherland, tied the rope on when he was hung). He, Mr. Todd, replied to us by declaring that the trial should not come on this term of the court, and that we (the State Witnesses) might return home, and rest contented. We left, and the next day after we were gone, Mr. Todd had Sutherland called to trial for the hanging of Henry Howard, declared the State ready, submitted the former evidence to the jury, and cleared him as before, throwed the other indictments out of the court that were obtained against men associated with Sutherland at the time of hanging and so the thing went off harmonious to his or their own wishes.[53]

Hopkins County court records do in fact show Southerland being tried and acquitted of murdering James K. Howard on Friday, October 26, 1866. Later the same day, with Maxey, Johnson, and Wright still acting for the defense, M. G. Settle also was tried and acquitted of murdering Henry Howard.[54]

A trial and acquittal for Southerland in the Henry Howard case on the following day is not mentioned in surviving court documents. Nor is it mentioned in a letter that Sam Bell Maxey wrote to his wife Marilda from Tarrant following the court action that Saturday. Maxey wrote:

> Today finished a very heavy week's work and so far I have been quite successful. Yesterday the case of Sutherland was taken up & argued by

Warren & Patterson for the State, & Johnson, Wright & myself for the defense & he was acquitted. Esq. Settle was next tried, & acquitted.

Today Merritt Branham was tried, Banks and Todd for the State, Culbertson & myself argued for defense & he was acquitted.

The first two cases were for the Howard & Hemby hanging; the last the Sulphur Springs hanging. I [told] Wright that Capt. Todd is satisfied he can't succeed in any of the cases and will on Monday dismiss all of them.

We have done very little Civil business, and so far I haven't collected a cent.

But if Todd does dismiss as I have no doubt he will Cox & Helmses' cases, McGlasson, Early, and the others, in certainty out of all I ought to collect something.[55]

Court records indicate that District Attorney Todd, in conjunction with Judge Mabry, did indeed dismiss many of the cases Maxey mentioned in his letter. In fact, the cases had already been dismissed on Saturday, before Maxey penned his letter that evening.[56] It seems likely that charges against Southerland in the Henry Howard case also were dismissed at this time, although court documents do not show it. Many court records are missing, however, including some pages of the records for this particular day. At any rate, the case against Southerland in the hanging of Henry Howard was a dead letter. It was never mentioned in any surviving court record from that day forward.

As mentioned by Maxey in the letter to his wife, Merritt Brannom was tried and acquitted on Saturday, October 27. Todd and Mabry then acted to dismiss all other charges against Brannom and most others who were accused in the 1863 hanging. Whether jurors would have convicted any of the defendants in either the 1862 or 1863 hangings if prosecutorial efforts had been vigorous is a question that is unanswered but moot; the available evidence indicates that the aim of the prosecution was not to convict, but to exonerate.

As the rose on the cake of the court session, Judge Mabry also rid the docket of civil suits filed against Elbert Early by survivors of James M. Millsaps and Joseph D. Campbell, both hanging victims, and Cicero F. Millsaps, who is thought to have been captured in Jernigan's Thicket but mysteriously disappeared from the record prior to the hanging. On Saturday, October 27, when he dismissed charges against numerous indicted men, Judge Mabry ordered the dismissal of lawsuits filed by "Minky" Millsaps, mother of James M. and Cicero F. Millsaps; Emeline Millsaps, wife of Cicero; and Rachel Campbell, mother of Joseph D. Campbell. Presumably Millsaps's wife Algeretta also would have filed a lawsuit if she had been alive; however, she was dead by January, 1866, according to family records. Mabry further ordered that the plaintiffs "be ruled for costs."[57]

Meanwhile, court proceedings with similar results were occurring elsewhere in northern Texas, notably in Cooke County, where William T. G. Weaver, a former Confederate army captain, had been elected to the bench in June, 1866. In the fall, Weaver presided over the trials of the first six jurors from the Great Hanging in Gainesville, with all six men being acquitted.[58]

❦

Actions in Hopkins, Cooke, and other counties soon brought down a torrent of criticism on the courts, including James W. Hemby's November advertisement in the *Paris Press* denouncing District Attorney Todd and the manner in which Charles H. Southerland's acquittal had been achieved. On April 13, 1867, another area man weighed in. M. L. Armstrong—the former state legislator who had spoken against secession along with Dohoney at the fateful meeting in Charleston in 1861—complained about both District Attorney Todd and Judge Mabry in a letter to Gen. Philip Henry Sheridan, who headed up the Reconstruction program in Texas and Louisiana.[59]

Sheridan's office may have responded by instructing Armstrong to direct complaints to Gen. Charles Griffin, who supervised operations within Texas, for on April 27, Armstrong and three other area men wrote to Griffin. In their long letter of complaint, Armstrong, George W. DeWitt, P. Miles, and J. M. Easley wrote:

> Dear Sir:
> The undersigned loyal union men from the counties of Lamar & Hopkins . . . respectfully beg leave to represent to you that in Febr. 1862 a mob headed by Rice Warren, James McGlasson, George Cox, Greenville Smith, G. W. & John Helm, Sutherland, and others murdered Henry Howard, Thomas Howard, and James Howard and John & Wm. [sic] Hemby's by hanging because, as was alleged, they were Union men, without trial. After the surrender of the rebels in 1865 and after the court had been organized in this state by the Provisional Governor Hamilton; the several parties who participated in these and other murders were indicted by the Grand Jurors of Hopkins County district

court; on application to the presiding Judge Gray, for bail, it was unhes-
itatingly denied the parties consisting of George Cox, [George W.]
Helm, Southerland and others [who] were committed and confined in
the Hopkins county jail. They remained there a short time and managed to effect their escape and left the country; Cox went to Mexico,
Helms and Southerland destination unknown; but shortly after the
State election in June 1866 Cox, Helms, & others returned (among
whom was Southerland) to Hopkins county and Lamar, and defied the
civil authorities. None of them were arrested; the sheriff and jailor both
being of the Rebel faction.

At the election in June past, Mabry was elected Judge of the 8th
judicial district, purely because he was devoted to the Rebel cause. . . .
He was one of the master spirits that precipitated the South into the
rebelion [sic]. He now professes as he did in 60 & 61, that secession is
and was right and the murder of Union men by Rebels is not worthy of
punishment . . . At the election aforesaid one George T. Todd, a captain of the Rebel army and son of Judge Todd who was member of the
secession convention, and a rabid secessionist, in 1861, was elected district atty. for the aforesaid 8th judicial district of which Hopkins county
forms a part. At the November term of said court for Hopkins county
judge Mabry presiding, Geo. T. Todd as district attorney; all the witnesses being present for the trial of the said Cox, Helm, Southerland &
others the said district attorney Todd informed the witnesses on the
part of the State that none of those cases would be tried this (that) term
of the court and directed them the witnesses to return to their homes,
which they accordingly did.

Then on the following day in the absence of these said witnesses,
these cases were called up by the said district attorney Todd and dismissed for want of testimony. Your attention is hereby requested to the
card of J. W. Hemby published in the Paris Press (which is herewith
transmitted) . . . to which no reply has ever been made either by Judge
Mabry nor district attorney Todd [and] the charges therein contained
are susceptible of proof to the letter by the entire Bar and many of the
citizens of Hopkins county. The indictments having been thus summarily disposed of said Cox returned to the county again, Greenville
Smith who escaped [to] Tennessee has returned and Southerland
whose name appears in the card of Hemby above referred to has long
since returned to his home in Lamar county and during the past winter
was twice attempted to be arrested for hog stealing but defies the Civil

authorities of the county and is still running at large. He after having committed murder in Missouri escaped to this State and is one of the worst of outlaws, and is a terror to the whole county in which he lives. There are numerous other cases that we could truthfully present but for the present we desist believing this will be sufficient to satisfy you that the ends of justice are not met, nor sufficient protection to the community afforded by the civil authorities in the hands in which they are now invested. And [we] beg further [to] have [leave] to assure you that the Loyal Union citizens white and Black in the counties bordering on Red River need prompt and efficient aid and protection. Many of thievery's worst class of men perhaps in the U.S. are amongst us such as followed the Rebel chiefs Shelby & Quantrell who murder steal and otherwise deprecate with impunity fearing nothing from the men by whom the laws are at present administered. . . .

Taking this view of our condition and desiring to assist the community in which we live (the Union portion) and with a view to relieve them and ourselves from such embarrassments and to "put down rebellion" we most respectfully but earnestly ask you to establish . . . a military commission in the county of Lamar or Hopkins for the purpose of bringing offenders to trial and punishment. And we beg leave to assure you that without some such aid as is herein indicated the Freedman will be detered from appearing at the polls and the assistance expected from them in restoring the Government [to] the Loyal Men of the state will undoubtedly be deprived of.

It is possible that Judge Mabry and district attorney Todd should be removed at once and others appointed in their stead, . . . and should [you] desire the people to recommend suitable persons from their district from your appointment they would most cheerfully do so.[60]

Even before these complaints were penned, General Sheridan had become gravely concerned about the state of affairs in Texas. He wrote to his superior, Gen. Ulysses S. Grant, saying, "The condition of Freedmen and Union men in remote parts of the State is truly horrible. The Government is denounced, the Freedmen are shot, and Union men are persecuted if they have the temerity to express their opinion." He also wrote Governor Throckmorton, saying, "There are more casualties occurring from outrages perpetrated upon Union men and freedmen in the interior of the state than occur from Indian depredations on the frontier." He accused Throckmorton of turning a blind eye to crimes against Unionists, whereupon Throckmorton condemned Unionists who complained of the crimes as a "howling crowd of canting, lying scamps."[61]

Throckmorton's attitude prompted John L. Haynes, president of the Texas Loyal League of Union Citizens, to say, "Whilst red handed murder stalks abroad in every county of the State, there he sets at Austin like an old hen on a bad egg, clucking away about 'occasional' crimes."[62]

The reports of violence against Unionists in North Texas contributed to a revolt in Congress against President Johnson's lenient Reconstruction policies. Beginning in March, 1867, Congress passed a series of Reconstruction Acts that ushered in the most punitive phase of Reconstruction, the period of Radical Reconstruction. One of the new reconstruction acts gave military commanders the power to remove officeholders "at all levels of state government." General Sheridan acted almost immediately, in July, 1867, to remove Governor Throckmorton from office as an "impediment to reconstruction," replacing him with Elisha Marshall Pease, whom Throckmorton had defeated in 1866.[63]

Complaints that had been surfacing about the judiciary also led military commanders to act against court officials. "By the end of November 1867, only three of the state's seventeen district judges . . . remained on the bench. Thirteen were removed, and one . . . resigned while facing certain removal," Randolph Campbell has noted.[64]

Hinche P. Mabry was among judges given the boot, on August 15, 1867. George T. Todd was kicked out as district attorney soon after, on November 18, 1867. Judge William T. G. Weaver, who had presided at trials of men accused in the Gainesville hanging, also was removed from office, on November 18, 1867.[65] However, the results of court actions during the tenures of these "impediments to reconstruction" were allowed to stand.

❧❦

No record exists of further prosecutions of anybody involved in either the 1862 or 1863 Hopkins County hangings. While charges in some cases were dismissed, others would simply fade away as far as court records are concerned. Only charges against two men would remain on the books for long—those against the fugitive John Jack Helms, accused of murder in the 1862 hangings, and those against the fugitive Council Goff, accused of murder in the 1863 hangings.[66]

The worst punishment wreaked on some of the defendants, as it turned out, was by their own lawyers. In 1867, the firm of Johnson & Townes sued George W. Cox, George W. Helms, and Charles H. Southerland for payment of their fees. (Presumably the lawyers won their case, although the outcome is not clear from court records.) Around the same time Maxey sued Cox and Southerland. He won his fee of $400, plus $57.90 interest, with the defendants being ordered to pay court costs and the sheriff being directed to auction off Cox's land to pay his share.[67]

Over in Gainesville, meanwhile, other cases stemming from the "Great Hanging" came to trial periodically for years afterward, with acquittals resulting in every instance. As in Hopkins County, some cases dragged on for years before finally vanishing from the record with no indication as to final disposition.[68]

The crackdown in the courts did have an effect, however. Some of the men indicted in the Hemby-Howard hanging apparently took the new get-tough attitude as their signal to leave the area once and for all. Greenville Smith, who was said to have fled to Tennessee and then returned, now left for Georgia. The 1870 census of the Rome, Georgia, area gives his occupation as overseer—a great comedown from his days as slave-owning planter and factory owner. George W. Cox, who was said to have fled to Mexico before reappearing in northeast Texas, now removed himself to Lampasas County in Central Texas. M. G. Settle moved to Los Angeles.[69]

Little is known about the subsequent lives of many of the men involved in the 1862 and 1863 hangings. At least one man who took part in the hanging of the Hembys and Howards was tracked down by the victims' friends, according to a story told to Judge Bowman by Aden Posey of Hopkins County. The man, whose name Posey could not recall, had moved "away down South of here" and was teaching school about a mile from his house. His pursuers found his wife at home and told her they were her husband's old friends. She directed them to the schoolhouse, where they found her husband and killed him.[70]

Many of the wartime vigilantes are believed to have lived out the remainder of their days in the Sulphur Forks watershed counties in relative anonymity. Dr. Thomas Searls of Sulphur Springs died in September, 1887, just short of his seventieth birthday.[71] James C. McGlasson, who is buried in McGlasson Cemetery near Roxton, was among the era's prodigious begetters; he and his wife Anna had ten children before James's death in 1881 at age fifty-one.[72] Elbert Early and his wife Mary had eleven offspring; he died in Durant, Oklahoma, at age ninety-two in 1904 and was buried in Ladonia Cemetery.[73] Merritt Brannom, known as "Captain," continued to farm in Hopkins County into his seventy-fifth year, when he fell from a wagon in January, 1900, sustaining an injury that was thought to be slight. "Cheerful and doing well one minute," he was dead soon after and lauded in his obituary as a man who "followed the path of duty as a lover of his country and his God."[74] It is not known what became of Council Goff, who was indicted along with Searls, McGlasson, Early, Brannom, and G. Smith for the 1863 Hopkins hangings. A distant relative who researched the family history learned that Goff was born in North Carolina around 1819 and that he was the brother of Edward Hill Goff of Hunt County—father of *Old-Timers of Hunt County* author C. W. Goff—but information about the Goff family is sketchy.[75]

Several of those linked to the Hemby-Howard hanging remained in the area and enjoyed long life. The 1880 census of the Forks delta, by then called Delta County, shows Charles H. Southerland residing in Precinct 1 along with wife Rachel and several children, including a six-year-old girl who was a grandchild.

Not far from Southerland in the 1880 census is George W. Helms, who not only had survived into his seventieth year but had come up in the world, now being a county commissioner. George W. and his second wife, Charlotte, age 60, are shown surrounded by an assortment of other Helms households, including that of John Jack's son G. W. "Pony" Helms, whom his grandparents raised. Other Helmses in the neighborhood include some of George W.'s many children—there were eight by his first marriage, three by his second. He had many grandchildren around him during a life that would not end until 1904.[76] One of the men with whom Helms spent time in jail, his arrested but unindicted neighbor David Simeon "Sim" George, had almost as many children as Helms—eight—and lived almost as long, dying in 1901 at age 84.[77] Outliving them all was Thomas Rufus McGuire, who lived on in Delta County until August, 1949, when he died at age 101.[78]

⬦⬦⬦

Some people connected with the Forks watershed hangings went on to earn a measure of fame, including E. L. Dohoney. After the war, he served in the Texas legislature and was the author of important laws, including one allowing local option elections on the sale of alcoholic beverages—the prohibitionist's proudest achievement, commemorated on his gravestone at Evergreen Cemetery in Paris. For a while, Dohoney also operated a Paris newspaper, *The North Texan*. Late in his career, he campaigned for state office, and lost, as a candidate for the Prohibition party and Greenback party. A man who found it difficult to resist losing causes, Dohoney once gave an excellent description of himself while contrasting his character with that of his beloved wife, the former Mary Johnson: "He is progressive on every line of life; she conservative; he heterodox; she orthodox; he a reformer and a crank; she a Christian and a fogy." Dohoney wrote a half-dozen books over the years, including *Man: His Origin, Nature and Destiny* (1884), *The Constitution of Man* (1903), *An Average American* (1907), and *Evolution of an Elder* (1916). He was stricken with paralysis in 1917 and remained an invalid until his death in March, 1919.[79]

Members of John Warren Hunter's family were dead or departed from the Forks delta by the time he returned there from Mexico after the war. He farmed a while in Arkansas before gaining an education through home study with the help of his wife, the former Mary Ann Calhoun, then went on to teach school in Hopkins County's Black Jack Grove and many other locales. An incident in Fredericksburg, where Hunter began teaching in 1878, served as a reminder that wartime bitterness was slow to fade. When he raised the American flag over the schoolhouse on Washington's birthday, two school trustees who were ex-Confederate soldiers ordered it removed. Hunter refused, whereupon he and one trustee fought it out with their fists while Mary Ann held the other at bay with a derringer. The one trustee finally was hauled away unconscious, while the other shook hands with John, and both teacher and flag stayed at the school. Hunter later turned to journalism, operating a newspaper in Menardville and Mason before joining the *San Angelo Daily Standard* as an editorial writer in 1905. In 1911, he and his son J. Marvin Hunter founded the short-lived *Hunter's Magazine,* which evolved into the long-staying *Frontier Times.* In addition to *Heel-Fly Time in Texas,* John Warren Hunter was the author of works that included the booklet *Rise and Fall of Mission San Saba.* He died in San Angelo in 1915.[80]

During the last years of the war, Church of God pastor Benjamin Ober found times "so turbulent in the Forks of Sulphur" that he and his wife, the former Elizabeth Barnett, sold their farm and moved back to the vicinity of Paris, beginning a decades-long odyssey marked by calamity and poverty. As recounted in his memoir, Ober was "penniless" by war's end, only managing to pay his debts by "giving some of my home furniture." Several endeavors failed to work out, for various reasons, including a stint editing the *Texas News* (precursor of the *Bonham News*) and an attempt to operate a sawmill at a location called Pine Woods, where the Obers were victimized by thieves, bandits, and a man to whom they leased the property.[81] Subsequently, Ober spent three years preaching in the Illinois Eldership and four in the Indiana Eldership before returning south,[82] where periodic missionary efforts in Arkansas and Texas were interrupted by a host of setbacks. A daughter died in the 1870s, leaving the Obers to raise her baby, and an attempt to start a prohibition newspaper in the Hunt County community of Caddo Mills in the early 1880s did not work out. Ober, who then moved with his family back to the Paris area, was reduced to picking cotton to raise money for food and rent. In 1894, son Richard, who had graduated from medical school in Indiana and taken up practice in Texas, was murdered while on a trip to sell livestock in the Indian Territory. His parents, who had gone to the Territory to meet him, were left "in a strange country penniless," after which, "we went into a dugout, made a scaffold to sleep on, and lived on a dust floor" during a very hard year.[83] Elizabeth, sick for many years, died in April, 1910, and Benjamin succumbed a little more than a year later, in September, 1911, while staying at the home of his granddaughter in Butler, Oklahoma. A succession of laudatory items followed in *The Church Advocate,* including a letter of praise from Ober's old associate Marple—then living in Lawton, Oklahoma, but still eschewing his given name of Enoch in favor of the initial E.—and a letter from one H. W. Allen, who reported that the old preacher's body had gone on serving the Lord even after its occupant's death. The "very worldly" undertaker who embalmed Ober was overcome by a feeling of strangeness when in the vicinity of the corpse, collapsed onto the floor, then arose with a shout to say he was saved.[84]

Another person connected with Forks watershed hangings also became well known—in fact very well known—but in his case, he was less famous than notorious.

⋘∘⋙

After his flight from Hopkins County in the fall of 1865, John Jack Helms, commonly called John Helms, traveled southward, eventually drifting into the cow camp of Shanghai Pierce under the name of Jack Helm. If he was seeking to conceal his identity and his indictment for murder, he was successful, for his early life remained a mystery to Texas historians prior to the research reflected in this book. "Jack Helm . . . is of unknown origin," *The Handbook of Texas* said of him. And historian C. L. Sonnichsen commented, "Helm is hard to trace. He had worked for cattle baron Shanghai Pierce down on the coastal plain before he became an officer, but nobody knew where or what he had been before that."[85]

"Helm" not only put his murder indictments behind him but his flight from the Confederate army as well; stories spread in Wharton County during his Rancho Grande days portrayed him as a Confederate war vet-

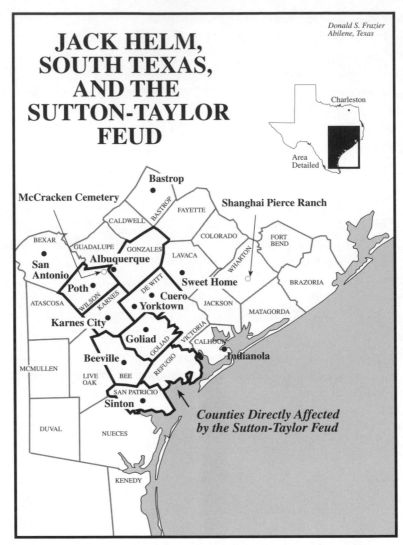

Major areas of John Jack Helm's activities in South Texas after leaving Charleston, Hopkins County, Texas, after the Civil War. Areas defined include counties affected by his employment as a "regulator" and as captain of the "state police." Map by Donald S. Frazier.

eran, with no mention of any desertion. Among the most curious of the ranch stories is one from a 1953 biography of Shanghai Pierce that dotes on Jack Helm as a suppressor of "Black insolence." The author wrote that Captain Jack returned to Texas after the war to learn that the black belt of Texas was not safe after the emancipation of the slaves. "[Helm] led in the thought that there must be no 'Black insolence.' But one day, when he was riding near Rancho Grande, a 'free nigger' mounted a stake-and-rider fence and began whistling 'Yankee Doodle' at the former Confederate. That was an error, not of marksmanship on the part of the Captain but of a musical selection on the part of the Negro. The first bullet struck the tune-maker 'square between the eyes,' and his bleached skeleton lay for years where the body fell, as a grim reminder to musically inclined Negroes."[86]

While Helm was settling in to ranching in Wharton County, tensions were heating up to the west, centering on the Central Texas counties of DeWitt, Gonzales, and Karnes, which were grouped southeast of Austin. Troubles in the area involved unreconstructed Confederates on one side and Union troops on the other. In a related development in the same area, unreconstructed Confederates who were part of the "Taylor party" carried on a feud with members of the "Sutton party," who allied themselves with Union troops and the Reconstruction government. This conflict eventually would evolve into the famed Sutton-Taylor Feud—Texas' longest-running and bloodiest feud, which at times could as accurately have been called the Helm-Taylor Feud.

The first trouble between Union troops and the clan led by the brothers Creed Taylor of Karnes County and Pitkin Taylor of DeWitt County occurred in 1866. Creed's son Buck and Pitkin's brother William killed a black sergeant at a relative's home, and Creed's son Hays killed a black soldier at a saloon. A number of the Taylors subsequently went "on the dodge" along with eight or ten other young men. The group had drifted northwestward into Mason County in the Texas Hill Country by November, 1867, when Hays and his brother Doby (or Doboy) faced off with Union troops in the town of Mason and killed two of the soldiers. The Taylors subsequently fled back to Creed's ranch in Karnes County.[87]

The origins of the Taylors' feud with the Suttons are cloudy, but the affair may have begun the following year with the killing of Buck Taylor and Dick Chisholm on Christmas Eve 1868 in the DeWitt County town of Clinton. One of the men involved in the killing was Bill Sutton.[88]

The two strands of the conflict—between the Taylors and the Reconstruction government, and the Taylors and the Suttons—began to merge in 1869 when Texas' civil and military affairs were controlled by Gen. Joseph Jones Reynolds. Reynolds decided to put together a band of "regulators" and employed a man named C. S. Bell to head them. How Bell had come to know Jack Helm is unknown, but he apparently did, for he hired

Helm as his chief deputy. In a statement to the *Victoria Advocate,* Helm would later recall that the regulators' assignment was "to assist in arresting desperadoes in Texas known as the 'Taylor party.'"[89] To this end, Bell and Helm went into the DeWitt County area in the summer of 1869 and deputized a large group of men who included Sutton allies; the Taylors' conflict with officialdom and their feud with the Suttons thereby became one.

The regulator campaign was very much a "Union operation"—authorized by General Reynolds and run by Bell, who wrote articles about the Civil War for *Bonner's New York Ledger* "in which he figured conspicuously as a Union spy and scout."[90] And the regulators' targets were unreconstructed Confederates. Helm, who stood accused of murdering five Unionists, made an odd fit with such a campaign. But he was not the only Texan who committed acts of violence against Unionists during the war, then switched sides afterward and operated against former Confederates. Also notorious in this regard was John Early, who led a brutal band of home guards during the war, lynching three Confederate deserters in Bell County. According to historian Richard Maxwell Brown, Early's "brutality was matched only by the shallowness of his Confederate allegiance—after the war he aligned himself with the military government of the victorious Union forces."[91]

Under the circumstances, Helm may have seen the wisdom of keeping silent about his past anti-Union activities. But it is possible that some of Helm's superiors both knew about the murder charges pending against him in Hopkins County and exerted their influence to have them dismissed. If this was not the case, then it was oddly coincidental that Helm signed on as a regulator around the spring of 1869 and during this very time a judge in Hopkins County ordered the murder charges that had been pending against him since 1865 "stricken from the Docket."[92]

Not long after Helm became Bell's deputy, Bell disappeared from the scene. Helm immediately moved into the top position and in the summer of 1869 led regulators during a series of raids against the Taylor clan and others. The raids ranged over Bee, San Patricio, Wilson, DeWitt, and Goliad Counties and were chronicled by the *Galveston News.* During July and August, the *News* reported in a September article, Helm's regulators "killed twenty-one persons and turned ten others over to civil authorities," with a great many of those killed being shot down while "attempting to escape."[93] In San Patricio County, the regulators killed two members of the Choate family—said to have been Taylor allies—and wounded one F. O. Skidmore, a Choate family neighbor. Skidmore subsequently wrote a letter of complaint about the regulators to the *Victoria Advocate*. The letter stated that "they conducted themselves in an extremely boisterous manner while at the house, appropriating whatever they desired, as if they had killed a robber chieftain and had a right to appropriate his effects. They left me nothing, not even my clothing and pocket change. They stole my saddle, six-shooter, and other things of less note."[94]

Reports of wholesale shootings and executions by Helm or his men began drawing criticism in the press as early as the fall of 1869. On September 14, for example, the *Galveston News* wrote: "This thing of putting down civil government and then employing 'regulators under military authority' to hunt up and execute people, according to their own notions, is not the best thing in the world."[95]

But Helm was popular with high officials. In July, 1870, the legislature passed a bill creating a state police force under authority of Gov. E. J. Davis, and the governor named Helm as one of the organization's four captains. Helm soon enlisted members of his old regulator band as deputies—including men who were Sutton allies.

Helm's band of state police soon aroused even more criticism than his regulators had. State senator B. J. Pridgen launched an attack on Helm in the *Austin Republican*, whereupon one F. E. Grothaus responded in the *State Journal* with an attack on Pridgen and a defense of Helm. "I have not heard one single Republican or law-abiding citizen complain of Jack Helm or his actions," Grothaus insisted. "On the contrary, they are highly pleased and perfectly satisfied with his services."[96]

Pridgen was not long in replying. On November 23, 1870, he shot back with a compendium of accusations in more than fifty column inches of small, dense print in the *Republican*. Among allegations:

> I know of at least twenty cases of murder by Helm and his party . . .
> For example: Helm with his men went to the house of a Mr. Bell of
> Goliad county—arrested him—took him off in the woods—killed him
> and left him to the mercy of scavengers generally and reported that "he
> attempted to escape." He arrested a Mr. Moore on the same day, treated
> him as he did Bell, and made the same report. They went to the house
> of a Mr. Jones, tore him from the embrace of his distressed wife and
> children, and when a little way from the house, *gallantly* dispatched
> him in the presence of his crying little ones, who had doubtless fol-
> lowed along in anxious expectation of what would be done. He, too,
> "attempted to escape." They then arrested a Mr. Pool, took him off in

the woods and left him lying in a Pool of blood and alleged that he, too, "attempted to escape."

The litany continued with allegations of the murders or attempted murders of assorted others (plus a theft and the levying of fees on the citizens of the Sweet Home community to pay the hotel bills of Helm and his posse). The *Republican* summed up Pridgen's report by commenting, "It is a little remarkable that Jack Helm's victims surrender at discretion, no matter whether he goes to their houses by night or by day, they lay aside their weapons and rely on him, as an officer, to look after their personal safety. But it seems that once in his possession a change quickly comes over the spirit of their dreams and they 'attempt to escape.'"[97]

In the context of such allegations, the old story about John Jack Helms using false promises to lure men from Jernigan's Thicket to their deaths seems completely plausible.

State Police captain Jack Helm was not prosecuted, however—because he was feared by citizens and protected by officials, Pridgen claimed—and whether allegations against him were true has never been established with certainty. His apologists note that State Police officers were viewed by many as hated symbols of Yankee rule, which would make Helm appear to be the object of unfair criticism. Ann Patton Baenziger took note of such views in an article on the State Police, commenting that "political partisans censured the force with little justification." However, she went on to say, "Some of the criticism . . . was deserved. One example of genuine guilt was that of State Police Captain Jack Helm."[98]

Helm was not actually present during two killings mentioned by Pridgen, those of Bill and Henry Kelly, sons-in-law of Pitkin Taylor, who also "attempted to escape." But the case received a huge amount of coverage in the state press, replete with accusing statements by the men's relatives, and Helm was blamed because the killings were laid to men under his command. Governor Davis yielded to public pressure, and Helm left the State Police sometime around the end of 1870. However, he won election as sheriff of DeWitt County around the same time and continued his career as an officer of the law.[99]

As regulator, State Police captain, and now sheriff, Helm allied himself with the Sutton clan in their feud with the Taylors and their friends. Among the latter was gunfighter John Wesley Hardin, whose cousin had married old Creed Taylor's daughter.[100]

In the spring of 1873, Hardin, according to his autobiography, attempted to play peacemaker between the Taylors and their old foes. This occurred shortly after Jim Taylor had shot and wounded Bill Sutton in the DeWitt County town of Cuero, leaving the leadership role on the Sutton side of the affair to Sheriff Helm. Around the first of April, Hardin had a meeting with Helm and his chief deputy, Jim Cox, with Helm attempting to persuade Hardin to switch sides as the price for dismissal of old criminal charges pending against the gunfighter. Hardin refused but exacted a promise from "Helms" (as he spelled the name) and Cox "that they and their mob must keep out of our country and leave us alone." The Helm-Sutton crowd was not long in breaking this vow, according to Hardin: "About the 23rd of April, 1873, Jack Helms and fifty men came into our neighborhood and inquired for [Taylor party-members] Manning [Clements], George [Tennile], and myself. They insulted the women folks and Jack Helms was particularly insulting to my wife because she would not inform him of some of the Taylor party."[101]

Insults to his wife notwithstanding, if Hardin is to be believed, he set up yet another peace parley with Helm. The meeting was to be in Albuquerque, Texas (then reckoned to be in Wilson County, but later discovered to be over the line in Gonzales County). Helm was using a blacksmith shop in Albuquerque to work on a Rube Goldbergesque cotton-worm destroyer of his invention; as the implement progressed along the rows, brushes supposedly would knock the worms to the ground, where the creatures would be crushed beneath a wheel.[102] Hardin recalled:

> On the 17th [of May, 1873], I was to meet Jack Helms at a little town called Albukirk in Wilson County. I went there according to agreement, a trusty friend accompanying me in the person of Jim Taylor. We [Hardin and Helm] talked matters over together and failed to agree, he seriously threatening Jim Taylor's life, and so I went and told Jim to look out, that Jack Helms had sworn to shoot him on sight because he had shot Bill Sutton and because he was a Taylor. Jim quickly asked me to introduce him to Helms or point him out. I declined to do this, but referred him to a friend that would. I went to a blacksmith shop and had my horse shod. I paid for the shoeing and was fixing to leave when I heard Helms' voice: "Hands up, you d—— s— of a b——."
>
> I looked around and saw Jack Helms advancing on Jim Taylor with a large knife in his hands. Some one hollered, "Shoot the d——d

scoundrel." It appeared to me that Helms was the scoundrel, so I grabbed my shotgun and fired at Capt. Jack Helms as he was closing with Jim Taylor. I then threw my gun on the Helms crowd and told them not to draw a gun, and made one fellow put up his pistol. In the meantime Jim Taylor had shot Helms repeatedly in the head, so thus did the leader of the vigilant committee, the sheriff of DeWitt, the terror of the country, whose name was a horror to all law-abiding citizens, meet his death. He fell with twelve buckshot in his breast and several six-shooter balls in his head. All of this happened in the midst of his own friends and advisors, who stood by utterly amazed.[103]

A La Grange newspaper carried another version of the encounter, described as a witness's account of "the assassination . . . of the notorious Jack Helm by the more notorious Wes Hardin and another party not known." The "stranger"—Jim Taylor—shot Helm in the chest with his pistol, the witness said, whereupon "Helm . . . rushed at him attempting to grapple with him. Just at this moment Hardin fired upon Helm with a double barrel shot gun shattering his arm. Helm then turned to go into the [blacksmith's] shop and the stranger pursued him shooting him five times about the head and face. Helm fell dead when Hardin and the stranger mounted their horses and rode away together remarking that they had accomplished what they had to do."[104]

In his autobiography, Hardin said, "The news soon spread that I had killed Jack Helms and I received many letters of thanks from the widows of the men whom he had cruelly put to death." He added: "Many of the best citizens of Gonzales and DeWitt counties patted me on the back and told me that was the best act of my life."[105]

Helm's body was taken to the McCracken Cemetery, located in Wilson County, and "buried shallow" so his wife could move him if she chose—which she never did. A rock was placed as a marker. In 1973, however, the deceased's great-granddaughter Billee Rhodes Smith secured a free government marker to place on the grave. It sits there still, in all its irony, a Confederate army tombstone.[106]

⋞⋟ CHAPTER 5 ⋞⋟

Forgetting

It seems barely possible that enough time has finally passed for Texans to look back on the Civil War with some small measure of objectivity. To be sure, the state's love affair with the Confederacy, which has threatened to block out all memory of the considerable Unionist sentiment that existed in many areas, continues. But if Texans are not working overtime at trying to give Unionists a fair shake historically, at least they are not putting in the long hours they once did on contrary measures. These efforts, which came under the heading of diligent, determined, selective remembering, went on for many years but are nowhere better illustrated than by the "United Daughters of the Confederacy Catechism for Children." The document, originally written in 1904 by Cornelia Branch Stone and later reprinted, was recited at Children of the Confederacy Clubs and distributed to schoolteachers as an "instructional aid." Two of the catechism's questions and responses, which perfectly capture the tone of the entire document, centered on slavery:

> Question: How were the slaves treated?"
> Response: With greatest kindness and care in nearly all cases, a cruel master being rare, and lost [sic] the respect of his neighbors if he treated his slaves badly. Self-interest would have prompted good treatment if a higher feeling of humanity had not.
> Question: What was the feeling of the slaves toward their masters?
> Response: They were faithful and devoted and were always ready and willing to serve them.[1]

The stuff of this catechism also is the stuff of much of our Texas history, unfortunately. For example, A. W. Neville's 1937 *History of Lamar County* informed generations of readers: "Negro slaves were seldom mistreated, despite Uncle Tom's Cabin and other authorities along that line. They were too valuable."[2]

Unsurprisingly, in times that gave birth to such views, contrasting accounts of the Confederacy and deeds done in its name were neither popular, welcome, nor in many cases acceptable. The longtime suppression of accounts about the Great Hanging at Gainesville, notably, is as notorious as the event itself.

An instructive version of the event, one of the major vigilante actions in American history, was written in 1884 by the Rev. Thomas Barrett, a juror who had mixed feelings about the proceedings. But Barrett encountered opposition when he published his story as a pamphlet. Historian Richard McCaslin wrote that "it became unsafe to have a copy of [Barrett's] publication, and the few copies that existed were secreted away." Only three copies were known to exist by 1961, when the Texas State Historical Association resurrected interest in the Gainesville hanging by reprinting Barrett's story.[3]

In this context, a monument to the Confederacy in Gainesville glares with even greater irony than Jack Helm's Confederate army tombstone. The inscription reads:

> God holds the scales of Justice;
> He will measure praise and blame;
> And the South will stand the verdict,
> And will stand it without shame.
> Oh, home of tears, but let her bear
> This blazoned to the end of time;
> No nation rose so white and fair,
> None fell so free of crime.[4]

It is possible that similar efforts were employed to suppress unpopular accounts of the 1863 hangings in Hunt and Hopkins Counties. If so, the efforts succeeded so well that no memory of the accounts is known to have survived. But very few accounts of any kind about these hangings exist from the half-century following the events in question. Not until the 1920s, when Judge Bowman began digging through records and collecting stories from old-timers, did much in the way of a body of evidence about the 1863 hangings begin to accumulate. But Bowman never pulled the dozens of accounts in his collection together into a coherent whole, nor did any historian of later years do so. Local historians who followed Bowman either neglected to mention the hangings altogether, mentioned only some of them,[5] or produced accounts containing inaccuracies,[6] while professional historians, in numerous articles for scholarly and popular magazines, limited their research almost entirely to Martin D. Hart's activities in Arkansas.

The "history of the history" is distinctively different for the 1862 Hemby-Howard hanging, in which falsehoods soon sprang up and came to be accepted as the truth by many area residents. In the revised scenario, the affair's civilian victims became deserters and terrorists, while the vigilantes who carried out the mob action were the instruments of legal executions, and the kangaroo court proceedings that preceded the hanging became a military court-martial. This is the version that appeared in 1935 in *Loose Leaves*, Ikie Patteson's history of Delta County, under the heading "legal executions." "During the Civil War, three citizens of the Charleston community were tried and found guilty by court martial, of treason against the Confederate Government. An elm tree on which they were hung still stands on the south bank of South Sulphur." She then related that in 1864, "the jury who had tried these men, were arrested and tried for murder. They were defended by Gen. Sam Bell Maxey, afterwards United States Senator, and D. B. Culberson, who served this Northeast Texas District as Congressman for twenty years. The jury came clear, and the three officials were never apprehended. One died in Rome, Georgia, one in Los Angeles, California, and the third on the Lampasas River."[7]

Variations on this version, some containing other errors, subsequently proliferated, including a reference to the affair in G. G. Orren's 1938 master's thesis, "The History of Hopkins County." Orren quoted one J. M. Reed as the source of the statement that "two Hembys and three Howards, northern sympathizers, were drafted into the Confederate army. They deserted and came home and terrorized the women and children. They were finally captured and hanged on Christmas day by authority of the Confederacy."[8] This version was still current in 1993, when June E. Tuck apparently drew on it in *Civil War Shadows in Hopkins County, Texas* as the source of the following: "As always, in a barrel of apples one will find a few rotten ones. In Hopkins County, there were two Hembys and three Howards that were northern sympathizers and had to be forced to join the Confederate Army. They deserted and came home. The people of the county had no use for them, and they in turn terrorized the county.

They were captured and hanged on Christmas day by the authority of the Confederacy."[9]

It should also be mentioned that Delta County historian Douglas A. Albright completely bought into the "court-martialed deserters" story. Albright, who spent years investigating the Hemby-Howard hanging, expended many futile hours in a search for an official record of this will-o'-the-wisp court-martial. He went to his grave at age eighty-four in 1990 still believing in its existence.[10]

How did such a long-running falsehood originate? Almost certainly with vigilante George W. Helms.

This supposition is based, in part, on the existence of another glaring flaw in the *Loose Leaves* account—namely, that the number of those hanged was three rather than five.

As should be re-emphasized here, *Loose Leaves* author Ikie Patteson was the wife of Cooper lawyer James Patteson, who talked with several of the vigilantes, was related to at least one of them, and provided Judge Bowman with much useful information about the case. In a letter of February 3, 1933, Patteson told Bowman, "I believe that all five of the men were executed on the same date . . . because Charley Southerland told me that was the number, but old man Helm placed them at three."[11]

So there it is. Either James Patteson (1856–1946), Ikie Patteson (1863–1947), or possibly both of them together apparently talked with George W. Helms at some point before Helms's death in 1904 and heard from him that three was the number of those hanged. While it cannot be established with certainty that Helms also was the source of the "court-martialed deserter" falsehoods, that seems probable. But this is not to say that Helms necessarily lied. As is the way in so many old-timers' stories, how he told it may actually have been the way he had come to remember it: No, it was not a vigilante action but a court-martial, and no those hanged were not vocal civilians but damnable deserters, and there were only three, not five, anyway.

Why Ikie Patteson believed this story is, however, an unsolved mystery. Her husband not only did not believe the part about the hanged men being three in number, he also never gave credence to the claim that the Hembys and Howards were tried by court-martial, as is clear from a statement Judge Bowman made about the affair in a letter to a Mr. Bagwell: "I know from my good friend Judge Jas. Patterson of Delta that this trial was a kind of citizens trial or Judge Lynch affair."[12] It is simply not known why Patteson's wife, years after her husband's correspondence with Bowman, included the falsehoods in her 1935 book.

It is also not known why two pro-victim versions of the affair, both published prior to *Loose Leaves,* remained ignored or undiscovered by area historians. Dohoney's *An Average American* was self-published in 1907, and, while it apparently was a commercial flop, the mere fact that its author lived in Lamar County should have worked to publicize its contents concerning a matter of such interest as the hanging of the Hembys and Howards. But there is no evidence that the Pattesons or any other regional historian ever was aware of the book's existence. The same is true of John Warren Hunter's "Heel-fly Time in Texas," which in 1911 was published in *Hunter's Magazine,* was re-published in 1924 in the successor magazine *Frontier Times,* and also was offered to that magazine's readers in book form. The most likely supposition is that Dohoney and Hunter's accounts *were* known, at least to a minority, around the time of their publication, but, being despised, were ignored; thus, they failed to become part of the source material relied on by later historians such as Albright and Tuck.

⟨≫⋅⋅≪⟩

But old Confederates and their apologists do not bear sole responsibility for the falling away from truth that occurred about the events in question. A *positive urge* seems to be at work in many families, including families of crime victims, which makes forgetting seem easier than remembering.

One clan of Hembys who live today in North Texas, Arkansas, and elsewhere trace their ancestry back to James E. Hembey—the family spelling—through four of his seven children who survived past childhood. Family historians Tom and Kathy Hembey of Garland, Texas, were surprised to learn from the authors that ancestor James had died by hanging. However, the evidence is there on the "Deaths" page of the family Bible, written by James's wife, Melinda Jane Oldham Hembey: "James E. Hembey departed this life February the 15 1862"—the date of the Hemby-Howard hanging.[13]

Many descendants of James's brother and companion in death, Jonathan Hemby, reside today in Central and South Texas, where some of Jonathan's children, including Zachry "Jack" Hemby, were raised by relatives. Nellie H. Olsen of Austin, who is among Jack Hemby's descendants, says family members have long been intrigued by the question of what happened to great-granddaddy Jonathan, and several have looked into the matter. A sister of Nellie's "thought our great-grandfather was killed at Helena when the Emmitt Butler murder took place"—an event that occurred in the 1880s—and a cousin of hers "said there once was a place called Hoff's Station . . . and that my great-grandfather was at this stagecoach station with a man named Hoff when they were raided by Mexican bandits and that the Mexicans killed the man named Hemby but Mr. Hoff escaped." Still another cousin, Annie Lee Hemby Adams, "said that she heard that our great-grandfather was approached during the night by Yankee soldiers to whom he gave corn and supplies. His neighbors were enraged because they felt he was a Yankee sympathizer and so they hung him. She did not know where this took place but she thought it was in Tennessee."[14]

As for Jonathan's widow, a curious legend about her has circulated within the family; it is said that Anna Pair Hemby became so distraught by her husband's death that she abandoned the children and turned to prostitution.[15]

Descendants of Joseph D. Campbell recall that he fought for the North and was hanged, although details of the family story are at odds with the evidence: "Joseph came home to attend the wedding of one of his sisters. During the party that followed, some of the Confederate followers took him and several others to the barn where they hanged them."[16]

Forgetfulness also has intruded into the family memories of the Fitzgerald-Randolph clan. While they do know that Thomas Randolph was captured in the spring of 1863 along with three Fitzgerald brothers-in-law, they do not accept that he did not escape along with the two of the Fitzgeralds. Furthermore, the story persists among descendants that he was not hanged. Instead, he "bought horses for the Cavalry and went to south Texas and was never heard from again."[17]

Howard descendant Wynema Blankenship of Krebs, Oklahoma, heard about our research project from a cousin, who had heard about if from another cousin. Wynema is descended from Henry T. Howard (whom the family misremembers as William Henry Howard, Sr.) through Henry's son William Henry (whom the family had believed was a "Junior") and William Henry's daughter Hazel, who was Wynema's grandmother.

"My grandmother," Wynema wrote, "had often told me of her dad's dad . . . being hung. . . . Grandma said she found a 'book' in her father's trunk that told of the hanging and when her father caught her reading it, the book later disappeared." (Hazel's father, William H. Howard, was a minister of the Church of God, following the path that his own father, Henry, had been hoping to pursue at the time he was hanged. Hazel, who was born in 1896, would have been about six years old at the time Church of God pastor Benjamin F. Ober penned his 1902 account of the hanging, a copy of which may have come into the hands of fellow pastor William H. Howard and may have been the book Hazel discovered in his trunk; alternatively, the book may have been Dohoney's 1907 *An Average American*.)

Wynema continued: "To the best of [my mother's] later memory, [Grandmother] said that [her grandfather] made some type of speech that he was told not to make and he was hung for it. She said that his two brothers defended him, and they were also hung. She remembered that one of them was James K. or J. and couldn't remember the third name. She thought the incident had happened in Kansas but couldn't remember for sure."[18]

⟞⟝

Some of those who read this book may be pointed toward remembering *the other side* of the story—not as kin of the hanged, but as kin of men who did the hanging (or carried out executions by other means). Relatives of the vigilantes may be able to take comfort from their own family stories about the hangings, which may portray the vigilantes as right-minded men who were justified in their actions. However, kin of vigilantes who were willing to talk with the authors invariably said they knew of no such stories. The *positive urge*, which led to forgetfulness within the families of hanged men, appears to have worked with even greater effect to wipe clean the slate of the past within the families of vigilantes.

In sum, many parts of the record are sketchy, but this much is clear: Men were murdered. Conditions surrounding some of the victims' deaths make them seem particularly poignant. An indelible impression remains of Henry T. Howard, the wagon rolling from beneath his feet as he delivers a prayer for his enemies; of Joseph D. Campbell and Thomas Greenwood, clasping hands as the nooses tighten around their necks; and of Frank Chamblee, far from friends in Jernigan's Thicket, on his knees, hands bound behind his back.

But those were hard times, full of sound and fury. As Judge Bowman commented in one of his letters, "Passion and prejudice ran high then. The Country was in the thrall of Civil war and it was difficult for men to act calmly and deliberately and to know what was the best to be done. Looking back to then from now we realize that many acts of violence were better left undone, but such is the result of all wars and especially Civil wars."[19]

But the final word on the matter is reserved for a person who was present during some of the events that have been chronicled here: Thomas Rufus McGuire, who served as a member of the jury that convicted the Hembys and Howards and who also may have witnessed the hanging of Joseph D. Campbell, Horace DeArman, Thomas Greenwood, and James M. Millsaps. He spoke about the hangings eight decades later.

On March 14, 1946, the *Dallas Morning News* published a story about retired Delta County farmer Thomas Rufus McGuyer (as the family then spelled its name). The writer said McGuyer "apologizes for the stern handling against men who agreed with Gen. Sam Houston in 1862 that Texas had no role on the side of the Confederacy. 'Some of those men . . . were hanged,' he said. 'These men shouldn't have been hanged. They were just expressing their own opinions, and they had a right.'" McGuyer is also on record with a further comment. In 1948, on the occasion of his hundredth birthday, he told the *Houston Press,* "Men do awful things when war is coming, and neighbor turns against neighbor. They hanged those people just because they sympathized with the Yankees."[20]

NOTES

Chapter 1

1. Matt White, telephone interview by Judy Falls, Mar. 17, 1998, and Matt White, e-mail to David Pickering, Mar. 18, 1998, Falls-Pickering Collection (hereafter cited as FPC).

   Matt White of Commerce, Tex., is a Paris Junior College history instructor and an avid naturalist with particular expertise in thickets. He believes the thickets of the Forks watershed prairie country and those in areas dominated by forests had different origins. On the prairie country, "which historically was a sea of grass," the thickets commonly owed their existence to "suppression of fire." But in forests, thickets "are and were caused by the removal of the upper canopy"—eliminating shade and allowing underbrush to take hold—"due to any number of natural or unnatural disasters such as lightning, tornado, hurricane, high winds, etc."

   The thickets of the Forks watershed are, for the most part, a thing of the past. However, there are patches of woodland here and there that knowledgeable people say must greatly resemble the thickets that existed in the area during the nineteenth century.

2. Hunt County lost a small strip of land in the south in 1870 to the newly created Rains County. Hopkins County, in addition to losing northern land to Delta County, also lost a small amount of land in the south to Rains County.

3. Delta County History Book Committee, *Delta County History*, p. 33; Frances Terry Ingmire, *Archives and Pioneers of Hunt County*, p. 38; Ikie Gray Patteson, *Loose Leaves: A History of Delta County*, p. 32.

4. Alfred Howell, letter to Morton Howell, May 14, 1854, Morton Boyte Howell Collection (hereafter cited as HC). The collection includes the letters of Alfred Howell, who immigrated to Texas from Virginia in 1852, and most of the letters were written to Alfred's brother Morton. He and Maude Howell Henderson donated the letters to the archives at Texas A&M University-Commerce.

5. J. W. Williams, "Moscoso's Trail in Texas," *Southwestern Historical Quarterly* 46 (Oct., 1942): 138–57. The Moscoso party may have been following part of the Old Chihuahua Trail, an ancient route used by Indians—if in fact the group

passed through northeast Texas. Several other possible routes also have been proposed by those who have studied expedition journals.

6. William Banta and J. W. Caldwell, Jr., *Twenty-seven Years on the Texas Frontier*, pp. 29–30.

7. L. L. Bowman, "Jernigan's Thicket," Bowman Papers (hereafter cited as BP). As noted by W. Walworth Harrison in *History of Greenville and Hunt County, Texas* (p. 412), L. L. Bowman had a long career as judge of the 8th Judicial District Court of Hunt County, also served as Greenville School Board chairman and Greenville city attorney, and was an avid local historian. During the 1920s and 1930s, Bowman interviewed many area old-timers about vigilante hangings during the Civil War, Reconstruction-era outlaws, and other matters. He donated his papers to the college that is now Texas A&M University-Commerce. Among principal documents that were resources for this research are "Jernigan's Thicket," a Bowman manuscript based on the recollections of Hicks Nowell and others; interviews with Erastus "Ras" Hopper, G. W. King, Jeff Mason, and Aden Posey; letters from W. B. Horton, lawyer James Patteson of Cooper, Tex., and lawyer T. A. Pettigrew of Charleston, Ark.; commentaries about a newspaper article describing hangings, postwar indictments and the genealogy of the Hart family; and various manuscripts Bowman collected from others, including Ben Briscoe's "Early History of Hunt County."

8. Banta and Caldwell, *Twenty-seven Years on the Texas Frontier*, p. 30.

9. A. W. Neville, "Backward Glances" column, *Paris News*, Oct. 14, 1942. (Complete collections of Neville's seven thousand columns are available in the Aikin Archives at Paris Junior College, Paris, Tex., and in the archives at Texas A&M University-Commerce.) Various retellers of the story seemed fascinated by all those ticks that made Jernigan's hours such a misery. Following his emergence from the thicket, he was said to have paid a local man "a fine mare" to pick the ticks off him (Bowman, "Jernigan's Thicket"). And Delta County historian Ikie Patteson, repeating the Jernigan story in the 1930s, got down to specifics about the ticks, "of which the jungle was full," informing her readers that they ranged "from the little seed tick, about one-fourth as large as an ordinary pin head, to what was called the dog tick, being about equal in size to a peanut after being hulled" (Patteson, *Loose Leaves*, pp. 176–77). Texas ticks made a big impression on many immigrants from the East. Hunt County pioneer Alfred Howell wrote home to his brother Morton saying, "my body is covered with tick bites; these are so very numerous that it is said there are a gallon of ticks to every square foot of ground in Texas" (Howell, letter to Morton Howell, May 5, 1852, HC).

10. Patteson, *Loose Leaves*, p. 152.

11. David Hackett Fischer, *Albion's Seed: Four British Folkways in America*, p. 633; Terry G. Jordan, "The Imprint of the Upper and Lower South on Mid-

Nineteenth-Century Texas," *Annals of the Association of American Geographers* 57, no. 4 (Dec., 1967): 668.

12. Terry G. Jordan, "A Century and a Half of Ethnic Change in Texas, 1836–1986," *Southwestern Historical Quarterly* 89 (Apr., 1986): 400–401. Jordan says deep Southerners of the slave-cotton culture were rare in pre-revolutionary Texas "both because the status of slaves was uncertain under Mexican law and because the large majority of early Anglo settlers came from southern mountain states, where slavery was uncommon." Starting in the late 1830s, with the legalization of slavery by the Republic, slave-owning planters from the coastal states began to arrive in Texas in large numbers; nearly 200,000 African Americans, almost a third of the total population, lived in the state by the time of the Civil War.

13. Jordan's "Imprint of the Upper and Lower South" focuses on Texans who were natives of four Upper South states—Tennessee, Kentucky, Missouri, and Arkansas—and four Lower South states—Alabama, Georgia, Mississippi, and Louisiana. Most immigrants to Texas were from these states. On p. 677, he rates Fannin, Hunt, and Lamar as three of thirty-seven counties where Upper Southerners were the dominant immigrant group, based on population birthplace figures of the 1870 and 1880 censuses. The others were Bandera, Bell, Blanco, Brown, Buchanan (Stephens), Burnet, Clay, Collin, Cooke, Dallas, Denton, Eastland, Ellis, Erath, Grayson, Hays, Hunt, Jack, Johnson, Kerr, Lampasas, Llano, Montague, Palo Pinto, Parker, Red River, San Saba, Shackelford, Tarrant, Throckmorton, Travis, Williamson, Wise, and Young Counties.

Jordan rates Hopkins County as one of sixty-seven counties where Lower Southerners were dominant. The others were Anderson, Angelina, Bastrop, Bee, Bosque, Bowie, Brazoria, Brazos, Burleson, Caldwell, Cass, Chambers, Cherokee, Comanche, Coryell, Falls, Fort Bend, Freestone, Goliad, Gonzales, Grimes, Hamilton, Hardin, Harris, Harrison, Henderson, Hill, Houston, Jackson, Jasper, Jefferson, Karnes, Kaufman, Lavaca, Leon, Liberty, Limestone, McLennan, Madison, Marion, Matagorda, Milam, Montgomery, Nacogdoches, Navarro, Newton, Orange, Panola, Polk, Refugio, Robertson, Rusk, Sabine, San Augustine, Shelby, Smith, Titus, Trinity, Tyler, Upshur, Van Zandt, Walker, Washington, Wharton, Wilson, and Wood Counties.

Jordan's further determination (pp. 671–72) that the Sulphur Forks delta was predominantly Upper Southern in origin is based on an analysis of immigration patterns reflected in the 1880 census of Delta County, which had been created in 1870 from the portions of Lamar and Hopkins Counties that lay in the Forks delta. The post–Civil War figures hold true for the time of the war as well, he believes.

14. Fischer, *Albion's Seed,* p. 754.

15. Jordan comments in "Imprint of the Upper and Lower South," pp. 668–69:

"There were . . . numerous slaveless yeomen to be found in the antebellum Lower South, just as there were select areas within the Upper South where the slave plantation had taken root. . . . Nevertheless, the generalization of a slave-cotton Lower South and a yeoman-noncotton Upper South is a valid one which few would dispute." The generalization also holds—despite exceptions—that Lower Southern immigrants to the Sulphur Forks watershed were either slaveholders or defenders of slavery while those from the Upper South were slaveless.

16. W. J. Cash, *The Mind of the South,* p. 90.

17. Randolph B. Campbell, *An Empire for Slavery: The Peculiar Institution in Texas, 1821–1865,* p. 229.

18. The Fannin County figures come from Tom Scott of the Fannin County Historical Museum (interview by Judy Falls, Apr. 12, 1997, FPC). Scott's 12.8 percent figure for Fannin County slaves is from his study of the original 1860 census record, which was damaged by water and is difficult to read. A slightly higher figure of 19 percent appears in Ron Tyler et al., eds., *The New Handbook of Texas,* 2:946. Figures for Lamar and Hopkins Counties are from Barnes F. Lathrop, "Migration into East Texas, 1835–1860," *Southwestern Historical Quarterly* 52 (July, 1948): 5. Figures for Hunt County are from Cecil Harper, Jr., "Slavery without Cotton: Hunt County, Texas, 1846–1864," *Southwestern Historical Quarterly* 88 (Apr., 1985): 389.

19. Jordan, "Century and a Half of Ethnic Change," p. 402.

20. James Marten, *Texas Divided: Loyalty and Dissent in the Lone Star State, 1856–1874,* pp. 13–14. A "Patrol Company" was organized in Hopkins County at this time, on Mar. 20, 1856, with G. H. Crowder as captain (June E. Tuck, *Civil War Shadows in Hopkins County, Texas,* p. 4).

21. Alfred Howell, letter to Morton Howell, May 1, 1854, HC.

22. C. H. Forney, *History of the Churches of God in the United States of America,* section on Texas Eldership.

23. Benjamin Ober, "Memoir" (manuscript, 1902, Ober Family Records, FPC) pp. 12–14.

24. Wesley Norton, "The Methodist Episcopal Church in North Texas in 1859 and 1860," *Southwestern Historical Quarterly* 68 (Jan., 1975): 328.

25. Richard Maxwell Brown, *Strain of Violence: Historical Studies of American Violence and Vigilantism,* p. 8.

26. Norton, "Methodist Episcopal Church in North Texas," p. 332.

27. Ralph Dice, "Lamar County and Secession" (research paper, Texas A&M University-Commerce, 1984), p. 24, in Steely Papers, University Archives, Texas A&M University-Commerce. (A copy is also available in FPC.)

28. DeMorse quoted in Richard B. McCaslin, *Tainted Breeze: The Great Hanging at Gainesville, Texas, 1862,* p. 23.

29. A. W. Sparks, *The War between The States As I Saw It: Reminiscent, Historical and Personal,* pp. 9–10.

30. Dice, "Lamar County and Secession," p. 24; Donald E. Reynolds, "Vigilante Law during the Texas Slave Panic of 1860," *Locus: An Historical Journal of Regional Perspective* 2 (spring 1990): 183.

31. *Marshall Texas Republican*, Aug. 25, 1860, quoted in Reynolds, "Vigilante Law during the Texas Slave Panic of 1860," pp. 183–84.

32. Reynolds, "Vigilante Law during the Texas Slave Panic of 1860," pp. 185–86. Reynolds also notes that "although some historians have accepted, at least partially, the original allegations of secessionist editors that there was an abolitionist plot, the fact remains that none of the 'evidence' upon which the vigilante convictions were based would stand up in a modern court of law."

33. Walter L. Buenger, *Secession and the Union in Texas*, p. 75.

34. Jordan, "Imprint of the Upper and Lower South," p. 686.

35. Georgia Lee Tatum, *Disloyalty in the Confederacy*, pp. 14–18.

36. The flag story is from John Black and H. P. Allen's "Civil War Experiences Reflect Life of Hardship," *Honey Grove Signal-Citizen*, July 2, 1976, p. 5. After the war, William Gambill, Jr., of Honey Grove would say in a letter to Union general Charles Griffin, "I was one of the crowd that helpt to raise a U.S. Flag in Honey Grove in the time of the beginning of our troubles. I was one of the crowd that burn the Cessation [sic] Flag at Honey Grove" (Gambill to Griffin, May 14, 1867, in United States, U.S. Army Continental Command Records, 1821–1920, Correspondence of the Office of Civil Affairs of the District of Texas, 5th Military District, and the Department of Texas, 1867–1870, Letters Received, A–G [hereafter cited as U.S. Army OCA Records]).

37. Robert S. Weddle, *Plow-horse Cavalry: The Caney Creek Boys of the Thirty-fourth Texas*, p. 22.

38. Neville, "Backward Glances," *Paris News*, Mar. 29–30, 1933. T. H. Hadden of Paris was twelve years old in 1862 when he rode along with his father, H. B. Hadden, and other men on their cotton-wagon trip. Many cotton-wagon trains from the Forks watershed followed an "eastern" route, down near the coast through the King Ranch and Brownsville. The Hadden party followed a western route through Dallas, Waco, and Austin to San Antonio. The western route was particularly popular during part of the war when Union troops held territory along the lower Rio Grande, forcing Texans to cross their cotton into Mexico at Laredo or elsewhere. But the San Antonio route also was used at other times, as described by Ronnie C. Tyler in "Cotton on the Border, 1861–1865," *Southwestern Historical Quarterly* 73 (Apr., 1970): 456–77. In the Alamo City, Texans could exchange their cotton for goods that merchants from Mexico had hauled up from the border, freeing the Texans to head back north immediately rather than continue on to Mexico.

39. Harrison, *History of Greenville and Hunt County*, pp. 126–27.

40. James L. Terry, letter to David Pickering, Mar. 31, 1996, FPC. Terry is the great-grandson of Thomas Henderson Terry. For figures on enlistment by Tex-

ans in the Union army, see Frank H. Smyrl, "Texans in the Union Army, 1861–1865," *Southwestern Historical Quarterly* 65 (Oct., 1961): 234–35.

41. Fugitives who took to the woodlands in North Texas were often called "bush men" or "brush men" by contemporaries, with "brush men" being the term most commonly used. See David Paul Smith, *Frontier Defense in the Civil War: Texas' Rangers and Rebels*, p. 199.

42. Weddle, *Plow-horse Cavalry*, p. 27.

43. Quoted in ibid., p. 97.

44. Loma Scroggins Patton, comp., "The Warm Heart" (manuscript, 1964, FPC), pp. 13–14.

45. Bowman, "Jernigan's Thicket."

46. Patton, "Warm Heart," p. 9.

47. Ibid. "Stevens Regiment" apparently was the Texas Twenty-second Cavalry Regiment, also called the First Indian-Texas Cavalry Regiment, which served in the Indian Territory May–Aug., 1862, and was dismounted in 1862. Originally commanded by Col. Robert H. Taylor, it was led during part of its service by Col. James G. Stevens (Stewart Sifakis, *Compendium of the Confederate Armies, Texas*, p. 79).

48. Ben Briscoe, "Early History of Hunt County," BP.

49. Quoted in Bowman, "Jernigan's Thicket."

50. Patton, "Warm Heart," p. 14.

51. Brig. Gen. Henry E. McCulloch to Capt. Edmund P. Turner, on the staff of Asst. Adjutant General Stephen D. Yancy, Sept. 16, 1863, in Robert N. Scott et al., eds., *The War of the Rebellion: A Compilation of the Official Records of the Union and Confederate Armies*, 26(2): 236.

52. O. M. Roberts, "Texas," in *Confederate Military History*, ed. Clement Evans, p. 105.

53. McCulloch to Gen. John P. Magruder, Oct. 21, 1863, in Scott, *War of the Rebellion: Official Records*, 26(2): 344–45.

54. Briscoe, "Early History of Hunt County."

55. T. U. Taylor, "The Lee-Peacock Feud," *Frontier Times* 4 (May, 1926): 19.

56. McCulloch to Henry Boren, Oct. 24, 1863, in Scott, *War of the Rebellion: Official Records*, 26(2): 352.

57. Smith, *Frontier Defense in the Civil War*, p. 77.

58. McCulloch, quoted in ibid., p. 80.

59. Ibid., p. 108.

60. Ibid., p. 109.

61. McCulloch to Col. James Bourland, Oct. 8, 1864, quoted in ibid., p. 127.

62. Gen. Edmund Kirby Smith to Maj. C. S. West, Oct. 7, 1864, in Scott, *War of the Rebellion: Official Records*, 41(3): 987.

63. Briscoe, "Early History of Hunt County."

64. McCulloch to Magruder, Dec. 18, 1863, quoted in Smith, *Frontier Defense in the Civil War*, p. 108.
65. Smith, *Frontier Defense in the Civil War*, pp. 78–79. About four hundred of the Missouri-based guerrillas under William Clarke Quantrill crossed into North Texas around October 1863, after committing notorious acts of butchery at Lawrence, Kans., and Baxter Springs, Indian Territory.
66. John Warren Hunter, "Heel-Fly Time in Texas: A Story of the Civil War Period," *Frontier Times* 2 (Apr., 1924): 39. (Unless otherwise stated, all "Heel-Fly" citations are from this issue of *Frontier Times*.) According to Cooper High School agriculture teacher Sam Bettes (Bettes, interview by Judy Falls, Feb. 19, 1998, FPC), the heel-fly is also known to Texas cattlemen as the cattle botfly or warble fly, which lays its eggs on the legs of cattle. The larvae burrow into the animals and can harm or even kill them before the insects re-emerge as winged adult flies. Horses and cattle, which seem to realize the flies are dangerous, become greatly excited when heel-flies are buzzing around the herd.
67. Brown, *Strain of Violence*, p. 128.
68. Three of the five men hanged in 1862 appear in the 1860 census. The records show zero personal property and land worth $250 for James E. Hemby; land worth $800 and $250 in other property for Jonathan Hemby; land worth $355 and $767 in other property for Henry T. Howard. Comparative figures for seven of the eight men indicted in the Hemby-Howard hanging are George W. Cox, land $4,000, other $5,180; George W. Helms, land $9,750, other $6,970; James C. McGlasson, land $5,000, other $5,500; M. G. Settle, land $1,100, other $2,460; Greenville Smith, land $3,200, other $15,000; Charles H. Southerland, land $1,280, other $350; and John Jack Helms, land $200, other $250.

Census records from 1860 are available for all four of the men hanged in Hopkins County in 1863. They show Joseph D. Campbell, land $1,092, other $1,200; Horace DeArman, land zero, other $300; Thomas Greenwood, land $1,110, other $685; and James M. Millsaps, land $400, other $300. Census figures are available for two of the five men indicted in the 1863 Hopkins County hanging. They show: Elbert Early, land $6,500, other $25,000; and Thomas Searls, land $1,200, other $5,500.

While nobody was indicted in the 1863 hangings in Hunt County, census records (U.S. Bureau of the Census, Eighth Census, 1860) exist for three of the five victims: Pleasant R. Fitzgerald, land $240, other $400; Austin H. Glenn, land $1,000, other $600; and Thomas Randolph, land zero, other $831.
69. The mean value of combined real and personal property for Texas men around this time was $6,393, according to Richard Lowe and Randolph Campbell in "Wealthholding and Political Power in Antebellum Texas," *Southwestern Historical Quarterly* 79 (July, 1975): 27–29. The authors of this book have used *average* worth—total worth divided by the number of people—rather than *mean*

value—the midpoint between the poorest and richest—but our figures and those of Lowe and Campbell provide a basis for approximate comparison.

70. Quoted in Brown, *Strain of Violence,* p. 108.

71. Kate Stone, *Brokenburn: The Journal of Kate Stone, 1861–1868,* ed. John Q. Anderson, pp. 225–26, diary entry for July 12, 1863; p. 234, entry for Aug. 16, 1863; p. 237, entry for Aug. 30, 1863.

Kate proclaimed Paris "a clean, pretty place" (p. 231, entry for Aug. 3, 1863), but just about everywhere else in the Forks watershed she saw ugliness. "And oh, the swarms of ugly, rough people, different only in degrees of ugliness. There must be something in the air of Texas fatal to beauty," she wrote in a famous comment (p. 223, entry for July 7, 1863). But she was deeply touched by one pitifully poor family, near Tarrant, who took the Stones in after their carriage broke a wheel and whose generosity is commemorated in a state historical marker at a roadside park five miles north of Sulphur Springs on state highway 19/154. Kate wrote of the place she termed "Rescue Hut" on Sept. 11, 1865. She explained that the house she visited was "the roughest two-room affair with six or eight people living in it, and with nothing to eat this last day but bread and milk and butter. They killed their last chicken for us yesterday, an old, old hen, but the people are as kind as they can be, and as hospitable. They give us of their best and are really sorry for us." Then Kate describes the "two women and a girl and not a scrap of ribbon or lace or any kind of adornment in the house. I never saw a woman before without a ribbon. They have not even a comb. They are the very poorest people I ever saw." Later Kate wrote that "the people who had sheltered us utterly refused all pay and were hurt at the idea— and they with absolutely nothing. Truly it is not the rich who are the most generous" (pp. 359–61).

72. Brown, *Strain of Violence,* p. 23.

73. Reynolds, "Vigilante Law During the Texas Slave Panic of 1860," p. 174.

74. After a vigilante hanging in Fannin County in 1861, editor F. W. Miner of the *Paris Press* editorialized against vigilantism. The *Paris Press* article of unknown date was reprinted in the Sept. 28, 1861, *Marshall Texas Republican.*

75. Dickson D. Bruce, *Violence and Culture in the Antebellum South,* pp. 2–3.

76. Bertram Wyatt-Brown, *Southern Honor: Ethics and Behavior in the Old South,* p. 369.

77. Ibid., p. 460.

78. Ibid., p. 371.

79. Cash, *Mind of the South,* pp. 42–43.

80. Bruce, *Violence and Culture in the Antebellum South,* p. 4.

81. Robert P. Ingalls, "Mob Violence," in *Encyclopedia of Southern Culture,* ed. Charles Reagan Wilson and William Ferris, p. 1508.

82. Reynolds, "Vigilante Law during the Texas Slave Panic of 1860," pp. 173–74.

Chapter 2

1. Terry G. Jordan, "Early Northeast Texas and the Evolution of Western Ranching, *Annals of the Association of American Geographers* 67, no.1 (Mar., 1977): 67–68.
2. James M. Millsaps, deed to wife and children, Hopkins County, Texas, Sept. 7, 1860, from Millsaps Family Records, FPC.
3. Jordan, "Imprint of the Upper and Lower South," p. 681.
4. In *Loose Leaves* (p. 152), Ikie Patteson states: "Of the early emigrants into the forks of Sulphur, those who took up lands in the northwest part . . . were from Southern states . . . and were principally old-time Southern aristocrats, . . . most of them being slave-holders. Those who settled in the extreme forks and in the southern part . . . were a mixture of people from both the South and the North. Yankees they were called." The Needmore community is located at the intersection of Farm Road 3132 and a dirt road between Barnett Creek and the West Fork of Jernigan Creek a mile and a half southwest of Yowell. Residents there organized the Jernigan Baptist Church in 1850. The post office was called Pecan for a while before being changed to Needmore in 1886 (Tyler et al., *New Handbook of Texas*, 4:962).
5. G. Ross Price, "A History of Charleston, Texas" (research paper, Texas A&M University-Commerce, 1952, FPC), p. 20.
6. Several children of James K. Howard described their family history and listed the children of Arington and Elizabeth Howard in applications for a share of the Eastern Cherokee settlement in Oklahoma in 1907 (Lance Hall, e-mail to Julie Clayton, Apr. 20, 1998, FPC). Also, the 1850 census shows James, Thomas, Henry, and five of their brothers and sisters, all in their teens or twenties, living together in their own household in a rural area of Travis County (Austin area). But the Howards may have been in Travis County only briefly—perhaps as farmworkers who came to help with the harvest. Later records show at least six of the siblings—Eliza, Elizabeth, James, Thomas, Henry, and Joseph—back in the Lamar-Hopkins area. Some other information on the family comes from Edna Evans LaFour (LaFour, e-mail to Julie Clayton, Oct. 14, 1996, FPC). Numerous land records for Howard family members exist in the Lamar-Hopkins area, including a deed that describes Henry as "son of A. Howard" (Delta County Deed Records, Volume W, pp. 276, 280), and a Sept. 19, 1863, statement by Elizabeth E. Howard verifying the authenticity of the signatures of her deceased brothers James, Henry, and Thomas on a deed. It reads: "They were her brothers" (Lamar County Deed Records, Book M, pp. 39–40).
7. Charles D. Spurlin, comp., *Texas Veterans in the Mexican War: Muster Rolls of Texas Military Units*, p. 65. Lance Hall lists the children of James K. and Lydia Howard as John T., born Sept. 13, 1855; Isaac Whitaker, born Mar. 13, 1857;

Mary Elizabeth, born Jan. 25, 1859; and Martha Jane, born June 22, 1861 (Hall, e-mail to Julie Clayton, Apr. 20, 1998).

8. Neither Thomas nor James K. Howard appears on the 1860 census. Benjamin Ober mentioned Thomas Howard's son M. in his "Memoir," p. 17.

9. The children of Henry T. and Harriet Howard, as shown in the Eighth Census, 1860, Hopkins County, Precinct 3, were William T., five, and Mary E. J., two. Paris attorney E. L. Dohoney said in his self-published memoir An Average American (p. 80) that Howard was a Baptist minister. Church of God pastor Benjamin Ober said in his "Memoir" (p. 17) that Howard was a licensed Cumberland Presbyterian Church pastor who switched to the Church of God in 1862. No records on Howard can be found in the Baptist or Presbyterian churches, but it is thought that Ober, as a fellow pastor, is probably the most accurate source concerning Howard's denomination. For more on the early area Cumberland church, see A. W. Neville, *The History of Lamar County*, p. 49.

10. A. W. Neville, *The Red River Valley, Then and Now*, p. 147.

11. Ibid., pp. 147, 74. Pioneer ministers in Texas commonly worked at other occupations in addition to preaching. Pastors of the Church of Christ, notably, were "chiefly men otherwise employed during the week who preached on weekends and during the summer months" (Tyler et al., *New Handbook of Texas*, 2:105).

12. Eighth Census, 1860, Schedule 4, Hopkins County, Precinct 3.

13. Ibid., Slave Schedules, Hopkins and Lamar Counties.

14. Hunter, "Heel-Fly Time in Texas," p. 33. "Heel-Fly," cited here from the 1924 *Frontier Times* version, previously appeared in *Hunter's Magazine* in 1911 with a somewhat different introduction. The introduction to the *Frontier Times* version apparently was written after Hunter's death in 1915, probably by his son J. Marvin Hunter. It states that the Hunter family resided in Sulphur Bluff (located outside the Forks delta on the south bank of South Sulphur River in Hopkins County). However, the Hunter family shows up in the 1860 census for Lamar County's Precinct 9, which included part of the East End of the Forks delta. J. W. Hunter, a fifteen-year-old male born in Alabama, is shown with his father, Thos., forty, and mother, J. D., thirty-two, both natives of Tennessee, and three younger siblings, all born in Mississippi—a girl, M. L., ten; a girl, W. A. E., eight; and a boy, W. E., six.

15. Marion Day Mullins, in *Republic of Texas: Poll Lists for 1846* (p. 75), lists James Hemby, J. W. Hemby, and Jonathan Hemby of Lamar County. The presumption that James W. and Jonathan Hemby were sons of James Hemby is based on anecdotal accounts among descendants of James W. Hemby (Richard Hunter, e-mail to David Pickering, Apr. 8, 1998).

16. Patteson, *Loose Leaves*, p. 186. The listed bridge fees are those charged after the Civil War by a "Mr. Harper," who constructed a bridge over South Sulphur River on the Bonham-Jefferson Road, where the DeSpain Bridge formerly stood.

17. Spurlin, *Texas Veterans in the Mexican War,* p. 65; Thomas H. Kreneck, "The North Texas Regiment in the Mexican War," *Military History of Texas and the Southwest* 12 (July, 1975): 110–17.

18. Betsy Mills, comp., and Elizabeth House, ed., *Lamar County, Texas, Marriage Records, 1841–1874,* p. 27; Mary Claunch Lane, "Biardstown School Site, Lamar County" (manuscript, FPC). The undated manuscript by Lane, of Paris, Tex., lists Jonathan Hemby as one of a number of people who taught at the Biardstown school, with classes being held "at an old log home of W. W. Biard; and then in the old Church of Christ." The Eighth Census, 1860, Lamar County, Precinct 2, shows Jonathan and Anna Hemby's children to be eleven-year-old Amanda, eight-year-old Miriam, four-year-old William Edward, and two-year-old John Z. Also living with the family was a Mary J. Kendall, fifteen.

19. James Patteson, letter to L. L. Bowman, Feb. 3, 1933, BP. The Cooper attorney's statement that James E. and Jonathan Hemby were brothers is the only known evidence, other than Hemby family stories, concerning their relationship.

20. Browne Elizabeth Millsap Myers, "The Millsaps," in *Pioneers of Hopkins County, Texas,* ed. Sylvia M. Kibart and Rita M. Adams, 2:25.

21. Tom and Kathy Hembey, "The Hembey Family History: Descendants of James E. Hembey and Melinda Jane Oldham" (manuscript, FPC). The 1860 census of Lamar County, Precinct 2, lists twenty-nine-year-old James Hemby along with his twenty-eight-year-old wife, Jane, who was a native of Illinois, and six children: ten-year-old Thomas, nine-year-old Mary, seven-year-old Julien, four-year-old John Miller, and three-year-old Nancy A., all born in Missouri, and six-month-old William Henry, who was born in Texas.

22. Lamar County Genealogy Society, "A History of the Church of Christ at Antioch, Lamar County, Texas," *Lamar County Genealogy & History* 14 (May, 1996): 14. Other Hembys on the list of early church members are A. M. Hemby, John Hemby, and William Hemby, while a list from 1866 includes "Ann Hemby." Both A. M. Hemby and Ann Hemby may have been Jonathan's wife/widow, Anna M. Pair Hemby.

23. Dohoney, *Average American,* p. 135.

24. Patteson, *Loose Leaves,* p. 156.

25. Mrs. L. F. Hooten, Sr., comp., "Delta County Scrapbook." The quoted material is taken from a hand-written entry for July 2, 1965, giving an account of Mrs. Hooten's interview with Mrs. Lula Lavenia Grant Bangs of the Cedar Creek community, who is a descendant of Forks watershed pioneer Joseph McElroy Griffith.

26. *Delta County History,* p. 31.

27. Neville, *History of Lamar County,* p. 81. The planters commonly sent the cotton down Red River from Wright's Landing in Red River County, but when the water was especially high they shipped out of Pine Hills (also called Pine Bluffs), about twenty-five miles farther upriver.

28. Ibid., pp. 84–85. As noted by Neville, the Red River Raft was demolished by the federal government in the 1870s in the belief that it would open the northern section of the river to easy navigation. In fact, however, the raft had been acting much like a dam. After the raft's demolition, the water level on upper Red River fell, ending steamer traffic to ports in Lamar County and killing the port of Jefferson as well.

29. *Delta County History*, pp. 27, 41; Patteson, *Loose Leaves*, p. 125; *Texas Almanac, 1861*, pp. 122–26.

30. Eighth Census, 1860, Slave Schedules, Lamar County. Members of one of the old-time families of the Forks watershed generally spell their surname "Patteson," but the name shows up in many documents as "Patterson." The authors employ the "Patteson" spelling for individuals known to belong to this family.

31. G. G. Orren, "The History of Hopkins County" (master's thesis, East Texas State University, 1938, FPC), p. 32; Frank H. Smyrl, "Unionism in Texas, 1856–1861," Southwestern Historical Quarterly 67 (Oct., 1964): 190. Also voting against secession, in addition to Lamar's delegates, were T. P. Hughes and E. Thomason of Williamson County; J. R. Johnson of Titus County; and J. D. Rains and A. P. Shuford of Wood County.

32. Dohoney, *Average American*, p. 78.

33. Ibid., p. 79.

34. Ibid., pp. 79–80. Dohoney gives the man's name as Thomas Howard, but he was writing about a half-century after the event. A newspaper item from 1862 and Ober's "Memoir" provide persuasive evidence that the man Dohoney was referring to was Henry Howard, brother of Thomas Howard.

35. Dohoney, *Average American*, pp. 74–75. Dohoney's comment about the Mississippi and its tributaries being "like the great aorta of the human system" brings to mind a comment by Dickson D. Bruce in *Violence and Culture in the Antebellum South* (p. 14): "Southerners generally held to organic conceptions of society. This could mean, and often did, that they viewed society as a system, like the body, of interdependent parts. It could also mean, as it did for a long time, that bodily metaphors controlled thinking about historical processes."

36. Dohoney, *Average American*, pp. 74–75.

37. *Marshall Texas Republican*, Mar. 2, 1861. Those listed as signers of the "Address to the People of Texas" were Senators "Martin D. Hart, I. A. Paschal, Emory Rains, and J. W. Throckmorton." The signers who were representatives to the state legislature were "M. L. Armstrong, Sam Bogart, L. B. Camp, W. A. Ellett, B. H. Epperson, John Hancock, J. L. Haynes, J. E. Henry, T. H. Mundine, A. B. Norton, W. M. Owen, Sam J. Redgate, Robert H. Taylor, and G. W. Whitmore." Those signers listed as Secession Convention Delegates were "Joshua F. Johnson of Titus County, John D. Rains and A. P. Shuford of Wood County, L. H. Williams, Geo. W. Wright, and Wm. H. Johnson of Lamar County."

38. In "Unionism in Texas" (p. 191) Smyrl states: "It was this election on February 23 that best reflects Unionist sentiment around the state. The anti-secession vote came mainly from two areas—the western counties centering around Austin and San Antonio, and the North Texas counties. Angelina County in East Texas also gave a majority against secession."

39. Roy Sylvan Dunn, "The KGC in Texas, 1860–1861," *Southwestern Historical Quarterly* 70 (Apr., 1967): 556. The KGC also had "castles," as the organization's chapters were known, in Alleyton, Austin, Bastrop, Booneville, Brenham, Caldwell, Cameron, Castroville, Chappell Hill, Columbus, Dallas, Eagle Lake, Gonzales, Helena, Houston, Huntsville, Independence, Jefferson, La Grange, Marshall, McKinney, Navasota, New Braunfels, Owensville, Pleasanton, Rusk, San Antonio, Seguin, St. Mary's, and Waxahachie.

40. Tyler et al., *New Handbook of Texas,* 3:1145–46.

41. Taylor's address to the legislature in Jan., 1861, is quoted in McCaslin, *Tainted Breeze,* p. 32.

42. Ibid., p. 36; *Marshall Texas Republican,* May 25, 1861.

43. Lost Lake Lodge Charter Book, records for 1861, 1865, 1867, State Archives of the Masonic Grand Lodge of Texas A. F. & A. M. Library and Museum of Texas, Waco (hereafter cited as Masonic Lodge Charter Book). Charter members of the lodge are listed as Greenville Smith, James Patterson [Patteson], John B. Craig, Garlin Anderson, Winnfield Williams, James Cole, John A. Trevilion, B. M. Patterson [Bernard M. Patteson], Saml Lunsford, G. W. Williams, and S. Jameson. (Some of the names are nearly illegible, particularly those taken to be Lunsford and Jameson.) The Masonic Hall owned by Greenville Smith is described in Patteson, *Loose Leaves,* p. 43.

44. Brown, *Strain of Violence,* p. 106.

45. McCaslin, *Tainted Breeze,* p. 61.

46. Tuck, *Civil War Shadows in Hopkins County,* pp. 13–14.

47. McCaslin, *Tainted Breeze,* p. 61.

48. Entry for John Jack Helm in Tommy Ruth Hargrave and Carroll Terrell Slack, comps., "Helms Family Records" (bound typescript, FPC). While the family currently uses the "Helm" spelling, the name is spelled "Helms" in numerous records from around the time of the Civil War. See *The Fayette County New Era* (La Grange, Tex.), Aug. 8, 1873.

49. F. O. Skidmore, letter to the *Victoria Advocate,* quoted by C. L. Sonnichsen in *I'll Die Before I'll Run: The Story of the Great Feuds of Texas,* p. 46.

50. Victor Rose, *The Texas Vendetta; or, The Sutton-Taylor Feud,* pp. 13–14.

51. Eighth Census, 1860, Hopkins County, Precinct 3.

52. *The Paris Advocate* article of unknown date was reprinted in the *Marshall Texas Republican* on June 15, 1861.

53. United States, *Biographical Directory of the United States Congress, 1774–1989: Bicentennial Edition.*

54. "Rep. H. S. Bennett of Mississippi speaking on behalf of a southerner as Speaker of the House," U.S. Congress, *The Congressional Globe*, appendix, 34th Congress, 1st sess. (Dec. 22, 1855), p. 50.

55. McCaslin, *Tainted Breeze*, pp. 26–27. See also Donald E. Reynolds, "Reluctant Martyr: Anthony Bewley and the Texas Slave Insurrection Panic of 1860," *Southwestern Historical Quarterly* 96 (Jan., 1993): 344–61.

56. Dohoney, *Average American*, p. 134.

57. Norton, "Methodist Episcopal Church in North Texas," p. 338.

58. Reynolds, "Reluctant Martyr," p. 350.

59. Dohoney, *Average American*, p. 79.

60. Tuck, *Civil War Shadows in Hopkins County*, pp. 4–5.

61. *Marshall Texas Republican*, May 25, 1861; Neville, "Backward Glances" column, *Paris News*, Oct. 15, 1937. The existence of Thomas Howard's card is known only because it was republished in a "Backward Glances" column. No copies are known to exist of most *Paris Press* issues.

62. Hayden's card was republished by Neville in a "Backward Glances" column that appeared in the *Paris News* on Oct. 10, 1937. (Note: In his *History of Lamar County* [p. 71], Neville wrote that Turner B. Edmondson, as he spelled the name, served as the first mayor of Paris following its incorporation in 1856.)

63. Neville included the Aug. 5, 1861, militia roster for Beat 2, Lamar County, in a "Backward Glances" column in the *Paris News* on Mar. 4, 1938. A roster from a militia organizational meeting in Hopkins County, Beat 3, on Aug. 24, 1861, is preserved in the Texas State Archives (Adjutant General Records, #RG 401, Military Rolls, Captain C. B. McGuyer [McGregor?], 9th Brig., Aug. 24, 1861).

64. Patteson, *Loose Leaves*, pp. 157–59; Texas Historical Marker for "Site of Old Camp Rusk," Delta County; Louise Horton, *Samuel Bell Maxey: A Biography*, p. 39. The Ninth Texas Infantry Regiment, under commanders other than Maxey, served in numerous major battles, including Shiloh, Corinth, Murfreesboro, Chickamauga, Perryville, Missionary Ridge, New Hope Church, Atlanta, and Mobile.

65. B. P. Gallaway, ed., *Texas: The Dark Corner of the Confederacy: Contemporary Accounts of the Lone Star State in the Civil War*, p. 6.

66. Sparks, *War between the States*, p. 17. Other Ninth Texas Cavalry companies were A Tarrant, C Grayson, D Tarrant, E Red River, F Titus, and I Titus.

67. George L. Griscom, *Fighting with Ross' Texas Cavalry Brigade C.S.A.: The Diary of George L. Griscom, Adjutant, 9th Texas Cavalry Regiment*, ed. Homer L. Kerr, p. 229.

68. Sparks, *War between the States*, p. 15.

69. Griscom, *Fighting with Ross' Texas Cavalry*, pp. 2–3.

70. Dohoney, *Average American*, pp. 134–35.

71. Griscom, *Fighting with Ross' Texas Cavalry*, p. 228. The regiment was still

called the Fourth Texas Cavalry when it went into winter quarters near Van Buren, Ark., in the vicinity of Fort Smith (Griscom, *Fighting with Ross' Texas Cavalry*, p. 12). The military records for John Jack Helms in the National Archives indicate he was absent from his regiment during Jan.–Feb., 1861. One card in Helms's files states that he appeared on a company muster roll for "Nov & Dec 1861," and another card says he appeared on the muster roll for "Mch & Apr 1862." There is no mention of service in Jan.–Feb.

Jim Elmore is thought to have been the J. C. C. Ellmore who was listed as a private in the Ninth Texas Cavalry's Company G (Griscom, *Fighting with Ross' Texas Cavalry*, p. 229) and appeared in the 1860 Hopkins County census as sixteen-year-old James C. C. Elmore (shown living near the Leech household and the several Helms households on the farm of his parents, William and Cyntha Elmore).

The allegation that John Jack's wife, Minerva, was having an affair with Jim Elmore is in Hargrave and Slack's "Helms Family Records." Delta County historian Douglas Albright heard a different version of the story, described in his undated manuscript "Criminal Cases of Delta County" (Delta County Public Library and copy in FPC). According to this version, John Jack deserted because his wife was having an affair with his brother-in-law, Alonzo Leech, husband of John Jack's sister Sarah Ann. The Helms family records give the name of Sarah Ann's first husband as Jim Lynch, rather than Alonzo Leech, but that may be incorrect. The Eighth Census, 1860, Hopkins County, Precinct 3, shows John Jack and his family living next door to Alonzo L. Leech and his wife, Sarah A., whose given name and age fit those of Sarah Ann Helms. The family records also indicate that John Jack was divorced from his first wife, time unspecified, and married Margaret Virginia Crawford in Jan., 1869, in Clinton, DeWitt County, Tex. He had two children by his first wife and three by his second.

72. Aden Posey, interview by L. L. Bowman (undated), BP.
73. Erastus "Ras" Hopper, interview by L. L. Bowman, Feb. 21, 1933, BP. (Note: Bowman's papers erroneously give the name as Harper instead of Hopper.) The use of celebratory explosions by North Texans is well documented. Troopers of the Ninth Texas Cavalry welcomed their commander back to camp in 1862 by "firing rifles by platoons and . . . anvils by the dozen" (Griscom, Fighting with Ross' Texas Cavalry, p. 12). Anvil firing involved filling the swage hole of one anvil with gunpowder, setting another anvil onto it, and blowing the top anvil into the air. Folklorist Frank C. Brown has made the interesting comment that "the shooting of firecrackers and the discharging of firearms at Christmastime are customs rarely, if ever, observed anywhere north of the Mason-Dixon line" (quoted in Fischer, *Albion's Seed*, p. 745).
74. Dohoney, *Average American*, p. 135.
75. *Marshall Texas Republican*, Oct, 26, 1861, Feb. 8, 1862, and Feb. 22, 1862.

76. Stone, *Brokenburn*, p. 85.

77. *Marshall Texas Republican*, Feb. 8, 1862.

78. Hendley Stone Bennett, Military Service Records, National Archives; Dohoney, *Average American*, pp. 95–96.

79. Brown, *Strain of Violence*, p. 111.

80. Eighth Census, 1860, Lamar County.

81. Brown, *Strain of Violence*, pp. 63–64.

82. Ibid., p. 64; Smith, *Frontier Defense in the Civil War*, p. 115; James M. McPherson, *Battle Cry of Freedom: The Civil War Era*, p. 240.

83. *Marshall Texas Republican*, Feb. 1, 1862.

84. Jotham H. Condit and Eben Condit, *Genealogical Record of the Condit Family,
Descendants of John Cunditt, a Native of Great Britain Who Settled in Newark,
N.J., 1678 to 1885*, pp. 212–13.

85. Dohoney, *Average American*, pp. 135–36. Some evidence that the Hembys and
Howards hid in Jernigan's Thicket comes from family stories gathered by Delta
County historian Douglas Albright. Also, old-timer Ras Hopper told Judge
Bowman that the Hembys and Howards were captured "in a thicket," although
he did not identify the thicket by name (Hopper, interview by Bowman). In
his "Memoir" (p. 16), Benjamin Ober does not specify where the capture took
place but seems to imply that it occurred in "a dense forrest (sic)" which was a
hiding place from "mobs" (a popular Texas synonym for vigilantes). He describes this place and vigilante activity that focused on it before going directly
into a description of the Hemby-Howard trial and hanging.

86. Benjamin Ober says in his "Memoir" (p. 17) that two other men were under arrest by the vigilantes along with the Hembys and Howards. It is thought the
two may have been captured along with the others in Jernigan's Thicket. Douglas Albright wove family stories about the hanging into a narrative account in
his manuscript "Criminal Cases of Delta County." Albright does not cite his
sources for the account, but story details appear to indicate that much of his
material apparently came from members of the Helms family or families of
other men accused of carrying out the hanging. One of the principal errors in
Albright's account is the assertion that the Hembys and Howards were deserters. No records indicate that the men were members of any active military
units, and their capture and death occurred before the Confederacy enacted
any conscription laws. The Confederate Congress passed its first conscription
act on Apr. 16, 1862.

87. John Warren Hunter, "Heel-fly Time in Texas," *Frontier Times* 2 (May, 1924):
43.

88. G. B. Ray, *Murder at the Corners*, p. 10.

89. Hopper, interview by Bowman.

90. Patteson, *Loose Leaves*, p. 39; Douglas Albright, interview by Judy Falls, Dec.,

1968, FPC; W. B. Miller, "History of Ben Franklin and Giles Academy," *Delta Courier* (Cooper, Tex.), Apr. 7, 1925.

91. Helen Hart Luckett, letter to Judy Falls, Apr. 23, 1997, FPC. Luckett, of Fort Worth, is a member of the Yates family. According to a family story from the Civil War, John Yates "was ordered to 'Go down to the Sulphur bottoms, . . . get the deserters, give them a military trial and hang them.' This is what he did!" Despite the references to "Sulphur bottoms," "deserters," and "military trial," none of which apply to the Hemby-Howard case, it is thought that the story is a memory-dimmed account of Yates's participation in the capture of the Hembys and Howards at Jernigan's Thicket, under orders from vigilantes who also were militia officers. That an attempt was made to arrest Yates on account of a hanging after the war, according to family stories, provides the strongest evidence of his involvement in the Hemby-Howard affair. As far as is known, no arrests were attempted in that area for any other Civil War hangings.

92. Hopper, interview by Bowman.

93. Albright, "Criminal Cases of Delta County."

94. *Austin Republican*, Nov. 23, 1870.

95. Hopper, interview by Bowman.

96. Ober, "Memoir," p. 17; Albright, "Criminal Cases of Delta County." The Albright account erroneously places W. S. Condit in the thicket with the Hembys and Howards, maintaining that he escaped back into the brush as the vigilantes were capturing the others. That story is contradicted by the accounts of Condit's fate in Dohoney's memoir and the Condit family history.

97. Several sources agree that the hanging site was on the south bank of South Sulphur River, in what is today Hopkins County. The sources include Ras Hopper, in his 1933 statement to Bowman; Patteson in *Loose Leaves*, p. 86; and James Patteson of Cooper, in his 1931 letter to Bowman. Patteson said his information came from Charles H. Southerland, one of the men indicted for the hangings. The south-bank hanging site also is given in "Criminal Cases of Delta County" by Albright, who possibly was told of the location by Charleston-area residents. No accounts specifically state that the trial site and hanging site were the same, but that may be inferred from the absence of any mention in accounts that the hanging site and trial site were separate locations.

98. Dohoney, *Average American*, p. 134.

99. Brown, *Strain of Violence*, p. 60. While some scholars today reserve the term "lynching" for hangings of blacks by whites, the authors have followed the practice of many scholars who apply the term to illegal hangings involving people of any race.

100. In *Tainted Breeze* (p. 71), McCaslin noted that vigilantes who carried out the Great Hanging in Gainesville in the fall of 1862 "sought to uphold at least the

spirit of American law by confirming each step through popular sovereignty, by involving many prominent members of the community, and by allowing the accused to have the same rights as a prisoner arraigned before a regular court."

101. Albright, interview by Judy Falls. The identity of the vigilante who visited the McGuire home is uncertain. Albright at one point mentions John Jack Helms as the man but elsewhere names him as D. S. "Sim" George, an in-law of McGuire's.

102. Dohoney, *Average American*, p. 133.

103. Wright Patman, *A History of Post Offices and Communities, First Congressional District of Texas*, p. 4.

104. Dohoney does not name the vigilantes but identifies an indicted man who fled to Georgia as the vigilantes' leader (Dohoney, *Average American*, p. 135). The man who fled to Georgia was Greenville Smith, according to his nephew James Patteson (Patteson, letter to Bowman, July 16, 1931, BP). Patteson also said he was told by Charles H. Southerland that Smith, G. W. Cox, and M. G. Settle were the trial officers and the jurors were Southerland, G. W. Helms, John Jack Helms, Thomas Rufus McGuire, and David Simeon "Sim" George. The indictments returned in the case in 1865 list Smith, Cox, Settle, Southerland, and the two Helmses and also James McGlasson and J. W. Stansbury. In 1867, Rice Warren was mentioned as a participant in the vigilante proceedings by men from Lamar and Hopkins Counties (George W. DeWitt, P. Miles, J. M. Easley, and M. L. Armstrong, letter to Gen. Charles Griffin, Apr. 28, 1867, U.S. Army OCA Records). The men also mentioned McGlasson, Cox, Smith, Southerland, and the two Helmses as participants.

105. Brown, *Strain of Violence*, p. 105.

106. Eighth Census, 1860, Hopkins and Lamar Counties.

107. Brown, Strain of Violence, p. 121.

108. Ober, "Memoir," p. 16.

109. Forney, *History of the Churches of God*, section on Texas Eldership.

110. Lamar County Genealogy Society, "History of the Church of Christ at Antioch," p. 14. As noted in Tyler et al., *New Handbook of Texas* (2:106), the Civil War had little adverse effect on the state's Churches of Christ.

111. Ober, "Memoir," p. 17.

112. Ibid.

113. Dohoney, *Average American*, pp. 35. For the popular saying about letting moss grow on one's back, see, for example, J. N. Carr's letter to his wife, quoted in chap. 1.

114. Richard W. Hunter, e-mail to David Pickering, Aug. 8, 1996, FPC. Hunter is a great-great-grandson of James Wesley Hemby. He heard the "Abraham Lincoln" story from his uncle Sanford Hemby, who said he got it from his grandfather—Richard Hunter's great-grandfather—Silas Wright Hemby.

115. Dohoney, *Average American*, pp. 134–35.

116. Ober, "Memoir," p. 17.

117. Ibid., pp. 17–18.

118. Dohoney, *Average American*, p. 134; Ober, "Memoir," p. 17.

119. Ober, "Memoir," p. 18. Several accounts say the men were hanged on the limb of a single tree, usually described as an elm. However, it is thought that Ober's account—more detailed than any other—is most accurate on this point. It is corroborated by a comment from Thomas Rufus McGuire printed in the *Houston Press* on Mar. 13, 1948; he said the hangings were carried out on "a pole between two trees."

120. Hunter, e-mail to David Pickering, Aug. 8, 1996. Hunter heard this story from his uncle Sanford Hemby.

121. Albright, "Criminal Cases of Delta County."

122. Robert Templeton, Thomas Peters, Dennis Calloway, Maggie Layer, and Nell Oliver, interviews by Judy Falls, June, 1998, FPC. In *Loose Leaves* (p. 169), Ikie Patteson said that Oxford's Bridge has changed names several times. Originally built by a Mr. Castleberry and called the Castleberry Bridge, it later was repaired by a Mr. Oxford and came to be called Oxford's Bridge until "after the war between the states [when it] was called the Redman Boyd Toll Bridge."

123. Skipper Steely, "Forty-seven Years" (manuscript, Steely Papers, University Archives, Texas A&M University-Commerce, 1988), p. 637.

124. Ober recalled the name as J. A. Connady, but Church of God records show the name as A. J. Canady (Forney, *History of the Churches of God*, section on Texas Eldership).

125. It is possible that jury holdout Cornelius B. McGuire was among Forks delta men who were pressured into joining the Confederate army. For whatever reason, he did not join up until very late in the game—on Apr. 18, 1864, when, at age forty-two, he became a private in Company G of the Twenty-third Regiment of Texas Dismounted Cavalry (Cornelius B. McGuire, Confederate Soldier's Discharge, McGuyer/Oats Family Records, FPC).

126. Ober, "Memoir," pp. 18–19.

127. Griscom, *Fighting with Ross' Texas Cavalry*, p. 13. The regiment reached Fayetteville, Ark., on Feb. 27, 1862. For a week or more afterward, dozens of men caught up to the regiment from behind, including many who were returning to the unit following furloughs in North Texas.

128. Sparks, *War between the States*, p. 53.

129. John Jack Helms, Military Service Records, National Archives. Griscom, who mentions mass desertions on some occasions, does not mention any on the date the regiment was dismounted. He states: "*Temporarily dismounted . . . now are wanted across the river to assist in fighting the big battle that is expected to take place at Corinth where forage is not obtainable in sufficient quantities to subsist all our stock . . . the Regt are not very well pleased but submit*" (*Fighting with Ross' Texas Cavalry*, p. 33). The regiment was later rehorsed and oper-

ated during the later years of the war as part of Ross's Texas Brigade, under Gen. Lawrence Sullivan "Sul" Ross, former Texas Ranger, future Texas governor, and Texas A&M college president.

130. Griscom, *Fighting with Ross' Texas Cavalry,* p. 228; Hargrave and Slack, "Helms Family Records." According to the Helms family records, Jim Elmore and Sarah Ann Helms Leech Elmore had three children before Jim died at age thirty-five of tuberculosis.

131. As James Marten has noted, "some home guard regiments harbored deserters from units sent east of the Mississippi." Such situations and other reprehensible features of militia companies contributed to scorn heaped on members of the units by many Southerners, including the sister of a Confederate soldier who derided home guardsmen as "feather beds" (Marten, *Texas Divided,* p. 97).

132. Hunter, "Heel-Fly Time in Texas," p. 33.

133. Ibid., pp. 33–37.

134. Masonic Lodge Charter Book, records of Lost Lake Lodge 255, Dec. 29, 1866, pp. 9, 11. At some point during the war, the lodge moved to the Giles Academy. In his "History of Ben Franklin and Giles Academy," W. B. Miller states, "The writer's search in the archives of the Grand Lodge failed to find why this lodge was moved from Smith's furniture factory at the lake to the Academy. The reports of T. H. B. Hockaday, secretary, failed to mention the matter."

135. J. J. Cunningham, *History of Paris Lodge No. 27, A. F. & A. M.: With a List of Other Lodges in the County, and Dates of Their Organization,* p. 45; Hendley Stone Bennett, Military Service Records.

136. Francelle Pruitt, "'We've Got to Fight or Die': Early Texas Reaction to the Confederate Draft, 1862." *East Texas Historical Journal* 36 (spring 1998): 4.

137. Griscom, *Fighting with Ross' Texas Cavalry,* muster rolls, pp. 209–38; James C. Bates, letter to Nancy Bates, May 10, 1862, and Bates, letter to Will Bramlette, May, 1862, from the letters of James Campbell Bates, Fink Family Collection, Henry Fink, Custodian (hereafter cited as Bates Papers).

138. In *An Average American,* Dohoney makes no mention of his failed attempt to secure a lieutenant colonelcy, saying instead that he was "discharged on account of physical disability" (p. 109).

139. Ibid., p. 80.

Chapter 3

1. McCaslin, *Tainted Breeze,* pp. 90–91, 94, 5–6.

2. In *Tainted Breeze* (p. 200), McCaslin gives the last recorded address for hanging victim Leander W. P. "Jacob" Lock as Lamar County (Eighth Census, 1860) and says that hanging victim Gilbert Smith was mustered into a Fannin County militia unit in July, 1861, although he apparently owned livestock in Cooke County (p. 203).

3. John F. Hart lived in Virginia and Indiana before coming to Texas, and his sons Martin D. and Hardin probably were born in Indiana, according to Tyler et al., *New Handbook of Texas*, 3:490. See also Banta and Caldwell, *Twenty-seven Years on the Texas Frontier*, p. 30. According to Sharon Jernigan Tingley, John Hart, nephew of John F. Hart, was married to Elvira Jernigan, sister of Curtis, William, and Felix (Tingley, e-mail to David Pickering, Jan. 8, 1998, FPC).

4. Elveta Phillips, *Fading Moments Recorded: A Brief Description and History of the Wieland Community*, pp. 16–17. "The Wieland Harts were all descended from Charles Hart, b. 1795 in Mercer County, Ky.," noted Milton Babb of Denton, Tex., whose ancestors include Harts from the Wieland community (Babb, e-mail to David Pickering, Jan. 28, 1998, FPC). These Harts came to the area from Kentucky via Illinois—a route similar to that of many other area Harts who came from Kentucky via Illinois or Indiana—but Babb has never been able to establish a common ancestry.

5. John F. Hart also had a brother named Meredith who "is said to have come to Texas even before John F. did," W. Walworth Harrison informed Carson Hart of Greenville in a letter (Harrison to Hart, Apr. 4, 1965, Hardin Hart File, W. Walworth Harrison Collection, Greenville Public Library, copy in FPC) (hereafter cited as Hart File, Harrison Collection). Harrison said Meredith Hart was one of the five commissioners named to organize Hunt County, but "we assume he left this part of the State and went on west." The John F. Hart clan of Fannin-Hunt and the Jonathan "Jackie" Hart clan of Fannin-Hopkins are thought to be branches of the same family, based on Judge Bowman's study of family relationships in "Hart Family," BP, and information in "Hart Family Records," compiled by Patsy White of Sugar Land, Texas, which were supplied to the authors by Hart relative Sharon Jernigan Tingley. (The records are in Vol. 3, World Family Tree CDs, WFT 2566, and also in FPC.) The records indicate that Miles H. Hart, who died around 1785 in Nelson County, Ky., was the father of one Josiah Hart (b. 1768) whose line led through son John F. Hart (b. 1790) to sons Hardin Hart (b. about 1814), Martin D. Hart (b. about 1821), and other descendants. Another of Miles H. Hart's sons, John Hart (b. 1759), left Kentucky for Illinois, where presumed son Jonathan "Jackie" Hart (born about 1799) is thought to have grown up and raised a family that included sons Jonathan G. "Fox" Hart (b. about 1831), James C. Hart (b. about 1839), daughter Martha (b. about 1837), and other children.

6. Tyler et al., *New Handbook of Texas*, 3:994; W. Walworth Harrison, letter to Mrs. Lutie Brown, Aug. 13, 1966, Hart File, Harrison Collection.

7. Steely, "Forty-seven Years," pp. 416–17, 426.

8. Rex Wallace Strickland, "History of Fannin County, Texas, 1836–1843, Part II," *Southwestern Historical Quarterly* 34 (July, 1930): 63.

9. Rex Wallace Strickland, "History of Fannin County, Texas, 1836–1843, Part I,"

Southwestern Historical Quarterly 34 (Apr., 1930): 271; Strickland, "History of Fannin County, Part II," p. 64.

10. Andy J. Middlebrooks and Glenna Middlebrooks, "Holland Coffee of Red River," *Southwestern Historical Quarterly* 69 (Oct., 1969): 149–50.

11. Silas Colville, letter to John Steele Young, July 10, 1842, quoted in Middlebrooks, "Holland Coffee of Red River," p. 150.

12. Tom Scott, "Fannin County: Two Centuries of Texas Legend," *Bonham Daily Favorite,* Sept. 1, 1985.

13. Graham Landrum, *Grayson County: An Illustrated History of Grayson County, Texas,* p. 70.

14. Harrison, letter to Brown, Aug. 13, 1966.

15. V. W. Grubbs, "Hunt County Pioneers: Judge Hardin Hart." *The Greenville Banner,* Apr. 12, 1911.

16. W. Walworth Harrison, "Hardin Hart" (manuscript, Hart File, Harrison Collection); Scott, "Fannin County: Two Centuries of Texas Legend." The Eighth Census, 1860, Hunt County, shows Martin D. Hart, thirty-nine, born in Indiana; wife, Mary, thirty-five, born in Missouri; and the following children, all born in Texas: John, seventeen; William, fourteen; Jincy [Jenny], eleven; Caius, seven; Louisa, six; and also one Hugh Hart, twenty-one, a "stock herder," who was presumably a relative. An undated note in the Greenville Public Library's Hart File, Harrison Collection, apparently by Hunt County historian Harrison, related information from the 1860 census for Martin D. Hart. According to this note, Hart had $18,000 worth of real estate and personal property worth $7,000. The author stated that "this real estate value was the highest I believe of any individual in Hunt County except M. H. Wright, who showed $32,470 in real estate and the same amount in personal property. When you consider that most of the real estate they had was rural and land was valued at perhaps a dollar an acre, it means these men had a tremendous acreage of Hunt County land. Several had higher personal property values than Martin Hart but only Wright had more land so far as I noticed."

17. Alfred Howell, letters to Morton Howell, Oct. 20, 1853, June 1, 1854, Apr. 17, 1855, and June 1, 1854, all in HC. Hardin Hart was well respected according to a 1911 biographical sketch (Grubbs, "Hunt County Pioneers: Judge Hardin Hart"). One of Hart's most notable qualities during several postwar terms as judge was "plain, blunt though expressive language." In a case of assault with a deadly weapon, involving one man's injuring another with a pocketknife, he instructed the jurors: "Gentlemen of the jury, you are charged that anything that will cut guts is a deadly weapon."

18. Ingmire, *Archives and Pioneers of Hunt County,* 1:36.

19. Many names on the handwritten muster roll of the Greenville Guards apparently are difficult to read, for transcribers have rendered some of them in strikingly different ways. The following list combines two different attempts at

transcription. Names as rendered on a typed list in the Bowman Papers are given first, followed, in parenthesis, by different versions of the names as they appear on a typed list found in the papers of Delta County historian Douglas Albright: Captain Martin D. Hart, 1st Lt. John W. Dise (John Dickson), 2nd Lt. Money Weatherford, 3rd Lt. Jackson Weatherford, 1st Sgt. Prior Hart, 2nd Sgt. Andrew (Anderson) Hart, 3rd Sgt. Andrew Lawson, 4th Sgt. Hardin W. Denney (Haden W. Dewry), 1st Cpl. Charles A. Gulivan (Sullman), 2nd Cpl. Gamuel P. Boyd (Samuel J. Boyd, Jr.), 3rd Cpl. K. T. Babb, 4th Cpl. A. Pool, and Privates I. R. (J. R.) Arnold, F. M. (G. M.) Arnold, C. C. Arnold, Frank Brown, Joseph C. Bacus (Baccus), I. M. Band (J. M. Bard), I. C. (J. C.) Baker, W. W. Bartholmen (Bartholomew), I. M. (J. M.) Babb, Leon (Levi) H. Brake, John Copeland, Oliver J. Christy (Chrisly), Isaa W. (Issac J.) Crabtree, W. D. Crabtree, W. (H.) Darling, W. I. Elter (W. J. Etter), Thomas Elliott, I. H. Gates (J. N. Gales), I. T. Gilspie (J. T. Gillespie), Wm. Graham (Grayham), Kelly Gilbreath, John Hart, L. M. Hamilton, Lyrus Hart (Syrus Heart), Stephen C. Hart (Heart), I. M. Hughey (J. M. Kelly), John Hopper, James Janiff (John James Joliff), Richard Janiff (Joliff), W. E. H. (W. E. M.) Jones, Wm. Long, Elby (Elley) Lawson, George F. Marshall, Wely N. Mainas (Wily N. Manos), I. W. (J. W.) Massey, E. I. (E. J.) Marshall, James McCokley (McCoulskey), Daniel McConkley (McCoulskey), Dusen (Duren) A. Moore, James Nance, John G. (W.) Norris, William Odell, Turner Odell, Ruben (Reubin) Odell, B. F. Primm (Pinson), I. F. (J. H.) Roberts, I. W. (J. M.) Robinson, Robert Hodges, William Hodges, Isiah (Josiah) Hart, J. W. Riley, Robert E. Glewart (Stewart), J. N. Glewart (J. W. Stewart), R. H. Scott, B. C. Sheppard (Shepherd), Wm. Pelts (Pitts), P. B. Purcell, Wm. H. Forbut (Torbert), Robert Taylor, Hugh Wadson (Wilson), James Welbanks (Wilbanks), I. W. Wardlon (J. W. Wardlow), George Wilson, W. H. Tart (W. C. Yost), John Bogus (Boggus), Wm Hart (Wm. Heart), James Wood, William C. Watson, W. H. Gart.

Harrison states in his *History of Greenville and Hunt County* (p. 122) that most of the Greenville Guards probably became Confederate soldiers—as did Guard Sgt. Prior Hart, who became a Confederate lieutenant—and none are known to have joined Martin D. Hart on the Union side. Harrison said most members of the Guards were "substantial citizens," including 2nd Lt. Money Weatherford, who was a Hunt County commissioner at the time.

20. Pleasant Fitzgerald, Military Service Records, National Archives; Martin D. Hart, Military Service Records, National Archives, cited by J. S. Duncan in "Commentary: 'Martin Hart, Civil War Guerrilla,'" *Military History of Texas and the Southwest* 11 (1973): 139–40. The Union pension applications by the widows of Martin D. Hart and Pleasant Fitzgerald, a trooper in Hart's band, clearly were jointly composed. The applications, filed at the same time by the two women who both resided in Hunt County, are identical in most details, in-

cluding wording, except where the stories of the two men differ. The supposition that Hart and his men were under suspicion from Confederate authorities when they fled from Texas is derived from two sources. One is the wording of a letter from E. L. Dohoney in Lamar County to a friend, saying Hart and his men had *"escaped* [italics added] from Hunt County" (Dohoney, letter to Capt. James C. Bates, Nov. 20, 1862, Bates Papers). The other source is a letter in the *Fort Smith (Ark.) New Era* of Dec. 17, 1864, under the heading "TEXANS LOOK HERE—INFORMATION WANTED!":

When the present rebellion broke out, I was a resident of Titus county, State of Texas, and about the 26th of August, 1862, *I, with several others, was ordered to be arrested* [italics added] on a charge of treason against the so-called Confederate States of America. I left Texas and came to Springfield, Missouri, in company with the brave, unfortunate and lamented Captain Martin D. Hart, consequently I was compelled to leave my wife and little son behind, but I think she will avail herself of the opportunity of coming out under the late order of Henry McCulloch. Her Christian name is Amanda Melvina. Now, if this notice should chance to meet the eyes of any person who can, and will give me any information, by letter or otherwise, of where she is, will confer a favor on me, for which I will ever feel grateful; also, if they could give her information of this notice, I will be very thankful. If she does get out and can reach Litchfield, Montgomery county, Illinois, she will find friends who will see that she does not suffer. I have been in the United States service over two years. My address:

William Gaston,
Q.M. Sergt. Co. E. 2 Bat. 6th Cav. Mo. Vol.
St. Louis, Mo. Nov. 26, 1864

21. A. B. Lewis, "Chasing Guerrillas in Arkansas," *Confederate Veteran* 29 (1921): 220.
22. William E. Sawyer, "Martin Hart, Civil War Guerrilla," *Texas Military History* 3 (fall 1963): 146.
23. Dohoney, letter to James C. Bates, Nov. 20, 1862, Bates Papers. The "Jack Hamilton" mentioned by Dohoney was Andrew Jackson Hamilton, a former Texas congressman and opponent of secession who had escaped from the state through Mexico after the outbreak of war and who had been appointed a general in the Union army. Immediately after the war, he would serve as provisional governor of Texas.
24. *Dallas Herald,* Dec. 6, 1862, quoted in Landrum, *Grayson County,* p. 70.
25. Emeline Fitzgerald, widow of Hart Company trooper Pleasant Fitzgerald, stated in her postwar application for a Union pension that her husband and other members of Hart's troop were attached to the First Regiment of Arkan-

sas Cavalry until Jan. 9, 1863, when "by order and with the consent of Generals Herron and Blunt" her husband and "nearly all members" of Hart's company started back to Texas with orders to recruit a Federal regiment "to be Styled the First Regiment of Texas Cavalry," leaving only Captain Hart, Lieutenant Hays, and ten men in Arkansas, and that the detachment "Came into Texas about the 25th day of January" (Pleasant Fitzgerald, Military Service Records, National Archives). That a part of Hart's company returned to Texas seeking recruits also was mentioned by old-timer G. W. King of Leonard, Tex., who said, "Fox [Jonathan] Hart . . . had taken part of Martin D. Hart's command and gone to Texas for recruits" (King, interview by Bowman, July, 1931, BP).

26. Thomas E. Jordon, "Captain Martin Hart's Date with Death," *Civil War Times* 36 (May, 1997): 42–43; Leo E. Huff, "Guerrillas, Jayhawkers and Bushwhackers in Northern Arkansas during the Civil War," *Arkansas Historical Quarterly* 24 (summer, 1965): 136.

27. Huff, "Guerrillas, Jayhawkers and Bushwhackers," p. 141.

28. Scott, *War of the Rebellion: Official Records,* 22(2): 774.

29. Lewis, "Chasing Guerrillas in Arkansas," p. 222.

30. T. A. Pettigrew, account of Hart's Charleston raid published by the *Fort Smith Times* around 1899, typewritten transcript, BP (hereafter cited as Pettigrew account of Hart's raid, *Fort Smith Times*). Pettigrew, who was seven years old at the time of the raids, was the grandson of Judge Thomas Aldridge. The boy was present at the Aldridge plantation when Hart's Company visited there without killing anyone.

31. Cecil Harper, "Martin D. Hart: Another Look at a Hanged Texas Unionist" (paper presented at the annual meeting of the Texas State Historical Association, Austin, Mar. 1, 1996, FPC).

32. Pettigrew placed the date of the plantation raids as Jan. 14, 1863 (Pettigrew account of Hart's raid, *Fort Smith Times*). But he placed the date of the raids at Jan. 12 in a letter to Judge Bowman on Aug. 24, 1931, BP.

33. Sawyer, "Martin Hart, Civil War Guerrilla," pp. 148–49; Pettigrew, letter to Bowman, Sept. 7, 1932, BP. In this letter Pettigrew described the intensity of the sentiment after the war regarding the murder of Col. DeRosey Carroll and Mr. E. M. Richardson. Pettigrew admits that the hostility and anger were so great in the area that Arkansas men who had been recruited by Hart's Company would not admit to it. "I know the names of four men who lived between the stream called Big Creek and the stream called Vache Grasse in Sebastian County, Ark., who were generally thought to be members of said band, but would not like to name them without positive proof. . . . Jeremiah Carter, owner of 160 acres of land adjoining Charleston, Ark., who died January or February, 1863, was according to depositions taken in the case of William vs. Carter . . . a member of this band."

34. Pettigrew told Bowman (letter, Sept. 7, 1932), "D. A. Carroll, a grandson of

Col. Carroll, states that he has made an investigation, and there is no doubt in his mind that McGoing is the man who shot Col. DeRosa [sic] Carroll. . . . McGoing was killed some six months after the death of Carroll by a small Confederate force who had captured the son of Bob Jones who lived half way between Charleston and Greenwood and spared young Jones's life on condition he would lead them to where McGoing was hiding." In his newspaper account of Hart's Charleston raid, Pettigrew quoted A. V. Reiff, who took part in the capture of Hart's Company, as saying, "I have talked with several witnesses who saw Lieut. Hays shoot down Col. Carroll and Mr. Ed Richardson." Pettigrew also quotes Reiff as saying, "I heard Captain Hart say on the gallows that Hays shot [Richardson and Carroll] by his order." A. B. Lewis, who also took part in the capture of Hart's Company, gave an account that differs from the others (Lewis, "Chasing Guerrillas in Arkansas," p. 220). He does not specify who killed Richardson but says Lieutenant Hays and another member of the party shot and killed Carroll. Based on the evidence, the authors think it possible that McGoing and Hays shot Carroll, and that Hays alone shot Richardson.

35. Pettigrew account of Hart's raid, *Fort Smith Times.*
36. Cameron quoted in Duncan, "Commentary: 'Martin Hart, Civil War Guerrilla,'" p. 138.
37. Thomas E. Jordon, "Captain Martin Hart" (manuscript, FPC), p. 17.
38. Sawyer, "Martin Hart, Civil War Guerrilla," pp. 150–51.
39. Huff, "Guerrillas, Jayhawkers and Bushwhackers," p. 127.
40. *Daily Arkansas Gazette,* Aug. 15, 1866, quoted in Huff, "Guerrillas, Jayhawkers and Bushwhackers," p. 148.
41. Pettigrew account of Hart's raid, *Fort Smith Times.*
42. Ibid.
43. Some accounts erroneously cite the unit as the Texas First Cavalry Battalion, a unit with which Crump previously had served (Sifakis, *Compendium of the Confederate Armies, Texas,* p. 40).
44. Lewis, "Chasing Guerrillas in Arkansas," p. 221; Pettigrew account of Hart's raid, *Fort Smith Times.*
45. Pettigrew account of Hart's raid, *Fort Smith Times.* Lewis had a different recollection. In "Chasing Guerrillas in Arkansas" (p. 221), he said the Confederates used "Richardson-Carroll" as "the countersign," possibly meaning they used the two names as sign and countersign.
46. Lewis, "Chasing Guerrillas in Arkansas," p. 222. Lewis's 1921 *Confederate Veteran* account, "Chasing Guerrillas in Arkansas," is one of the most often-quoted sources about the activities of Hart's Company in Arkansas. But the article does not inspire trust in its accuracy, since it contains some obvious errors and may contain others that are not obvious. Notably, Lewis gives Martin Hart's first name as Wilson, says Fox Hart was his brother (whereas the two

were cousins), says Fox was killed in Arkansas (whereas he lived through the war), says the Harts were from Greene County, Texas (instead of Hunt County), and is off by a month in some dates, citing events of Jan., 1863, as having occurred in Dec., 1862.

47. Pettigrew account of Hart's raid, *Fort Smith Times.*

48. When the *Texas Republican* printed this article about the capture, on Jan. 29, 1863, the news had not yet arrived in Marshall that Martin D. Hart and J. W. Hays already had been hanged.

49. Sawyer, "Martin Hart, Civil War Guerrilla," p. 150.

50. Huff, "Guerrillas, Jayhawkers and Bushwhackers," pp. 141, 128.

51. Pettigrew, letter to Bowman, Sept. 7, 1932.

52. Quoted in Jordon, "Captain Martin Hart's Date with Death," p. 46.

53. The number of men who returned to Texas is inferred from an account saying that Hart's Company contained thirty men when it attacked a Union force in early January (Sawyer, "Martin Hart, Civil War Guerrilla," p. 147) and from Emeline Fitzgerald's statement in her postwar pension application that "nearly all" the troop was sent back to Texas later, with only Captain Hart, Lieutenant Hays, and ten men remaining in Arkansas (Pleasant Fitzgerald, Military Service Records).

54. Bowman, "Jernigan's Thicket."

55. Lewis, "Chasing Guerrillas in Arkansas," p. 222. Pettigrew, in his account of Hart's raid, gives a different version of the hanging, quoting former Confederate officer A. V. Reiff: Charles Carroll "climbed the tree and tied the rope to a limb, that hung Hart . . . Carroll Armstrong tied the rope to the limb that swung Hays into eternity."

56. The existence of the Hart's Company muster roll, which apparently has not survived, is mentioned by Ras Hopper of Hopkins County. He told Judge Bowman (Hopper ["Harper"], interview by Bowman) that he attended the trial of the men captured that year in Jernigan's Thicket and that those conducting the trial had a muster roll of Hart's troop. Since the Young Man attended this trial, according to Hicks Nowell of Hunt County (Bowman, "Jernigan's Thicket"), it seems possible that the Young Man was the person who supplied the muster roll.

57. Reba Bayless Boyer, comp., *Monroe County, Tennessee, Records, 1820–1870,* 1:16, 35.

58. The scissors story is from "Capt. Merit Brannom: Biographical Sketch of an Interesting Man, an Eventful Career—Reminiscences of That Time That Tried Men's Souls," a turn-of-the-century biographical sketch from an unknown newspaper, probably in Hopkins County, included in the Millsaps Family Records, FPC. The information about education in the Glenn family is from Austin H. Glenn descendant Fred Odom. Thomas Tyre Glenn was a doctor while son Joseph was a schoolteacher, both before the war. Afterward, daughters

Rhoda and Margaret became schoolteachers, while Austin, Jr., became a farmer-preacher (Fred Odom, e-mails to David Pickering, Aug. 27, 1996, and Mar. 30, 1997, FPC).

59. Odom, e-mail to Pickering, Mar. 30, 1997. The information about Austin H. Glenn, Jr.'s 1862 service comes from his own application for a Union pension in 1915. Although he was approved for a Union pension based on other service, the 1862 claims were disallowed after a government search of records failed to substantiate them. However, there is little doubt that Austin, Jr., actually did serve from 1862 as he stated. Disapproval of Union pension claims was common, even in cases where no doubt existed concerning a man's Union service—as, notably, for claims by the widows of Martin D. Hart and Hart Company trooper Pleasant Fitzgerald (Military Service Records of Austin H. Glenn, Jr., Martin D. Hart, and Pleasant Fitzgerald, National Archives).

60. Austin H. Glenn, Jr., Military Service Records.

61. *Marshall Texas Republican,* Apr. 4, 1863; L. L. Bowman, comments on Brannom and Searls indictments, BP.

62. Odom, e-mail to Pickering, Aug. 27, 1996.

63. L. L. Bowman, annotation of article in *Dallas Herald,* Apr. 15, 1863, BP. In his comments on the *Herald* article, which was a reprint of a *Marshall Texas Republican* article about Hunt and Hopkins Counties hangings, Bowman quotes one Charley Dial as saying, "Parson Glenn . . . was a Protestant Methodist preacher and . . . an abolitionist. . . . With Glenn was also hung Trace Chain Smith, said to have been given this name because he was accused of stealing some trace chains at one time."

64. Frances Terry Ingmire and Robert Lee Thompson, *Johnny Rebs of Hunt County, Texas,* p. 8.

65. Bowman, annotation of *Dallas Herald* article; Bowman, comments on Brannom and Searls indictments.

66. In his comments on the Brannom and Searls indictments, Bowman said of Glenn and Smith, "These two men were buried at a point south east from the old France Fore home on the ridge north from Lone Oak." That location may accord with a description of Austin Glenn's burial place given by his daughter Rhoda in a letter to her niece, Frances Crenshaw, on Oct. 14, 1920 (cited by Odom, e-mail to Pickering, Aug. 27, 1996). Rhoda said her father was buried on the family farm "12 or 15 miles SE of Greenville, and 8 miles SW of Black Jack Grove [today's Cumby] and 5 miles N of Lone Oak."

67. Bowman, annotation of *Dallas Herald* article; Bowman, comments on Brannom and Searls indictments; Jerry Green, telephone interview by Judy Falls, June 27, 1998, FPC.

68. DeArman Family Records, from Patricia DEArman Fite of Houston, FPC.

69. Horace DeArman married Martha C. Hart on Aug. 16, 1854, in Fannin County, according to Hart Family Records. The Eighth Census, 1860, Fannin

County, Precinct 6, Garrett's Bluff, shows H. DeArman, a thirty-year-old, Tennessee-born farmer; his wife, M., twenty-one, born in Illinois; and a two-year-old Texas-born son, Jonathan J.

70. In his comments on the Brannom and Searls indictments, Bowman cites one Bruce McMahan, who was related to the DeArmans, as his informant for the story of DeArman's horseshoeing accident and recovery on the Glenn farm.

71. McCulloch to Magruder, Oct. 21, 1863, in Scott, War of the Rebellion: Official Records, 26(2): 344–45.

72. Bowman, "Jernigan's Thicket."

73. Jordan, "Early Northeast Texas and the Evolution of Western Ranching," pp. 66–87; James M. Millsaps, deed to wife and children, FPC.

74. U.S. Bureau of the Census, Seventh Census, 1850, Fannin County; Eighth Census, 1860, Hopkins County.

75. Eighth Census, 1860, Hopkins County, Beat 5.

76. Muster Roll for Beat No. 8, Hopkins County, including election of officers, on Aug. 17, 1861, Millsaps Family Records, FPC.

77. Beth Gunn, The Fitzgeralds: From Tennessee to Texas, p. 14.

78. Fox and Jim Hart's father, Jonathan "Jackie" Hart, died around 1859. The household of their mother is listed in the Eighth Census, 1860, Hopkins County, Beat 5, showing fifty-eight-year-old Synthia A. Hart, a "stock raiser" born in Tennessee with real estate valued at $600 and other assets totaling $1,500, and various other members of the household. The same census shows numerous other Harts in the area, including son James C. Hart, a twenty-one-year-old farm laborer who was born in Illinois and owned real estate valued at $830 and other property totaling $930; wife Emeline, eighteen, who was born in Kentucky; and two-month-old son Stephen, who was born in Texas.

79. Joseph D. Campbell, who apparently was Joseph D. Campbell, Jr., appears with his parents and siblings in the Seventh Census, 1850, Hickman County, Tennessee. It lists Joseph D. Campbell, born 1785 in Tennessee; wife Rachel, born 1783 in South Carolina; son Joseph D., born 1833 in Tennessee; and four daughters, all born in Tennessee: Margaret, born in 1831; Frances, born in 1835; Virginia, born in 1840, and Mary, born in 1842. The Eighth Census, 1860, Hopkins County, Beat 5, lists Joseph D. Campbell, twenty-eight-year-old Tennessee-born farmer; a "housekeeper" named Rachel, age fifty-six, who was born in Tennessee (Campbell's mother, although her age and birthplace do not fit those given in the Tennessee census); a fourteen-year-old male named Armsted W., who was born in Tennessee and was said to be Joseph's brother; and a Mary Z., a twenty-year-old "domestic" (probably Joseph D.'s sister Mary) whose birthplace is not legible.

80. The Eighth Census, 1860, Hopkins County, Beat 5, lists Thomas Greenwood, thirty-eight, a Kentucky-born farmer; wife Mary, thirty-two, born in Illinois; daughters Frances, fifteen, Sarah A., twelve, and Mary, eight, all born in Illi-

nois, and Charity, two, born in Texas; and sons James, ten, and Thomas, seven, both born in Texas. A twenty-year-old Illinois-born farm laborer named William Stafford also was part of the household.

81. Myers, "The Millsaps," pp. 24–26. The Eighth Census, 1860, Hopkins County, Precinct 5, lists James Millsaps, twenty-eight, Georgia-born farm laborer; wife Algeretta, twenty-four, born in Missouri; sons Americus, three, and William, seven months, both born in Texas.

82. The Eighth Census, 1860, Hopkins County, Precinct 5, lists Cicero Millsaps, thirty, day laborer born in Georgia, no land, other property valued at $4,000; Emeline, twenty, born in Texas; Jacob Millsaps, thirty-four, day laborer born in Georgia; Minta Millsaps, sixty-three, "domestic" born in South Carolina; and John Potter, nineteen, day laborer born in Texas.

83. Bowman, "Jernigan's Thicket."

84. Ibid.; Bowman, analysis of Hart family genealogy, BP; Janice Jernigin Kiker, "William Jernigin, Founder of Commerce," Commerce Journal, Oct. 31, 1982; Tingley, e-mail to David Pickering, Jan. 8, 1998.

85. Friends of the Commerce Public Library, *The Handbook of Commerce, Texas 1872–1985*, pp. 97–98; Bowman, analysis of Hart family genealogy; Bowman, "Jernigan's Thicket." "According to Hart Family Records, Elvira Jernigan was first married to John Hart; after his death she married Josiah Hart Jackson" (Tingley, e-mail to Pickering, Jan. 8, 1998).

86. Accounts differ as to the formula for jury selection. Hicks Nowell told Bowman ("Jernigan's Thicket") that four men were selected from among the vigilantes, including Jason Wilson and three others whose names he did not recall. The four picked one hundred names, after which the brush men were allowed to choose twelve men from the hundred to serve as their jurors. Ras Hopper had a different recollection. He said the agreement called for the vigilantes to pick a dozen men from Hunt County, a dozen from Hopkins County, and a dozen from Lamar County, with the brush men being allowed to choose twelve men from the thirty-six to act as their jurors (Hopper, interview by Bowman).

87. Bowman, "Jernigan's Thicket." Ras Hopper said, "These men first agreed to be conveyed to the stockade at Tyler, but later protested this as they thought that they would not get any consideration" (Hopper, interview by Bowman). Hopper's account, which is at odds with others in several respects, agrees with the Petty statement about the trip to Tyler.

88. Bowman, "Jernigan's Thicket"; Weddle, *Plow-horse Cavalry*, pp. 102–103.

89. Bowman, "Jernigan's Thicket."

90. Family members who filed postwar lawsuits against Elbert Early, one of the men indicted for murder in the hangings, included Cicero Franklin Millsaps's widow, Emeline. Some evidence also exists that Cicero was the "Tid" mentioned in Hicks Nowell's account. Browne Elizabeth Millsap Myers of Austin says that Cicero's brother Fuller named one of his sons after Cicero and that

this boy, who was born after the war, went by the nickname of "Tid"—thus, there is a strong presumption that the namesake uncle had the same nickname as his nephew. Adding to the considerable uncertainty about the matter is the likelihood that Hicks Nowell got confused in his old age about which Millsaps brother was "Tid" and which was "Jim." Hicks said Tid gave Hicks's father, Bernard, his weapons, with instructions to pass them on to his sons and that Tid had "two sons." However, Cicero, the presumed Tid, had no sons while James had two young boys. Hicks also said that the guns passed from Bernard to himself and that he later gave them to another brother of James and Cicero, Jake Millsaps, who agreed "to deliver them to the sons of Tid Millsaps when they were grown." It is surely significant that Jake Millsaps was the family member who raised *James's* two sons after James's death in 1863 and his widow's death in 1866. Almost certainly it was to these boys that Jake handed on the weapons (Myers, letter to David Pickering, Feb. 22, 1997, FPC).

Further complicating the issue of the identity and the fate of Cicero are a number of Hopkins County documents. Hopkins County Marriage Records, Vol. 2, p. 131, lists the issuance of a marriage license to "Emmeline Millsapps and Wm. Neal" on October 26, 1867. Then the Hopkins County District Clerk Civil Minutes Record, Vol. C, 1866–1871, Case # 918, p. 246, shows that Emeline is granted a divorce from Cicero Millsaps on October 31, 1868. In 1869 the Hopkins County Deed Records, Book N, p. 91, has a listing of owners of Minta Millsaps' land; "Emeline Neil" is listed, apparently for Cicero's share of his mother's land. Another marriage record, found on p. 328 of the Hopkins County Marriage Records, shows that Emeline married Zachariah Lawson on Sept. 8, 1870. Still unanswered is why Emeline filed a lawsuit against Early, why she married William Neal and then sought a divorce from Cicero in 1868, and what happened to Cicero.

91. The location of the house was identified by Hopkins County historian John Sellers (Sellers, e-mail to Pickering, Feb. 15, 1998, FPC), based on Ras Hopper's statement to Judge Bowman in Feb., 1933, that "The house in which these men were tried stood close to where the Stand Pipe [water tower] in Sulphur Springs now stands on Main Street."

92. Bowman, "Jernigan's Thicket."

93. Hopper, interview by Bowman.

94. Pate, quoted in Orren, "The History of Hopkins County," p. 56.

95. Hopper, interview by Bowman.

96. Jeff Mason, undated interview by L. L. Bowman, BP. Mason said the men were tried in Tarrant, instead of Sulphur Springs, but most evidence supports the Sulphur Springs location, including a letter referring to "the Sulphur Springs hangings" that was written after the war by attorney Samuel Bell Maxey (Maxey to wife Marilda, Oct. 27, 1866, Samuel Bell Maxey Papers, Archives Division, Texas State Library, Austin, Tex.). Note: Maxey misdated the

letter as Oct. 26 and gave no year, but events mentioned in the letter clearly show it was written Saturday, Oct. 27, 1866). Aden Posey of Sulphur Springs (interview by Bowman) also placed the hanging site at "this side of White Oak," and Hopper (interview by Bowman) said the hanging site was "on the west side of the road at the present old Tedford place." The location of the hanging site within today's Sulphur Springs city limits was made by Hopkins County historian John Sellers (Sellers, telephone interview by Judy Falls, Dec. 28, 1997, FPC).

97. Jacklyne Houston Conces and Ashley Wysong, interview by Judy Falls, Apr. 11, 1997, FPC.

98. Bowman's "Jernigan's Thicket" is flawed in its math. Although five men were said to have been hanged, it is stated: "the two Millsaps boys were buried at Horton and a rail pen now encloses the place where they were buried. The other two were buried at Shiloh in Delta County."

99. The name of the doctor who visited the *Marshall Texas Republican* is not altogether legible, but appears to be something on the order of Dr. I. L. Woods. The *Republican*'s article of Apr. 4, 1863, about the hangings was reprinted by the *Dallas Herald* on Apr. 15, 1863.

100. Reynolds, "Reluctant Martyr," pp. 356–61.

101. Thomas Greenwood will, Hopkins County Will Book 1, pp. 343–44, Hopkins County Courthouse.

102. Hopkins County Minutes of the District court, 8th Judicial District, Book B, p. 633. The lawsuits are listed as No. 798 "Minky" Milsapps vs. Elbert Early, No. 799 Emeline Millsaps vs. Elbert Early, and No. 800 Rachel Campbell vs. Elbert Early. The Elbert Early in question is presumed to have been Elbert Early of Fannin County, the only man of that name known to have been living in the area at that time and a person who fits the profile of a vigilante leader. An E. B. Early applied for a Confederate pension in 1901 while living at Cumby, in Hopkins County (Tuck, *Civil War Shadows in Hopkins County*, p. 303), but it is not known if his first name was Elbert, and no evidence can be found indicating that he resided in the area during the Civil War.

103. Muriel Champion Burleson, ed., *A History of Ladonia, Texas, 1836–1997*, p. 19, entry for "Elbert Early" by Mary Early Dishner and Honey Sue Lanham Dodge.

104. Smith, *Frontier Defense in the Civil War*, p. 65.

105. Burleson, *History of Ladonia*, p. 19; Steely, "Forty-seven Years," pp. 434–35; Neville, "Backward Glances" column, *Paris News*, Aug. 30, 1932; Neville, *History of Lamar County*, p. 43; Eighth Census, 1860, Fannin County.

106. Clay Randolph, e-mail to Pickering, June 12, 1998. Randolph heard the story about the feud over hay from other members of the Fitzgerald-Randolph clan.

107. Frank B. Norris, interview by L. L. Bowman, Oct. 9, 1929, BP. "Old Doc Nicholson" was perhaps the man referred to by J. B. Gober in his paper "Early His-

tory of Hunt County," BP. He wrote: "Wm. Bramley, Jordon Balshr, James Terry, the Taxams, Dr. Nicholson, others were the early settlers around Hog Eye or Mt. Carmel, as the church was called." Hogeye is located in northern Hunt County, near the Fannin County line.

108. Gunn, Fitzgeralds, p. 11.

109. Ibid., p. 12.

110. Tyler et al., *New Handbook of Texas,* 6:507–508.

111. Randolph, e-mail to Pickering, June 12, 1998.

112. Gunn, *Fitzgeralds,* p. 14.

113. The Eighth Census, 1860, Hunt County, shows John Stubbs, forty-six; wife Elizabeth, forty-two; and eight children who, like the parents, were born in Tennessee: daughters Sarah, eighteen; Mary, twelve; Nancy, ten; and Nicy, six; along with sons Thomas, sixteen; John, fourteen, George, six; and Nicholas, four; Norris, interview by Bowman; Gunn, Fitzgeralds, p. 65.

114. Norris, interview by Bowman; Gunn, *Fitzgeralds,* pp. 27–28.

115. Norris (interview by Bowman), only mentions the capture of Newman, Randolph, and one Fitzgerald. The capture of the two other Fitzgeralds is described by Gunn (*Fitzgeralds*, pp. 27–28), based on family stories. It is possible that "Fate" and James Star Fitzgerald escaped before "Plez" Fitzgerald, Thomas Randolph, and Newman were brought together where Norris saw them.

The Eighth Census, 1860, Fannin County, shows R. Butler, forty-five, and wife E. A., forty-four, both born in Virginia, along with daughters Mary M., nineteen, and Lucy L., twelve, both born in Missouri, son Barness, sixteen, born in Missouri, and son Matthias, five, born in Texas.

116. *Marshall Texas Republican,* Feb. 26, 1863; Mark M. Boatner III, *The Civil War Dictionary,* p. 24.

117. Eighth Census, 1860, Hunt and Titus Counties.

118. Gunn, *Fitzgeralds,* pp. 27–28.

119. Ibid., pp. 25–29.

120. Ibid., pp. 57–58.

121. Ibid., pp. 80–81.

122. Ibid., pp. 54–55.

123. Ibid., p. 27.

124. Frank B. Norris, interview by Bowman, Oct. 9, 1929, BP; W. B. Horton, letter to Bowman, Nov. 4, 1927, BP.

125. Horton, letter to Bowman, Nov. 4, 1927.

126. Ibid.

127. Pleasant Fitzgerald, Military Service Records; Gunn, *Fitzgeralds,* p. 28; Bowman, annotation of *Dallas Herald* article; Green, interview by Falls. When the Ten Stitchers launched their operation is uncertain. Bowman's narrative accounts mention the vigilante raid on the Glenn farm, the vigilante raid on

Jernigan's Thicket, then the Ten Stitchers' operation, which leads to the presumption that the actions in question occurred in that order. But Emeline Fitzgerald placed the capture of her husband at around the beginning of March. If this is correct, and the Apr. 11 date she gave for the hanging of her husband also is correct, then it is possible that Fitzgerald, Randolph, and Newman were captured *before* the men from Glenn's farm and Jernigan's Thicket but not hanged until *after* those other lynchings had occurred. This scenario is possible, but far from certain. Many questions about the Hunt-Hopkins hangings of 1863 simply cannot be resolved.

128. Stone, *Brokenburn*. John Q. Anderson states in his introduction to this book that Amanda Stone owned 1,260 acres of cotton land and about 150 slaves at the Brokenburn plantation in northeastern Louisiana, about thirty miles northwest of Vicksburg, Mississippi. In the spring of 1863, the family fled with most of its slaves from advancing Union troops. In July, Amanda Stone arrived in the western Forks delta with daughter Kate, twenty-two, son Jimmy, sixteen, son Johnny, fifteen, and daughter Amanda Rebecca, thirteen. Not accompanying the family were three older sons, William, Coleman, and Walter, all of whom served with the Confederate military. Coleman and Walter both died while on duty in Mississippi, and Jimmy also would serve in the war, enlisting in 1864. The Stones brought 130 slaves to Texas, which probably made them the largest slaveholders in the Forks delta and among the largest in the state of Texas. Ralph A. Wooster, in "Notes on Texas' Largest Slaveholders, 1860," *Southwestern Historical Quarterly* 65 (July, 1961): 72, reports on a study of 1860 slave schedules that turned up only 51 planters in Texas who owned more than 100 slaves. None of those planters lived in the Sulphur Forks watershed.

129. The identity of "Mr. Smith" has long been a subject of curiosity. That Kate Stone said his home was in Lamar County, toward the western end of the Forks delta, has led some researchers to believe Mr. Smith was Greenville Smith. But there are some problems with the "Greenville Smith solution." Kate locates Mr. Smith's home out on the prairie, while Greenville Smith's home apparently was in Ben Franklin. Also, she refers to his home as "a rough two-room shanty," which seems out of keeping with Greenville Smith's substantial wealth.

But if Mr. Smith was not Greenville Smith, who was he? Most likely a member of the clan headed by one of the four pioneer Smith brothers. The Smith brothers have escaped the attention of researchers because their property was in Hopkins County, not Lamar, albeit their land was just across the county line. Strong evidence that one of this Smith clan was "Mr. Smith" is provided by data from the Eighth Census, 1860, Hopkins County, and a diary entry (Stone, *Brokenburn*, p. 238, entry for Aug. 30, 1863). Kate states that near-neighbor Mrs. Vaughn, who was Mrs. Smith's cousin, had died, leaving six children, including "the two older children, Kitty and Bobby." This neighbor surely was the Elizabeth Vaughn, twenty-seven, who appears as a near-neighbor of the Smith brothers in the 1860 census along with her husband, farmer Augustus Vaughn, thirty-eight, and their then-five children: *Keturah,* ten; *Robert,* nine; Edwin, seven; Tully, three; and Sarah, eleven months (italics added).

The Smith brothers, all of whom were 6-foot-4-inches or taller and weighed more than 250 pounds, were interesting characters who are commemorated by a state historical marker in Delta County near the Antioch community. Charles H. Smith, age forty-four (at the time of the 1860 census), was a well-known beekeeper nicknamed "Honey" Smith. Mira J., a year younger, was a blacksmith. The others were Benjamin, thirty-four, and Gilford, thirty.

Mira J. had a large family including two sons of particular interest. Moses, age seventeen in 1860, became a tanner and was known for his buckskin suits. Henry, age sixteen in 1860, became a blacksmith like his father. While almost any adult male of this Smith clan might well have been "Mr. Smith," Moses and Henry seem particularly notable as candidates. In 1863, with Moses at age twenty and Henry at age nineteen, either could have been a married man living with his young family in a "two-room shanty," and such a shanty might well have been just across the county line, in Lamar, from the homes of other members of the Smith clan.

130. Stone, *Brokenburn,* p. 223, diary entry for July 7, 1863.

131. Ibid., pp. 226–27, diary entry for July 12, 1863. Kate erroneously thought the killings had occurred "within the last couple of weeks."

132. Ibid., p. 227, diary entry for July 12, 1863.

133. Ibid., p. 229, diary entry for July 26, 1863.

134. Ibid., pp. 240–41, diary entry for Sept. 11, 1863.

135. Beth Gunn gives additional information about Sally in *The Fitzgeralds* (p. 29): "Sally not only lost her husband and father in tragic ways, but also lost [her and Cy's] only two children. Sally was undoubtedly a true pioneer woman. Shortly after the Civil War, as a widow, she drove a herd of cattle all the way to St. Louis, Missouri. She had the help of her brothers Bud and Hiram, and two younger Hart boys, brothers of her dead husband. The cattle belonged to all of them. She drove a buggy and took little daughter Dell along on the first trip. While in St. Louis she met her second husband, Ben F. O'Brien. They were later married back in Texas. On another cattle drive to St. Louis, two of the O'Brien children went along."

136. Weddle, *Plow-horse Cavalry,* pp. 102–12.

137. Smith, *Frontier Defense in the Civil War,* p. 107.

138. James C. Hart died Oct. 6, 1876, in Cumberland County, Illinois, according to probate papers involving land he owned in Delta County; the papers were discovered in Delta County records by Judge Bowman and are included in the Bowman Papers. According to unconfirmed information in a 1997 posting on

the Internet from an unknown sender, Jonathan G. "Fox" Hart was married in 1865 or 1866 to one Martha Butts and died Jan. 13, 1889, in Scott County, Ark., where his widow survived him until Feb. 2, 1919.

139. Weddle, *Plow-horse Cavalry*, pp. 102–12. Dr. Penwell wrote home from Illinois, "I fear Jack Rutherford and Bill Leachman did not get through." He recalled that the Harts who accompanied him were "Fox and John" although they almost certainly were Fox and Jim. That Fox and Jim Hart fled "to the north" together was mentioned by G. W. King in his interview by Bowman. (Aden Posey confused the names of the brothers as Fox and Tom Hart in his interview by Bowman but said the two escaped together and "went back north.")

140. Odom, e-mail to Pickering, July 14, 1997, FPC.

141. Odom, e-mail to Pickering, Mar. 30, 1997; Boatner, *Civil War Dictionary*, p. 485.

142. Odom, e-mail to Pickering, Mar. 7, 1997, FPC.

143. Gunn, *Fitzgeralds*, pp. 48–53. "Chism's Regiment" apparently was the Texas Second Cavalry Regiment Partisan Rangers, which was commanded during part of its service by Col. Isham Chism. It served in Louisiana during the Red River Campaign in the spring of 1864, taking part in the battles of Mansfield and Pleasant Hill (Sifakis, *Compendium of the Confederate Armies*, p. 45).

144. Gunn, *Fitzgeralds*, pp. 65, 57.

Chapter 4

1. Briscoe, "Early History of Hunt County."
2. Patton, "Warm Heart," pp. 13–14.
3. Bowman, "Jernigan's Thicket."
4. Patton, "Warm Heart," pp. 10, 15.
5. Ibid., pp. 14–15. Sterling Rodney Scroggins's tale of Frank Chamblee's death also includes a family story about hidden treasure. It was said that Chamblee owned a bucketful of gold, dating from his horse trading in prewar days, and he kept this gold-filled bucket buried in the ground. He went out one night, dug up the bucket, recounted the hoard, then reburied it in a different spot. Frank planned to tell Mary Ellen where he had rehidden the gold, but the arrival of his old foes forced him back to the thicket. Scroggins's tale concludes following his description of Frank's escape and Mary Ellen serving supper to his enemies:

> She did not hear anything of him for some time. . . . Then a man came to see her, with a message, and asked for her to come with him, at once. He takes her to one of the men who had eaten supper with her. This man was dying and he wanted to make a confession. His brother, the other man, was already dead. These boys were Bill and Frank Jurnigan . . . Bill told her

that 3 weeks after they had been to her house they had come upon Frank (Chamblee) by accident. He was on his knees, praying, when they saw him. They shot him there and buried him where he fell. She asked about the money. They had known of no money. Then she asked where they had buried him. He said "Jurnigan's Thicket," but got no further, as the man was dead. She never found the grave nor the money.

Note: Felix Jernigan died in 1876 and William Jernigan in 1880, according to Sharon Jernigan Tingley (Tingley, e-mail to Pickering, Jan. 8, 1998, FPC).

6. Bud Rush, an area old-timer, is quoted by Bowman in "Jernigan's Thicket" as saying, "John Nail killed" Chamblee. The accuracy of Rush's recollection is placed in doubt by his further assertion that "Martin D. Hart was with Nail," since Hart had been dead two years or more by the time of Chamblee's death. Rush apparently was referring to the John Nail shown in the Eighth Census, 1860, Fannin County, Precinct 4, Honey Grove post office. The entry shows Jno. Nail, twenty-nine, a farmer with land worth $4,000 and other assets totaling $2,000 who was a native of Tennessee; wife, R. A., twenty-four, born in Missouri; sons John, six, and Robert, four, and daughter Josephine, two, all born in Texas; and other members of the household—M. Vick, a fourteen-year-old male native of Kentucky; Ann Nail, a forty-five-year-old woman who was born in South Carolina and owned property worth $1,000; and a male farmhand named Ora Miller, twenty-four, who was born in Germany.

7. Sparks, *War between the States,* pp. 120, 123.

8. The *Paris Press* article of unknown date was reprinted in the *Marshall Texas Republican* on Oct. 20, 1865.

9. William L. Richter, "'The Revolver Rules the Day!': Colonel DeWitt C. Brown and the Freedman's Bureau in Paris, Texas, 1867–1868," *Southwestern Historical Quarterly* 93 (Jan., 1990): 303–32; Harrison, *History of Greenville and Hunt County,* pp. 128–35; Ray, *Murder at the Corners;* Taylor, "The Lee-Peacock Feud"; Barry A. Crouch and Donaly E. Brice, *Cullen Montgomery Baker: Reconstruction Desperado;* James Smallwood, "Swamp Fox of the Sulphur," *True West* 38 (Oct., 1991): 20–23 and (Nov., 1991): 38–41; T. U. Taylor, "Ben Bickerstaff, the Noted Desperado," *Frontier Times* 2 (Oct., 1924): 9–10.

10. *Cincinnati Commercial,* Jan., 1869, quoted in Allen W. Trelease, *White Terror: The Ku Klux Klan Conspiracy and Southern Reconstruction,* p. 138.

11. Those who attended the Paris meeting, according to an Aug. 4, 1865, account in the *Marshall Texas Republican,* were E. L. Dohoney, W. H. Johnson, Rice Maxey, F. W. Miner, and G. W. Wright of Lamar; R. H. Taylor and Sam G. Galbraith of Fannin; Hardin Hart and M. H. Wright of Hunt; William M. Ewing, L. A. Lollar and Josiah Smith of Hopkins; B. W. Gray and Henry Jones of Titus; and T. G. Wright of Red River.

12. William Gambill, Jr., letter to Gen. Charles Griffin, May 14, 1867, U.S. Army OCA Records.

13. Harrison, *History of Greenville and Hunt County,* pp. 134–35. Others appointed to posts by the administration of Governor Hamilton included Dohoney's colleague on the anti-secession stump, M. L. Armstrong, who was named district clerk in Lamar County, and T. R. H. Poteet, one of the men threatened by the Sons of Washington, who was named Lamar County treasurer (Neville, *History of Lamar County,* p. 132).

14. Dohoney, *Average American,* p. 123.

15. Ibid., pp. 125–29.

16. If records of indictments in the Hunt County hangings had existed, it seems likely that Judge Bowman, who served on the bench there, would have learned about them during his extensive historical research. No such indictments are mentioned in his papers.

17. Dohoney, *Average American,* p. 135.

18. *Dallas Herald,* Sept. 16, 1865.

19. *Delta County History,* p. 156; James Patteson, letter to Bowman, July 16, 1931, BP. Robert McFarland, a Tennessee native, is listed in the Eighth Census, 1860, Charleston area, as "McFarlin." The Ninth Census, 1870, for the same area gives the spelling as "McFarland." McFarland, who was forty-eight in 1860, was listed with a wife, Nancy, born in Missouri, also age forty-eight, and no children.

20. *Dallas Herald,* Oct. 2, 1865.

21. Hopkins County Minutes of 8th Judicial District Court, Book B, p. 598. The document in question lists grand jurors who were being paid on Nov. 3, 1865, for their recent service. This is the only grand jury list appearing in Hopkins County court records for the fall 1865 court session, and it is thought that those on the list were the grand jurors who returned indictments in both the 1862 and 1863 hangings. One grand juror who served in the Union army was "V. C. Ratton" (Volney C. Rattan) of the Forks delta (Steely, "Forty-seven Years," pp. 393, 405), while it is possible that the grand jury list's "Thos Garrett" was the Thomas P. Garrett listed as a Union army veteran in Tuck's *Civil War Shadows in Hopkins County,* p. 310. At least one grand juror, J. S. (James Shelton) Ashley, was a relative, through marriage, of a hanged man. According to Campbell-Millsaps family records (FPC), Ashley married Margaret Campbell Marrs, sister of the hanged Joseph D. Campbell, after her first husband, James Marrs, was killed in the war, circumstances unknown, around Dec., 1862. Others on the grand jury list included Z. R. Terrell, an early Charleston postmaster (Price, "History of Charleston," p. 17), foreman F. M. Rogers, O. C. McCloy, R. M. Cade, G. W. Downing, W. Thrasher, J. S. Hamilton, Sam W. Smith, F. E. Finney, J. S. Dixon, J. B. Morton, J. C. Dillingham, and H. W. Shrade.

22. Hopkins County Minutes of 8th Judicial District Court, Book B, p. 602, Nov. 3, 1865.

23. James Patteson, letter to Bowman, Feb. 3, 1933, BP.

24. Steely, "Forty-seven Years," p. 387; Neville, "Backward Glances" column, *Paris News,* July 12, 1933; Dice, "Lamar County and Secession," p. 35.

25. Griscom, *Fighting with Ross' Texas Cavalry,* pp. 211–37.

26. Dohoney, *Average American,* pp. 125–26; Price, "History of Charleston," p. 14.

27. *Delta County History,* p. 111.

28. Eighth Census, 1860, Hopkins County, Precinct 7.

29. The Hemby-Howard hanging indictments are listed in the *Hopkins County Minutes of 8th Judicial District Court,* Book B, pp. 599–610. Neville wrote about the gunpowder case in which Stansberry testified in a series of "Backward Glances" columns that ran in the Paris News, June 6–8, 1949.

30. The indictments in the 1863 hanging are mentioned in Hopkins County Minutes of 8th Judicial District Court, Book B, pp. 593–98; Bowman, comments on Brannom and Searls indictments.

31. Ikie Patteson states in *Loose Leaves* (p. 47) that "part, if not all, of the following men took part [in the Indian battle] and probably some of them were among the wounded: Captains Manuel Mathers and Barker (this Captain Barker's son was afterwards county surveyor of Hopkins County), Lieutenant Merritt Brannom, Messrs. Ab. Neatherly, Henry Stout and Wilkshire Bailey."

32. "Capt. Merit Brannom." This newspaper biographical sketch was in materials sent by Browne Myers (now in Brannom File, FPC). It apparently was published at the time of Brannom's death in 1900 and tells of his service as a private; he also is listed as a private in the muster rolls for the Ninth Texas Cavalry's Company K (Griscom, *Fighting with Ross' Texas Cavalry,* p. 236). He is incorrectly listed as a second lieutenant in a 1919 obituary of Jesse C. Garrett, who also was a member of Company K (June E. Tuck, *Hopkins County Obituaries Prior to 1939,* 1:155). According to muster roll information (Griscom, *Fighting With Ross' Texas Cavalry,* p. 236), those elected to serve as officers for Company K were James P. Williams, captain; Moses B. Bowen, first lieutenant; Charles C. Mount, second lieutenant; and Hamilton C. Dial, third lieutenant. In "Brannom's" military records for Ninth Texas Cavalry service, from the National Archives in Washington, D.C., the name is spelled variously as Merit Brannom, M. B. Branom, and M. Brannon. His given name appears in various local records as Merit and Merritt, and his surname as Branom, Brannom, Brannon, and Branham. His state archives military records for service in the TST Second Cavalry Regiment's Company I give the name as "Meredith Brannon."

33. George W. Cox and Greenville Smith, Military Records, Texas Confederate Muster Roll Index, Texas State Archives.

34. Hopkins County Minutes of 8th Judicial District Court, Book B, pp. 593–610.

35. Smith's flight to Tennessee is mentioned in DeWitt et al., letter to Gen. Charles Griffin, Apr. 28, 1867, U.S. Army OCA Records. John Jack Helms's link to Shanghai Pierce's spread is described in Sonnichsen's *I'll Die Before I'll Run,* Chris Emmett's *Shanghai Pierce: A Fair Likeness,* and elsewhere.

36. C. W. Goff, a relative of Council Goff, said that those who took part in the hangings included "pioneer citizens of Hunt Co." and that some left the county "and remained away for several years until personal animosities died out and Federal soldiers no longer patrolled" (quoted in Clara Colder Buckett, comp., "Old-Timers of Hunt County, Texas."

37. DeWitt et al., letter to General Griffin. The jailbreak story is from B. J. "Knob" Chapman of Klondike, Tex., grandson of George and Genova Chapman of the Tarrant area of Hopkins County (Chapman, letter to Pickering, Sept. 11, 1997, FPC). The sequel to the story involves a third person who was present on the night of the escape, B. J. Chapman's father, longtime Sulphur Springs barber John Chapman (1889–1980), who on the night in question was about four years old. When Genova arrived at the jail with Johnny on her saddle, she lifted him down off her horse with instructions to stand quietly. After she overturned the building, she reached down and lifted the boy back up—leaving two tiny bootprints in the mud. The next day, the sheriff rode up to the Chapman home in a buggy, carrying a shovelful of mud that bore the imprints of the boy's boots. But Genova spotted sheriff and shovel coming, added two and two, gathered up her son's little boots before the sheriff reached the door, and threw them into the cistern. "Johnny has no boots" was her reply when the sheriff asked to see them.

38. Posey, interview by Bowman.

39. Dice, "Lamar County and Secession," p. 35; Patteson, *Loose Leaves,* p. 157; James Patteson, letter to Bowman, July 16, 1931. The young food-bringer James Patteson, who would grow up to become Cooper attorney James Patteson, was a major source of information about the Hemby-Howard hangings, based on his childhood experiences and conversations as an adult with surviving vigilantes. Ikie Gray Patteson, who wrote the 1935 Delta County history *Loose Leaves,* was James Patteson's wife.

40. DeWitt et al., letter to General Griffin.

41. Dohoney, *Average American,* p. 136.

42. McCaslin, *Tainted Breeze,* pp. 162–63.

43. Ibid., p. 168.

44. Ibid., p. 169.

45. Randolph B. Campbell, "District Judges of Texas in 1866–67, an Episode in the Failure of Reconstruction," *Southwestern Historical Quarterly* 93 (Jan., 1990): 360.

Hinche Parham Mabry (1829–84) was a Jefferson lawyer who served two terms in the legislature before the war. Initially opposed to secession, he joined Company G of the Third Texas Cavalry Regiment as a captain (Tyler et al., *New Handbook of Texas*, 4:359). In the *New Handbook of Texas*, Mabry is listed as being a general. However, according to Bruce S. Allardice in *More Generals in Gray*, some discrepancies exist in the records regarding Mabry's appointment to general. Mabry is probably one of those generals who was appointed but never confirmed by President Davis in the latter part of the war. Interestingly, "Mabry was, also less honorably, a leader in the local Ku Klux Klan affiliate (the "Knights of the Rising Sun") during Reconstruction. After one particularly notorious lynching, Mabry had to flee to Canada to escape prosecution" (pp. 146–47). George T. Todd (1839–1913) was born in Virginia and came to East Texas in 1840 with his family, which settled in Jefferson. George served as a captain with Company A, First Texas Infantry, Hood's Texas Brigade. After being wounded at Antietam, he finished his service as adjutant of the Third Texas Cavalry Regiment, in which Mabry earlier had served (Tyler et al., *New Handbook of Texas*, 6:514).

46. Dohoney, letter to Bates, Nov. 20, 1862, Bates Papers.
47. McCaslin, *Tainted Breeze*, p. 170.
48. DeWitt et al., letter to General Griffin.
49. Ober, "Memoir," p. 18; DeWitt et al., letter to General Griffin. The *Paris Press* article of unknown date was reprinted in the Sept. 28, 1861, *Marshall Texas Republican*.
50. James W. Hemby, letter to *Paris Press*, Nov. 5, 1866, U.S. Army OCA Records.
51. In *An Average American* (p. 136), Dohoney says attorneys involved in the trial included "Gen. S. B. Maxey, Col. W. H. Johnson, Major W. B. Wright, Col. D. B. Culberson, Col. N. W. Townes and others." Other information comes from Maxey, letter to wife Marilda, Oct. 27, 1866, Samuel Bell Maxey Papers.
52. James W. Hemby, Military Service Records, National Archives.
53. James W. Hemby, letter to *Paris Press*.
54. Hopkins County Minutes of the 8th Judicial District Court, Book B, p. 628, Oct. 26, 1866.
55. Maxey, letter to Marilda Maxey, Oct. 27, 1866.
56. Hopkins County Minutes of the 8th Judicial District Court. The proceedings of Saturday, Oct. 27, 1866, are mentioned starting on p. 635 and ending on p. 639 of Book B; pp. 636–37 are missing.
57. Ibid., Book B, p. 633. See also Myers, letter to Pickering, Feb. 22, 1997, FPC.
58. McCaslin, *Tainted Breeze*, p. 171.
59. M. L. Armstrong, letter to Gen. H. P. Sheridan, Apr. 13, 1867, U.S. Army OCA Records.
60. DeWitt et al., letter to General Griffin. George W. DeWitt held numerous offices in Lamar County over the years, including presiding justice (as county judges were then called), deputy district clerk, county clerk, and district clerk.

He was elected to some of these offices and appointed to others by officials of the state's Reconstruction government (Neville, *History of Lamar County*, pp. 142, 146).

61. Quoted in McCaslin, *Tainted Breeze*, pp. 173–74.

62. Ibid., p. 178.

63. Ibid., p. 176; Tyler et al., *New Handbook of Texas*, 6:486.

64. Campbell, "District Judges of Texas," pp. 374–75.

65. Ibid., p. 375. After being removed from the bench, Mabry practiced law in Jefferson until 1879, when he moved to Fort Worth. Camp Mabry in Austin was named for his son, Woodford Haywood Mabry, who served for a while as Texas adjutant general. George T. Todd went on to represent the 11th district in the Texas House during the 17th Legislature (Tyler et al., *New Handbook of Texas*, 4:359–60, 6:514).

66. In 1867 and 1868, Hopkins County Minutes of the 8th Judicial District Court, Books C and D, contain periodic entries for the murder indictments against John Jack Helms and Council Goff, with entries typically reading, "This case continued for Service."

67. The lawsuit by Johnson & Townes against George W. Cox, George W. Helms, and Charles H. Southerland was ongoing on Dec. 9, 1867, according to court records. On May 3, 1867, the court ordered judgment for the firm of "R. & S. B. Maxey vs. G. W. Cox, G. W. Helms and C. H. Southerland." The case against George W. Helms was dismissed, presumably because he had paid up.

68. McCaslin, *Tainted Breeze*, p. 186.

69. Albright, "Criminal Cases of Delta County."

70. Posey, interview by Bowman.

71. Hopkins County Genealogy Society and Sulphur Springs Cemetery Society, *Sulphur Springs City Cemetery: Old City Cemetery*. Searls (Sept. 15, 1817–Sept. 3, 1887) is buried in the Sulphur Springs Old City Cemetery.

72. McGlasson File, Aikin Archives, Paris Junior College, Paris, Tex., and FPC.

73. Falls, e-mail to Pickering, Apr. 7, 1998, FPC, summarizing information gleaned from Falls's contacts with Honey Lanham Dodge of Dallas.

74. Tuck, *Hopkins County Obituaries Prior to 1939*, 1:296.

75. Melba Goff Allen, e-mail to Judy Falls, Apr. 4, 1998, FPC.

76. U.S. Bureau of the Census, Tenth Census, 1880, Delta County, Precinct 1; Hargrave and Slack, "Helms Family Records."

77. *Delta County History*, p. 156.

78. McGuyer/Oats Family Records.

79. Neville, *History of Lamar County*, pp. 186–87; Dohoney, *Average American*, p. 174; Tyler et al., *New Handbook of Texas*, 2:670–71.

80. Tyler et al., *New Handbook of Texas*, 3:787–88; Hunter, "Heel-Fly Time in Texas," pp. 33–35.

81. Ober, "Memoir," pp. 20–28.

82. *The Church Advocate* (published by the Church of God in Harrisburg, Pa.), Oct. 11, 1911.

83. Ober, "Memoir," pp. 36–42.

84. *The Church Advocate,* Oct. 18, 1911.

85. Walter Prescott Webb et al., eds., *The Handbook of Texas,* 1:794; Sonnichsen, *I'll Die Before I'll Run,* p. 44.

86. Emmett, *Shanghai Pierce,* p. 66. The story about Helms's murder of the black man also appears in Hargrave and Slack's "Helms Family Records," which states that the incident occurred in Hopkins County.

87. Sonnichsen, *I'll Die Before I'll Run,* pp. 39–41; Tyler et al., *New Handbook of Texas,* 6:162.

88. Sonnichsen, *I'll Die Before I'll Run,* pp. 53–54.

89. Ibid., p. 44.

90. Ibid., p. 43.

91. Brown, *Strain of Violence,* p. 242.

92. The charges against Helm, along with those against Council Goff, were dropped on May 2, 1869, according to Hopkins County Minutes of the 8th Judicial District Court, Book D, pp. 297–98. It is possible that Helm continued to face charges afterward in some county other than Hopkins, which would explain a mysterious blurb that appeared in the *Daily Herald* of San Antonio on Apr. 28, 1871: "The *Round Rock Sentinel* says the notorious Jack Helm recently passed through that place going to Northern Texas, to stand trial for some indictment against him."

93. Quoted in Sonnichsen, *I'll Die Before I'll Run,* pp. 45–46.

94. Ibid.

95. *Galveston News,* Sept. 14, 1869.

96. *Austin Daily State Journal,* Nov. 13, 1870.

97. *Austin Republican,* Nov. 23, 1870.

98. Ann Patton Baenziger, "The Texas State Police during Reconstruction," *Southwestern Historical Quarterly* 72 (Apr., 1969): 477.

99. Tyler et al., *New Handbook of Texas,* 3:547–48.

100. Webb et al., *Handbook of Texas,* 2:693.

101. John Wesley Hardin, *The Life of John Wesley Hardin As Written by Himself,* p. 81.

102. Tyler et al., *New Handbook of Texas,* 1:94–95; Karon Mac Smith, *On the Watershed of Ecleto and the Clear Fork of Sandies,* 2:177.

103. Hardin, *Life of John Wesley Hardin,* pp. 82–84.

104. *The Fayette County New Era* (La Grange, Tex.), Aug. 8, 1873.

105. Hardin, *Life of John Wesley Hardin,* p. 84.

106. Karon Mac Smith, *On the Watershed of Ecleto and the Clear Fork of Sandies,* 1:11. Billee Rhodes Smith (Mrs. Dale Smith) also donated material on her ancestor John Jack Helms/Jack Helm and other family members to Texas Tech Univer-

sity; this material is identified as Mrs. Dale Smith, Genealogical Material, 1927–1972, Southwest Collection, Texas Tech University (microfilm).

Chapter 5

1. Decca Lamar West, ed., *Catechism on the History of the Confederate States of America*, pp. 11–12.
2. Neville, *History of Lamar County*, p. 106.
3. McCaslin, *Tainted Breeze*, pp. 7, 190–91. See Thomas Barrett, *The Great Hanging at Gainesville*, preface by H. Bailey Carroll.
4. Ibid., p. 192. The second and final verse of the Gainesville monument's inscription is borrowed, slightly altered, from P. S. Worsley's dedicatory poem to Robert E. Lee in Worsley's translation of *The Iliad*. As noted by Douglas S. Freeman in *R. E. Lee, A Biography*, 4:260, Worsley's full poem, which he sent to Lee in 1866, reads:

> *The grand old bard that never dies,*
> *Receive him in our English tongue!*
> *I send thee, but with weeping eyes,*
> *The story that he sung.*
> *Thy Troy is fallen, thy dear land*
> *Is marred beneath the spoiler's heel.*
> *I cannot trust my trembling hand*
> *To write the things I feel.*
> *Ah, realm of tombs!—but let her bear*
> *This blazon to the last of times:*
> *No nation rose so white and fair,*
> *Or fell so pure of crimes.*
> *The widow's moan, the orphan's wail,*
> *Come round thee; yet in truth be strong!*
> *Eternal right, though all else fail,*
> *Can never be made wrong.*
> *An angel's heart, an angel's mouth,*
> *Not Homer's, could alone for me*
> *Hymn well the great Confederate South,*
> *Virginia first, and Lee.*

5. See E. B. Fleming, *Early History of Hopkins County, Texas*, p. 102, which mentions neither the 1862 nor 1863 hangings, and Tuck, *Civil War Shadows in Hopkins County*, which does not mention the 1863 hanging. Gladys St. Clair mentions the 1863 hanging of "Millsap, De Ormand, Greenwood and Campbell" in *A History of Hopkins County, Texas* (p. 30), but makes no mention of the

related Hunt County hangings. In *History of Greenville and Hunt County* (p. 23), Harrison mentions the 1863 Hopkins County hanging and one group hanging in Hunt County but fails to mention the hanging of Glenn and Smith in Hunt County.

6. Frances Terry Ingmire briefly discusses the career of Martin D. Hart in *Archives and Pioneers of Hunt County* (1:36–37), including the following mention of the local hangings: "A large supply of guns and ammunition was discovered in Jernigan Thicket about eight miles northeast of Greenville. It was confiscated and three of Hart's men were captured and hung on a big oak tree." That is followed by the curious comment: "At the time Colonel Martin D. Hart was shot, six of his men had been caught and hung." A. W. Neville of Paris was not on target in *The Red River Valley, Then and Now* (pp. 108–109) when he wrote about the hangings. "During the war between the sections the [Jernigan's] Thicket was a hiding place for bushwhackers and Union sympathizers who perpetrated many outrages on the families of the men in the Confederate Army. When those men came back those who could come—they rounded up a gang of guerrillas and there was a hanging near Sulphur Springs after semblance of a trial in the form of a court martial. Then when Federal soldiers came to take charge of Texas some of the more prominent in the court martial found it advisable to leave the country until things quieted and the soldiers went away."

Neville's account may have been the source of an account by C. W. Goff of Hunt County, who repeated the same story about men in Jernigan's Thicket committing crimes against soldiers' families during the war and saying soldiers returned to hang these "bushwhackers" and "skulkers" after war's end (Goff quote in Buckett, "Old-Timers of Hunt County," p. 30).

W. Walworth Harrison's version is, for the most part, the most reliable of any, but it gives the name of the man hanged along with Fitzgerald and Newman as Barker, based on one old-timer's account (while the preponderance of evidence indicates that the man was Randolph), gives the place of the three men's capture as Jernigan's Thicket rather than Mustang, and does not go into great detail (*History of Greenville and Hunt County*, pp. 121–23).

7. Patteson, *Loose Leaves*, p. 86.

8. Orren, "The History of Hopkins County," p. 46.

9. Tuck, *Civil War Shadows in Hopkins County*, p. 31.

10. Douglas A. Albright, who worked for the Corps of Engineers in Fort Worth for many years, served as chairman of the Delta County Historical Society on many occasions between the 1960s and the time of his death.

11. James Patteson, letter to Bowman, Feb. 3, 1933, BP.

12. Bowman, undated letter to Mr. Bagwell, BP.

13. Tom and Kathy Hembey, comps., "The Hembey Family History," Hembey Family Records, FPC. Records show that Jane, who had already borne six chil-

dren, was pregnant with another at the time James E. Hemby was hanged. In early October 1862, seven and a half months after her husband's death, a boy named Elexander was "borned," the family Bible shows in an entry penned by Jane. Elexander did not survive much over a month; another entry shows he "departed this life" Nov. 15, 1862.

14. Nellie H. Olsen, letter to the authors, Apr. 4, 1996, FPC.
15. Nellie H. Olsen, telephone interview by Judy Falls, Apr. 4, 1996, FPC.
16. Conces and Wysong, interview by Falls.
17. Gunn, *Fitzgeralds*, pp. 27, 55. Randolph descendants' uncertainty concerning the fate of their ancestor is due, in part, to differences of opinion among Hunt County old-timers as to the name of the man hanged along with Fitzgerald and Newman. Eighty-nine-year-old W. B. Horton told Bowman the third man's name was Barker but gave no details about him (Horton, letter to Bowman). But two other old-timers, eighty-nine-year-old G. W. King and eighty-four-year-old Frank B. Norris, said that the third man's name was Randolph. In addition, Norris provided enough details about Randolph to make his information persuasive: Randolph had married a Fitzgerald; he was the brother-in-law of the hanged Fitzgerald and of Brad Fitzgerald, who brought food to Mustang Thicket. Records bear out the accuracy of Norris's memory concerning one detail: he said the courthouse in which the prisoners were held was "about twenty feet square" while the official plan for the structure places its size at twenty feet by twenty-two feet (King, interview by Bowman, July, 1931, BP; Norris, interview by Bowman; courthouse plan, signed by Wm. Richey, Apr. 16, 1847, from the "Rat Book" records of the Chief Justice of Hunt County, copy in FPC).
18. Wynema Blankenship, letter to Julie Clayton, Oct. 17, 1997, FPC.
19. Bowman, letter to Mr. Bagwell.
20. *Dallas Morning News,* Mar. 14, 1946. The *Morning News* article was published on what the newspaper believed to be McGuyer's hundredth birthday (Headline: "Texan 100 Years Old . . ."). However, McGuyer, who was born Mar. 14, 1848, according to the family Bible (McGuyer/Oats Family Records), actually turned 98 in 1946. Two years later, McGuyer's true hundredth birthday was celebrated in the *Houston Press,* on Mar. 13, 1948. This article indicates that "Uncle Rufe," as he came to be known, may have witnessed both the 1862 and 1863 Hopkins hangings. It states: "It's Rufus McGuyer's 100th birthday and Mr. McGuyer is the only man still alive who saw those nine men, five from Charleston and four from White Oak across the Sulphur, hanged to a pole between two trees." McGuyer died in August 1949, age 101.

BIBLIOGRAPHY

David Pickering and I have donated our collection of research materials to the University Archives, Texas A&M University–Commerce. Included in this collection are e-mail printouts and correspondence with academic researchers and family historians; materials collected from various historical societies and genealogy centers; information collected from other libraries; notes from interviews with families; copies of National Archives records; military records from the Texas State Archives; records from Lamar, Delta, and Hopkins Counties; Hopkins County Court records; family genealogies; unpublished manuscripts; and newspapers (including a set of the *Marshall Texas Republican* from February, 1861, to December, 1865).

The Delta County Public Library in Cooper, Texas, has a partial set of the materials from this Falls-Pickering Collection, primarily those items related to family histories and genealogies.

It is important to note that I have collected many materials that were not used but are historically valuable to families and researchers. It is my hope that other researchers can benefit from having these materials in a central location. Finally, I am of the opinion that there is much valuable information related to people mentioned in this book that is in private family collections, and it is my hope that these families will provide the University Archives at Texas A&M University–Commerce or the Delta County Public Library the opportunity to copy these documents that relate to the history and heritage of northeast Texas.

—Judy Falls

Collections

Bates, James Campbell. Papers. Fink Family Collection, Henry Fink, Custodian, Dallas, Tex.

Bowman, L. L. Papers. University Archives, Texas A&M University-Commerce, Commerce, Tex.

Falls, Judy, and David Pickering. Falls-Pickering Collection. University Archives, Texas A&M University-Commerce, Commerce, Tex.

Harrison, W. Walworth. Collection. Greenville Public Library, Greenville, Tex.

Howell, Morton Boyte. Collection. University Archives, Texas A&M University-Commerce, Commerce, Tex.

Masonic Lodge Charter Book. Records of Lost Lake Lodge for 1861, 1865, 1867. State Archives of the Masonic Grand Lodge of Texas A. F. & A. M. Library and Museum of Texas, Waco, Tex.

Maxey, Samuel Bell. Papers. Archives Division, Texas State Library, Austin, Tex.

McGlasson File. Aikin Archives, Paris Junior College, Paris, Tex.

Smith, Mrs. Dale. Genealogical Material, 1927–1972. Southwest Collection, Texas Tech University, Lubbock, Tex. Microfilm.

Steely, Skipper. Papers. University Archives, Texas A&M University-Commerce, Commerce, Tex.

Government Documents

Adjutant General Records. RG 401, Military Rolls. Texas State Archives, Austin, Tex.

Bennett, Hendley Stone. Military Service Records. National Archives, Washington, D.C.

Brannon, Merit (sic). Military Service Records. National Archives, Washington, D.C.

Delta County Deed Records. Volume W. Delta County Courthouse, Cooper, Tex.

Fitzgerald, Pleasant. Military Service Records. National Archives, Washington, D.C.

Glenn, Austin H., Jr. Military Service Records. National Archives, Washington, D.C.

Hart, Martin D. Military Service Records. National Archives, Washington, D.C.

Helms, John Jack. Military Service Records. National Archives, Washington, D.C.

Hemby, James W. Military Service Records. National Archives, Washington, D.C.

Hopkins County Deed Records. Book N. Hopkins County Courthouse, Sulphur Springs, Tex.

Hopkins County District Clerk Civil Minutes Record. Vol. C, 1866–1871. Hopkins County Courthouse, Sulphur Springs, Tex.

Hopkins County Marriage Records. Vol. 2. Hopkins County Courthouse, Sulphur Springs, Tex.

Hopkins County Minutes of the 8th Judicial District Court. Hopkins County Courthouse, Sulphur Springs, Tex.

Hopkins County Property Tax Rolls. Texas State Archives, Austin, Tex.

Hopkins County Will Book. Hopkins County Courthouse, Sulphur Springs, Tex.

Lamar County Deed Records. Book M. Lamar County Clerk's Office, Paris, Tex.

Lamar County Property Tax Rolls, 1842–1865. Texas State Archives, Austin, Tex.

Lamar County Transcribed Deeds, Book 1. Delta County Clerk's Office, Cooper, Tex.

Muster Roll and Election Returns. Beat No. 3, Hopkins County, Ninth Brigade Texas State Troops. Texas State Archives, Austin, Tex.

Scott, Robert N., et al., eds. *The War of the Rebellion: A Compilation of the Official Records of the Union and Confederate Armies.* 70 vols. in 128 books. Washington, D.C.: Government Printing Office, 1880–1901.

Texas Confederate Muster Roll Index. Texas State Archives, Austin, Tex.

United States. *Biographical Directory of the United States Congress, 1774–1989.* Bicentennial Edition. Washington, D.C.: Government Printing Office, 1989.

United States Army. Records of the U.S. Army Continental Command, 1821–1920. Correspondence of the Office of Civil Affairs of the District of Texas, 5th Military District, and the Department of Texas, 1867–1870. Letters Received, A–G. Group RG393, Roll 5, Microcopy M1188. National Archives, Washington, D.C. Microfilm.

United States Bureau of the Census. Eighth Census, 1860. National Archives, Washington, D.C. Microfilm.

———. Ninth Census, 1870. National Archives, Washington, D.C. Microfilm.

———. Seventh Census, 1850. National Archives, Washington, D.C. Microfilm.

———. Tenth Census, 1880. National Archives, Washington, D.C. Microfilm.

United States Congress. *The Congressional Globe,* appendix. 34th Congress, 1st sess., 1855.

Books

Adams, Florence Chapman. *Hopkins County and Our Heritage.* Wolfe City, Tex.: Henington Publishing Co., 1976.

Allardice, Bruce S. *More Generals in Gray.* Baton Rouge: Louisiana State University Press, 1995.

Banta, William, and J. W. Caldwell, Jr. *Twenty-seven Years on the Texas Frontier.* 1893. Rev. ed. Council Hill, Okla.: L. G. Park, 1933.

Barrett, Thomas. *The Great Hanging at Gainesville.* Preface by H. Bailey Carroll. 1885. Reprint, Austin: Texas State Historical Association, 1961.

Barton, O. S. *Three Years with Quantrill: A True Story Told by His Scout John McCorkle.* 1914. Reprint, Norman: University of Oklahoma Press, 1992.

Benner, Judith Ann. *Sul Ross: Soldier, Statesman, Educator.* College Station: Texas A&M University Press, 1983.

Boatner, Mark M., III. *The Civil War Dictionary.* Rev. ed. New York: Vintage Books, 1991.

Boyer, Reba Bayless, comp. *Monroe County, Tennessee, Records, Volume I, 1820–1870.* Easley, S.C.: Southern Historical Press, 1969.

Brown, Richard Maxwell. *Strain of Violence: Historical Studies of American Violence and Vigilantism.* New York: Oxford University Press, 1975.

Bruce, Dickson D. *Violence and Culture in the Antebellum South.* Austin: University of Texas Press, 1979.

Buenger, Walter L. *Secession and the Union in Texas.* Austin: University of Texas Press, 1984.

Burleson, Muriel Champion, ed. *A History of Ladonia, Texas, 1836–1997.* Ladonia, Tex.: Ladonia Historical Preservation Society, 1997.

Campbell, Randolph B. *An Empire for Slavery: The Peculiar Institution in Texas, 1821–1865.* Baton Rouge: Louisiana State University Press, 1989.

Cash, W. J. *The Mind of the South.* 1941. Reprint, New York: Vintage Books, 1991.

Castel, Albert. *William Clarke Quantrill: His Life and Times.* New York: Frederick Fell Inc., 1962.

Clark, James Lemuel. *Civil War Recollections of James Lemuel Clark.* Edited by L. D. Clark. College Station: Texas A&M University Press, 1984.

Condit, Jotham H., and Eben Condit. *Genealogical Record of the Condit Family, Descendants of John Cunditt, a Native of Great Britain Who Settled in Newark, N.J., 1678 to 1885.* 1885. Revision by Condit Family Association. Newark: The Essex Press, 1916.

Crouch, Barry A., and Donaly E. Brice. *Cullen Montgomery Baker: Reconstruction Desperado.* Baton Rouge: Louisiana State University Press, 1997.

Cunningham, J. J. *History of Paris Lodge No. 27, A. F. & A. M., with a List of Other Lodges in the County, and Dates of Their Organization.* Paris, Tex., 1935.

Delta County History Book Committee. *Delta County History.* Dallas: Taylor Publishing Co., 1991.

Dohoney, Eben Lafayette. *An Average American.* Paris, Tex., 1885.

Emmett, Chris. *Shanghai Pierce: A Fair Likeness.* Norman: University of Oklahoma Press, 1953.

Falls, Judy, Sylvia Wood, et al. *Voices in the Wind: The Cemetery Records of Delta County.* Cooper, Tex.: Friends of the Library, 2000.

Fischer, David Hackett. *Albion's Seed: Four British Folkways in America.* New York: Oxford University Press, 1989.

Fleming, E. B. *Early History of Hopkins County, Texas.* 1902. Reprint, Wolfe City, Tex.: Henington Publishing Co., 1976.

Forney, C. H. *History of the Churches of God in the United States of America.* Harrisburg, Pa.: Board of Directors of the Publishing House and Book Rooms of the Church of God, 1914.

Freeman, Douglas Southall. *R. E. Lee, A Biography.* 4 vols. 1935–1936. Reprint, New York: Charles Scribner's Sons, 1947.

Friends of the Commerce Public Library. *The Handbook of Commerce, Texas, 1872–1985.* Wolfe City, Tex.: Henington Publishing Co., 1985.

Gallaway, B. P. *The Ragged Rebel: A Common Soldier in W. H. Parsons' Texas Cav-alry, 1861–1865.* Austin: University of Texas Press, 1988.

———, ed. *Texas: The Dark Corner of the Confederacy: Contemporary Accounts of the Lone Star State in the Civil War.* 1968. 3d ed., Lincoln: University of Nebraska Press, 1994.

Gaustad, Edwin Scott. *A Religious History of America.* San Francisco: Harper, 1990.

Griscom, George L. *Fighting with Ross' Texas Cavalry Brigade C.S.A.: The Diary of George L. Griscom, Adjutant, 9th Texas Cavalry Regiment.* Edited by Homer L. Kerr. Hillsboro, Tex.: Hill Junior College Press, 1976.

Gunn, Beth. *The Fitzgeralds: From Tennessee to Texas.* Arlington, Tex.: Privately printed, 1976.

Hare, David Hugh "Dick." *The Tell of Time: People, Places, and Things of Sulphur Bluff and Hopkins County, Texas.* Pioneer Book Publishers, 1972.

Hardin, John Wesley. *The Life of John Wesley Hardin As Written by Himself.* 1896. Re-print, Norman: University of Oklahoma Press, 1961.

Harrison, W. Walworth. *History of Greenville and Hunt County, Texas.* Waco: Tex-ian Press, 1976.

Hodge, Floy Crandall. *History of Fannin County, Vol. II.* Hereford, Tex.: Pioneer Book Publishers, 1974.

Hopkins County Genealogy Society and Sulphur Springs Cemetery Society. *Sul-phur Springs City Cemetery: Old City Cemetery.* Sulphur Springs, Tex., 1989.

Horton, Louise. *Samuel Bell Maxey: A Biography.* Austin: University of Texas Press, 1974.

Ingmire, Frances Terry. *Archives and Pioneers of Hunt County.* Vol. 1. Creve Coeur, Mo.: Privately printed, 1975.

Ingmire, Frances Terry, and Robert Lee Thompson. *Johnny Rebs of Hunt County, Texas.* St. Louis, Mo.: Privately printed, 1977.

Jordan, Jerry Wright. *Cherokee by Blood: Records of Eastern Cherokee Ancestry in the U.S. Court of Claims, 1906–1910.* Vol. 3. Bowie, Md.: Heritage Books, Inc., 1988.

Jordan, Terry G. *Trails to Texas: Southern Roots of Western Cattle Ranching.* Lincoln: University of Nebraska Press, 1981.

Landrum, Graham. *Grayson County: An Illustrated History of Grayson County, Texas.* Fort Worth: University Supply & Equipment Co., 1960.

Lonn, Ella. *Desertion during the Civil War.* New York: The Century Co., 1928.

Marten, James. *Texas Divided: Loyalty and Dissent in the Lone Star State, 1856–1874.* Lexington: University Press of Kentucky, 1990.

Martin, Bessie. *Desertion of Alabama Troops from the Confederate Army: A Study in Sectionalism.* New York: Columbia University Press, 1932.

McCaslin, Richard B. *Tainted Breeze: The Great Hanging at Gainesville, Texas, 1862.* Baton Rouge: Louisiana State University Press, 1994.

McPherson, James M. *Battle Cry of Freedom: The Civil War Era.* New York: Oxford University Press, 1988.

Mills, Betsy, comp., and Elizabeth House, ed. *Lamar County, Texas, Marriage Records 1841–1874.* Paris, Tex.: Genealogy Society of North Texas, 1993.

Monaghan, Jay. *Civil War on the Western Border, 1854–1865.* 1955. Reprint, Lincoln: University of Nebraska Press, 1984.

Mullins, Marion Day, comp. *Republic of Texas: Poll Lists for 1846.* Baltimore: Genealogical Publishing Co., 1874.

Neville, A. W. *The History of Lamar County.* 1937. Reprint, Paris, Tex.: North Texas Publishing Co., 1986.

———. *The Red River Valley, Then and Now.* Paris, Tex.: North Texas Publishing Co., 1948.

Nunn, W. C. *Texas under the Carpetbaggers.* Austin: University of Texas Press, 1962.

Paludan, Phillip S. *Victims: A True Story of the Civil War.* Knoxville: University of Tennessee Press, 1981.

Patman, Wright. *A History of Post Offices and Communities, First Congressional District of Texas.* Texarkana, Tex., 1968.

Patteson, Ikie Gray. *Loose Leaves: A History of Delta County.* Dallas: Mathis Publishing Co., 1935.

Phillips, Elveta. *Fading Moments Recorded: A Brief Description and History of the Wieland Community.* Greenville, Tex.: Greenville Herald Banner, 1972.

Ramsdell, Charles William. *Reconstruction in Texas.* 1910. Reprint, Austin: University of Texas Press, 1970.

Ray, G. B. *Murder at the Corners.* San Antonio: The Naylor Co., 1957.

Rose, Victor. *The Texas Vendetta; or, The Sutton-Taylor Feud.* 1880. Reprint, Houston: Frontier Press of Texas, 1956.

Sifakis, Stewart. *Compendium of the Confederate Armies, Texas.* New York: Facts on File, 1995.

Smith, David Paul. *Frontier Defense in the Civil War: Texas' Rangers and Rebels.* College Station: Texas A&M University Press, 1992.

Smith, Karon Mac. *On the Watershed of Ecleto and the Clear Fork of Sandies: Volume I.* Seguin, Tex.: Tommy Brown Publishing Co., 1983.

———. *On the Watershed of Ecleto and the Clear Fork of Sandies: Volume II.* Seguin, Tex.: Tommy Brown Publishing Co., 1988.

Sonnichsen, C. L. *I'll Die Before I'll Run: The Story of the Great Feuds of Texas.* Lincoln: University of Nebraska Press, 1988.

Sparks, A. W. *The War between the States As I Saw It: Reminiscent, Historical and Personal.* 1901. Reprint, Longview, Tex.: D & D Publishing, 1987.

Spurlin, Charles D., comp. *Texas Veterans in the Mexican War: Muster Rolls of Texas Military Units.* Victoria, Tex.: Privately printed, 1984.

St. Clair, Gladys. *A History of Hopkins County, Texas.* Waco, Tex.: Texian Press, 1965.

Stone, Kate. *Brokenburn: The Journal of Kate Stone, 1861–1868.* Edited by John Q. Anderson. Baton Rouge: Louisiana State University Press, 1955.

Tatum, Georgia Lee. *Disloyalty in the Confederacy.* 1934. Reprint, New York: AMS Press, 1970.

Texas Almanac, 1861. Galveston, Tex.: Galveston News, 1860.

Trelease, Allen W. *White Terror: The Ku Klux Klan Conspiracy and Southern Reconstruction.* New York: Harper & Row, 1971.

Tuck, June E. *Civil War Shadows in Hopkins County, Texas.* Marceline, Mo.: Walworth Publishing Co., 1993.

———. *Hopkins County Obituaries Prior to 1939.* Vol. 1. Sulphur Springs, Tex.: Privately printed, 1995.

Tyler, Ron, et al., eds. *The New Handbook of Texas.* 6 vols. Austin: Texas State Historical Association, 1996.

Webb, Walter Prescott, et al., eds. *The Handbook of Texas.* 3 vols. Austin: Texas State Historical Association, 1952, 1976.

Webster's Biographical Dictionary. Springfield, Mass.: G. & C. Merriam Co., 1961.

Weddle, Robert S. *Plow-horse Cavalry: The Caney Creek Boys of the Thirty-fourth Texas.* Austin: Madrona Press, 1974.

West, Decca Lamar, ed. *Catechism on the History of the Confederate States of America.* 1904. Reprint, Texas Division of the United Daughters of the Confederacy, 1934.

Wilson, Charles Reagan, and William Ferris, eds. *Encyclopedia of Southern Culture.* Chapel Hill: University of North Carolina Press, 1989.

Wooster, Ralph A. *Texas and Texans in the Civil War.* Austin: Eakin Press, 1995.

Wright, Marcus J., and Harold B. Simpson. *Texas in the War, 1861–1865.* Hillsboro, Tex.: Hill Junior College Press, 1965.

Wyatt-Brown, Bertram. *Southern Honor: Ethics and Behavior in the Old South.* 1982. Reprint, New York: Oxford University Press, 1983.

Articles and Papers

Albright, Douglas A. "Criminal Cases of Delta County." Manuscript. Delta County Public Library, Cooper, Tex.

———, comp. "Delta County Cemetery Records." Manuscript. Delta County Public Library, Cooper, Tex.

———, comp. "Texas State Historical Markers, Delta County." Manuscript. Delta County Public Library, Cooper, Tex.

Alverson, Allene. "E. L. Dohoney and the Constitution of 1876." Master's thesis, Texas Technological College, 1941.

Baenziger, Ann Patton. "The Texas State Police during Reconstruction." *Southwestern Historical Quarterly* 72 (April, 1969): 470–91.

Black, John, and H. P. Allen. "Civil War Experiences Reflect Life of Hardship." Honey Grove Signal-Citizen, July 2, 1976.

Buckett, Clara Colder, comp. "Old-Timers of Hunt County, Texas." Bound typescript. Privately printed, 1983.

Buenger, Walter L. "Secession Revisited: The Texas Experience." *Civil War History*
30 (December, 1984): 293–305.

———. "Texas and the Riddle of Secession." *Southwestern Historical Quarterly* 87
(October, 1983): 151–82.

Campbell, Randolph B. "Carpetbagger Rule in Reconstruction Texas, an Enduring
Myth." *Southwestern Historical Quarterly* 97 (April, 1994): 587–96.

———. "District Judges of Texas in 1866–67, an Episode in the Failure of Reconstruction." *Southwestern Historical Quarterly* 93 (January, 1990): 357–77.

———. "Political Conflict within the Southern Consensus: Harrison County,
Texas, 1850–1880." *Civil War History* 26 (September, 1980): 218–39.

Dice, Ralph. "Lamar County and Secession." Research paper, East Texas State University, 1984.

Duncan, J. S. "Commentary: 'Martin Hart, Civil War Guerrilla.'" *Military History
of Texas and the Southwest* (1973): 137–42.

Dunn, Roy Sylvan. "The KGC in Texas, 1860–1861." *Southwestern Historical Quarterly* 70 (April, 1967): 543–73.

Grubbs, V. W. "Hunt County Pioneers: Judge Hardin Hart." *The Greenville Banner*, April 12, 1911.

Hargrave, Tommy Ruth, and Carroll Terrell Slack, comps. "Helms Family Records." Bound typescript. Falls-Pickering Collection.

Harper, Cecil. "Martin D. Hart: Another Look at a Hanged Texas Unionist." Paper
presented at the annual meeting of the Texas State Historical Association, Austin, March 1, 1996.

———. "Slavery without Cotton: Hunt County, Texas, 1846–1864." *Southwestern
Historical Quarterly* 88 (April, 1985): 387–405.

Harris, William C. "The Southern Unionist Critique of the Civil War." *Civil War
History* 31 (March, 1985): 39–56.

Hooten, Mrs. L. F., Sr., comp. "Delta County Scrapbook." Delta County Museum,
Cooper, Tex.

Huff, Leo E. "Guerrillas, Jayhawkers and Bushwhackers in Northern Arkansas during the Civil War." *Arkansas Historical Quarterly* 22 (summer, 1965): 126–48.

———. "Heel-fly Time in Texas: A Story of the Civil War Period." *Frontier Times*
2 (April, 1924): 33–48, (May, 1924): 33–48, (June, 1924): 33–47.

Jordan, Terry G. "A Century and a Half of Ethnic Change in Texas, 1836–1986."
Southwestern Historical Quarterly 89 (April, 1986): 385–417.

———. "Early Northeast Texas and the Evolution of Western Ranching." *Annals of
the Association of American Geographers* 67, no. 1 (March, 1977): 66–87.

———. "The Imprint of the Upper and Lower South on Mid-Nineteenth-Century
Texas." *Annals of the Association of American Geographers* 57, no. 4 (December,
1967): 667–90.

————. "Population Origins in Texas, 1850." *Geographical Review* 59, no. 1 (January, 1969): 83–101.

Jordon, Thomas E. "Captain Martin Hart's Date with Death." *Civil War Times* 36 (May, 1997): 40–46.

Kiker, Janice Jernigan. "William Jernigin, Founder of Commerce." *Commerce Journal*, October 31, 1982.

Kreneck, Thomas H. "The North Texas Regiment in the Mexican War." *Military History of Texas and the Southwest* 12 (July, 1975): 110–17.

Lamar County Genealogy Society. "A History of the Church of Christ at Antioch, Lamar County, Texas." *Lamar County Genealogy & History* 14 (May, 1996): 14–16.

Lathrop, Barnes F. "Migration into East Texas, 1835–1860." *Southwestern Historical Quarterly* 52 (July, 1948): 1–31.

Lewis, A. B. "Chasing Guerrillas in Arkansas." *Confederate Veteran* 29 (1921): 220–22.

Lowe, Richard, and Randolph Campbell. "Wealthholding and Political Power in Antebellum Texas." *Southwestern Historical Quarterly* 79 (July, 1975): 21–30.

McCaslin, Richard B. "Conditional Confederates: The Eleventh Texas Cavalry West of the Mississippi River." *Military History of the Southwest* 21 (spring, 1991): 87–99.

————. "Wheat Growers in the Cotton Confederacy: The Suppression of Dissent in Collin County, Texas, during the Civil War." *Southwestern Historical Quarterly* 96 (April, 1993): 526–39.

McIlhaney, Jackie, ed. "From Missouri to Texas in 1845: Martin Austin Gauldin's Journal." *Southwestern Historical Quarterly* 83 (October, 1979): 151–65.

Middlebrooks, Andy J., and Glenna Middlebrooks. "Holland Coffee of Red River." *Southwestern Historical Quarterly* 69 (October, 1969): 145–62.

Miller, W. B. "History of Ben Franklin and Giles Academy." *Delta Courier* (Cooper, Tex.), April 7, 1925. Reprinted in *Cooper Review*, June 6, 1963.

Myers, Browne Elizabeth Millsap. "The Millsaps." In *Pioneers of Hopkins County, Texas, II*. Edited by Sylvia M. Kibart and Rita M. Adams. Sulphur Springs, Tex.: Hopkins County Genealogical Society, 1989.

Neville, A. W. "Backward Glances." *Paris (Tex.) News*, 1930–49.

Norton, Wesley. "The Methodist Episcopal Church in North Texas in 1859 and 1860." *Southwestern Historical Quarterly* 68 (January, 1965): 317–41.

Orren, G. G. "The History of Hopkins County." Master's thesis, East Texas State Teachers College, 1938.

Parrish, T. Michael. Comments on "Hanging Time in the Confederacy." Annual meeting of the Texas State Historical Association, Austin, March 1, 1996.

Price, G. Ross. "A History of Charleston, Texas." Research paper, East Texas State Teachers College, 1952.

Pruitt, Francelle. "We've Got to Fight or Die: Early Texas Reaction to the Confederate Draft, 1862." *East Texas Historical Journal* 36 (spring, 1968): 3–17.

Rable, George C. "Bourbonism, Reconstruction, and the Persistence of Southern Distinctiveness." *Civil War History* 29 (June, 1983): 135–53.

Reynolds, Donald E. "Reluctant Martyr: Anthony Bewley and the Texas Slave Insurrection Panic of 1860." *Southwestern Historical Quarterly* 96 (January, 1993): 344–61.

———. "Vigilante Law during the Texas Slave Panic of 1860." *Locus: An Historical Journal of Regional Perspective* 2 (spring, 1990): 173–86.

Richter, William L. "'The Revolver Rules the Day!' Colonel DeWitt C. Brown and the Freedman's Bureau in Paris, Texas, 1867–1868." *Southwestern Historical Quarterly* 93 (January, 1990): 303–32.

Roberts, O. M. "Texas." In *Confederate Military History*, vol. 11. Edited by Clement A. Evans. Atlanta: Confederate Publishing Co., 1899.

Sawyer, William E. "Martin Hart, Civil War Guerrilla." *Texas Military History* 3 (fall, 1963): 146–53.

———. "The Martin Hart Conspiracy." *Arkansas Historical Quarterly* 23 (summer, 1964): 154–65.

Scott, Tom. "Fannin County: Two Centuries of Texas Legend." *Bonham Daily Favorite*, September 1, 1985.

Smallwood, James. "Black Texas during Reconstruction: First Freedom." *East Texas Historical Journal* 14 (spring, 1976): 9–19.

———. "Disaffection in Confederate Texas: The Great Hanging at Gainesville." *Civil War History* 22 (December, 1976): 349–60.

———. "Swamp Fox of the Sulphur." *True West* 38 (October, 1991): 20–23, (November, 1991): 38–41.

Smart, Morris. "Camp Rusk, Home of the Texas Ninth Infantry Regiment." Paper presented to the Delta County Historical Survey Committee, Cooper, Tex., 1986.

Smyrl, Frank H. "Texans in the Union Army, 1861–1865." *Southwestern Historical Quarterly* 65 (October, 1961): 234–50.

———. "Unionism in Texas, 1856–1861." *Southwestern Historical Quarterly* 67 (October, 1964): 172–95.

Steely, Skipper. "Forty-seven Years." Manuscript, 1988. University Archives, Texas A&M University-Commerce.

Strickland, Rex Wallace. "History of Fannin County, Texas, 1836–1843. Part I." *Southwestern Historical Quarterly* 34 (April, 1930): 262–98.

———. "History of Fannin County, Texas, 1836–1843. Part II." *Southwestern Historical Quarterly* 34 (July, 1930): 38–68.

Taylor, T. U. "Ben Bickerstaff, the Noted Desperado." *Frontier Times* 2 (October, 1924): 9–10.

———. "The Lee-Peacock Feud." *Frontier Times* 4 (May, 1926): 19–28.

Tyler, Ronnie C. "Cotton on the Border, 1861–1865." *Southwestern Historical Quarterly* 73 (April, 1970): 456–77.

Watson, Judy. "The Red River Raft." *Texans* 5 (spring, 1967): 68–76.

Williams, J. W. "Moscoso's Trail in Texas." *Southwestern Historical Quarterly* 46 (October, 1942): 138–57.

Wooster, Ralph A. "An Analysis of the Membership of the Texas Secession Convention." *Southwestern Historical Quarterly* 62 (January, 1959): 322–34.

———. "East of the Trinity: Glimpses of Life in East Texas in the Early 1850s." *East Texas Historical Journal* 13 (fall, 1975): 3–7.

———. "Notes on Texas' Largest Slaveholders, 1860." *Southwestern Historical Quarterly* 65 (July, 1961): 72–79.

INDEX

abolitionists, 10–13, 38, 43–46, 49, 52, 76, 149, 172
Adams, Annie Lee Hemby, 142
"Address to the People of the State," 38, 40, 73, 105, 156
agriculture, 28–30, 40
Alabama, 8, 29, 84, 113
Albright, Douglas, 56, 140–41, 159–62, 167, 189
Albuquerque (Albukirk), Tex., 135
Aldridge, Thomas, Judge, 77, 169
Alexander, Mrs., 24
Allen, H. W., 129
Alvarado, Luis de Moscoso, 5
American flag stories, 14, 149
American Revolution, 53
amnesty, 20
Anderson, Garlin, 157
Anderson, John Q., 178
Angelina County, 157
anti-abolitionist, 10–11
Antioch, Tex., 179
Antioch Church of Christ, 33, 60, 155
anvil firing, 159
Appalachian chain, 6
Arkansas, 41, 46, 48, 50, 63–64; Hart's activities in, 169–71; mentioned, 5–7, 69, 72–73, 75–80, 82, 87–89, 93–94, 99–100, 110, 128–29
Arkansas Post, 94
Armstrong, Callie (Carroll), 80, 171
Armstrong, M. L., 36–38, 42, 122, 156, 162, 182, 185
Arnold, C. C., 167
Arnold, F. M. (G. M.), 167
Arnold, I. R. (J. R.), 167

arson, 11–12
Ashley, J. S. (James Shelton), 182
Askew, Richard L., 35
Atlas, Tex., 56
Austin, Tex., 22, 35, 39, 52, 177, 125, 131, 174
Austin (Tex.) Republican, 133–34
Average American, An (Dohoney), 35–38, 128, 141, 143, 154, 156, 160, 162, 164, 185

Babb, I. M. (J. M.), 167
Babb, Milton, 165
Babb family, 167
Bacus (Baccus), Joseph C., 167
Baenziger, Ann Patton, 134
Bagdad, Mex., 65
Bagwell, Mr., 140
Bailey, Wilkshire, 183
Baker, Cullen, 105
Baker, I. C. (J. C.), 167
Ball, Joseph H., 82, 99
Ball, Missouri Ann Glenn, 99
Balshr, Jordon, 177
Band, I. M., 167
Bangs, Lula Lavenia Grant, 155
Banta, William, 5
Baptist Church, 10
Bard, J. M., 167
Barker, Captain, 183
Barrett, Thomas, 138
Bartholmen (Bartholomew), W. W., 167
Bates, James C., 66–67, 117, 164, 168
Bee County, 132
Bell, C. S., 131–32
Bell, E. E., 94
Bell, Mr., 133
Bell County, 132

Bell Rangers, 94

Ben Franklin, Tex., 33, 113, 116, 178

Bennett, Hendley Stone, 34, 40, 43–45, 52, 58, 61, 66, 158

Benton County, Ala., 84

Bettes, Sam, 151

Bewley, Anthony, Rev., 44–45, 90

Bexar County, 9, 31–32, 39

Biard, W. W., 155

Biardstown, Tex., 32–33, 36, 56, 60, 63

Biardstown School, 155

Bickerstaff, Ben, 105, 116

Big Creek Thicket, 4

Black Cat Thicket, 4–5, 18, 103

"Black Insolence," 130–31

Black Jack Grove, 12, 128, 172

Black Republicans, 38

Blackwell, Erastus, 110–12

Blankenship, Wynema, 142–43

Blunt, General, 169

Blythe, William T., 35

Bogart, Sam, 156

Bogus (Boggus), John, 167

bois d'arc apples, 112

Bois d'Arc (Bonham, Tex.), 69

Bonham, Tex., 11, 17–18, 20–21, 34, 69, 84, 98, 106–107, 112

Bonham-Jefferson Road, 34, 154

Bonham (Tex.) News, 128

Bonner, W. J., 35

Bonner's New York Ledger, 132

borderers, 6–7. *See also* Upper South; Upper Southerners

Boren, Henry, 20

Boston Tea Party, 53

Bourland, James, 41, 91–92

Bourland's Border Regiment, 91

Bowen, Moses B., 183

Bowie County, 9, 107

Bowman, L. L., 5, 17, 50, 55, 79, 83, 88–89, 91, 96, 103–104, 111, 113, 126, 138, 140, 143, 146, 159–60, 166, 172, 174–76, 179–82

Boyd, Gamuel P. (Samuel J., Jr.), 167

Brackeen, J. M., 10

Bradley, C. J., 30

Bradley County, Tenn., 93

Brake, Leon (Levi) H., 167

Bramley, Wm., 177

Brannom, Merritt, 113–16, 118, 121, 126–27, 171, 183

Bray, Lydia D., 95

Briscoe, Ben, 17–18, 21, 103, 146

Brogdan Springs, 49

Brokenburn plantation, 97, 178

Brokenburn; The Diary of Kate Stone, 24, 51–52, 97–98, 152, 178–79

Brown, Frank, 159, 167

Brown, Richard Maxwell, 11, 23–24, 40–41, 53, 58, 132

Brown, Wm. S., 110–11

Brownsville, Tex., 65

Bruce, Dickson D., 25, 156

Brush Battalion, 20–21

brush men, 15–16, 18, 20–22, 48, 55–56, 84, 86–87, 98–99, 150, 161, 174, 180

Bryant, N. G., 110–11

Buenger, Walter L., 13

Bunyan, Emaline, 95

Burnside, Milly, 78–79

bush men, 150

bushwackers, 83, 189

Butler, Emmitt, 142

Butler, Okla., 129

Butler, Ransom, 94

Butler family, 177

Butts, Martha, 180

Caddo Creek, 18

Caddo Mills, Tex., 129

Cade, R. M., 182

Calhoun, Mary Ann, 128

California, 40

Calloway, Dennis, 163

Cameron, Alexander, 77

Cameron County, 65

Camp, L. B., 156

Campbell, Armsted, 173

Campbell, Frances, 173

Campbell, Joseph D., Sr., 173

Campbell, Joseph D.: burial site of, 89–90,

176; capture of, 87–88, 91; family history, 85, 142, 151, 173, 182; hanging of, 88–91, 174–76; mentioned, 85, 91, 108, 113, 121–22, 143; postwar judicial proceedings, 91, 108–24; and vigilante trial, 88. *See also* Campbell-DeArman-Greenwood-Millsaps hanging; Eighth Judicial District; postwar judicial proceedings

Campbell, Margaret, 173

Campbell, Mary, 173

Campbell, Mary Z., 173

Campbell, Rachel, 85, 89, 91, 122, 173–76

Campbell, Randolph B., 9, 125, 151

Campbell, Tex., 83

Campbell, Virginia, 173

Campbell-DeArman-Greenwood Millsaps hanging: burial site of victims, 89–90, 176; capture of, 87–88, 91; hanging of, 88–91, 175–76; mentioned, 97–98, 144, 188–90; postwar judicial proceedings, 91, 108–24; and vigilante trial, 88. *See also* Eighth Judicial District; postwar judicial proceedings

Camp Mabry, 185

Camp Reeves, 114

Camp Rusk, 48

Camp Wharton, 114

Canady, A. J., 63, 163

Caney Creek, 15

Carpenter, T. C., 110–11

Carr, Helen, 15

Carr, J. N., 15, 162

Carroll, Charlie, 80

Carroll, D. A., 169–70, 171

Carroll, DeRosey, 76, 78, 80, 169–70

Carter, Jeremiah, 169

Cash, W. J., 8, 25–26

Cason, Basil, 71

Cass County, 93, 95, 107

Castleberry, Mr., 163

Castleberry Bridge, 163

Cedar Creek, Tex., 155

Central National Road, 34, 81

Chamblee, Frank: death of, 103–104, 143,

180–81; family history, 16; stories about, 16–17, 23, 102–104, 180–81

Chamblee, Mary Ellen Terry, 16–17, 21, 102–103, 180

Chapman, B. J., 184

Chapman, Genova Ladosky, 115, 184

Chapman, George Elias, 115, 184

Chapman, John, 184

Charleston, Ark., 76, 78–79, 146, 169–70

Charleston, Tex., 29–30, 36–38, 41–43, 48, 56–59, 65, 108, 111–13, 120, 122, 161, 182

Charleston-Tarrant Road, 57

Chesapeake, Va., 8

Childs, James W., 98–99

Chisholm, Dick, 131

Chism, Isham, Col., 180

Chism's Regiment, 100, 180

Choate Family, 132

Christian Advocate and Journal, 45

Christy (Chrisly), Oliver J., 167

churches, 6, 9–11, 30, 33, 41, 44, 54, 56, 59–60, 63, 81–82, 102, 106–107, 128–29, 143, 153–55, 162–63, 172

Church of Christ, 33, 60, 154–55, 162

Church of God: beliefs of, 10–11, 107; and *The Church Advocate,* 10, 129, 187; members of, 106–107, 154, 163; mentioned, 128–29, 143; and slavery beliefs, 10–11

Cincinnati, Ohio, 51, 105

Civil War battles: Antietam, 185; Atlanta, 158; Chickamauga, 158; Corinth, 48, 158, 163; Elkhorn Tavern, 63; Fishing Creek, 51–52; Mansfield, 180; Missionary Ridge, 158; Mobile, 158; Murfreesboro, 158; Nashville, 48; New Hope Church, 158; Pea Ridge, 48, 63; Perryville, 158; Pleasant Hill, 180; Shiloh, 48, 63, 158

Civil War Shadows in Hopkins County, Texas, 139, 182

Clark, John, 111

Clark, Joshua, 110–11

Clarksville, Tex., 5

Clarksville (Tex.) Northern Standard, 12

Clay County, 39

Clayton, Julie, 153–54
Clements, Manning, 135
Clinton, Tex., 131, 159
Coffee, Colville & Company, 71
Coffee, Holland, 71
Cole, James, 157
Collin County, 20, 30, 39, 105, 117
Columbus, Miss., 43
Colville, Silas, 71
Comet, Charles V., 12
Commerce, Tex., 87, 174
Commerce (Tex.) Journal, 174
Committee of Safety, 11
Condict, John, 110–11
Condit, Jane, 54
Condit, William Spangler, 50, 54–55, 62, 110, 161
Condit family, 47, 54–55, 62, 110, 161
Confederate States of America (CSA): army of, 17–18, 20–23, 48–52, 61–64, 66–67, 74–76, 78, 82, 91, 93, 99–100, 104, 106, 112, 114, 116, 119, 150–51, 158–59, 163–64, 170–71, 180, 183, 185; flag of, 64, 149; leaders of, 17–18, 20–23, 48–52, 56, 64, 66–67, 76, 78, 91, 100, 106, 107, 114, 117, 119, 122, 150–51, 164, 170, 180, 183, 185; mentioned, 105–106; and Northern Sub-District of Texas, 17–18, 20–23, 107; supporters of, 8–9, 35–36, 38–45, 47–51, 55, 57–59, 61–65, 73–78, 81–93, 100–101, 105–106, 113–14, 116–19, 122–27, 129–34, 168–70, 174, 178, 183, 185, 187; and Trans-Mississippi Department, 21–22. *See also individual military units;* conscription; impressment laws
Connady, J. A., 163
conscientious objector, 106
conscription: 64; Confederate, 14, 106; and CSA Conscription Act: April 6, 1862, 66–67, 160; mentioned, 18, 22, 55
Constitution of Man, The (Dohoney), 128
Cooke County, 39, 68, 73, 91, 116, 122, 164
Cooper, Tex., 4, 58, 111–12, 146
Copeland, John, 167
Copperheads, 53

Cornell, Colonel, 51
Corpus Christi, Tex., 65
cotton: growing of, 8–9, 28, 34, 147, 178; hauling/shipping of, 34, 65, 106, 149, 155–56; mentioned, 38, 40; and plantations, 9, 34, 148; producers of, 9, 65; and slavery, 8–9, 28, 147; wagons of, 15, 65, 149
cotton-worm destroyer, 135
Cow Hill, Tex., 87
Cowleech Fork, 83
Cox, George W., 42, 58, 108, 113–16, 118, 121–23, 125–26, 151, 162, 186
Cox, Jim, 135
Cox, R. M., 42–43, 46–47, 49
Crabtree, Isaa W. (Isaac J.), 167
Crabtree, Lydia, 30
Crabtree, W. D., 167
Craig, John B., 110, 112–13, 157
Craig, Tex., 112
Craig and Denton, 112
Craig Prairie, 112
Craig-Tranquil Methodist Episcopal Church South, 112
Crawford, Margaret Virginia, 159
Crenshaw, Frances, 172
Crowder, G. H., 148
Crump, R. P., 78, 170
Cuero, Tex., 135
Culbertson, D. B., 121, 139, 185
Cumberland County, Ill., 179
Cumberland Presbyterian Church, 30, 60, 154
Cumby, Tex., 12, 176. *See also* Black Jack Grove
Cunningham, J. E., 59

Dagley, William B., 31
Dagley Lake, 83
Dagley's Mill, 83
Daily (Tex.) Herald, 187
Daingerfield, Tex., 34
Dallas, Tex., 12, 33–34, 46
Dallas County, 12, 33–34, 46
Dallas Herald, 75, 108–109, 172

Dallas Morning News, 144

Danville, Ky., 100

"dark corner of Confederacy," 24

Darling, W. (H.), 167

Davis, E. J., 133–34

Davis, Jefferson, 61, 66, 185

DeArman, Horace: capture of, 87–88, 91; family history, 83–85, 151, 172–73; hanging of, 88–91, 174–76; mentioned, 108, 113, 121; and postwar judicial proceedings, 91, 108–25; occupation of, 84, 173; and vigilante trial, 88. *See also* Campbell-DeArman-Greenwood-Millsaps hanging; Eighth Judicial District; postwar judicial proceedings

DeArman, James, 83–84

DeArman, Jonathan J., 173

DeArman, Martha Hart, 172–73

DeArman, Polly, 83–84

"Declaration of the Causes which Impel the State of Texas to Secede," 9

Delta County, 3–4, 6, 8, 15, 23, 28–30, 33–34, 36–38, 40–43, 48, 56–59, 65, 69, 88, 90, 108–109, 111–14, 120, 122, 127, 140, 144–45, 147, 176, 179

DeMorse, Charles, 12

Denney, Hardin W., 167

Denton, Tex., 12, 165

Denton County, 12

Denton's School House, 35

Des Arcs, Ark., 64

deserters, 17–18, 20–23, 48, 94, 99, 105, 132, 139–40, 161

DeSoto, Henry, 5

DeSpain Bridge, 34, 154

DeWitt, George W., 122, 162, 185

DeWitt County, 131–32, 134–36, 159

Dewry, Haden W., 167

Dial, Charley, 172

Dial, Hamilton C., 183

Dial, Tex., 92

Dickson, John, 167

Dillingham, J. C., 182

Dimsdale, Thomas, 23

Dise, John W., 167

Dishner, Mary Early, 176

Dixon, J. S., 182

Dixon, Simp, 116

Dixon, Tex., 83

Dodge, Honey Lanham, 176, 186

Dohoney, Eben Lafayette: career of, 35, 127–28; and Hemby-Howard hanging, 44, 57–58, 60, 108, 162; mentioned, 42, 44, 50, 54, 74–75, 105–106, 141, 143, 154, 156, 161, 168, 181–82; military service of, 48, 66, 106, 164; participation in Noble legal case, 106–107; and postwar judicial proceedings, 108–109, 117, 122, 185; and secession, 35–38, 108; writings of, 37–38, 108, 128

Dohoney, Mary Johnson, 127

Downing, G. W., 182

Drennan, Elbert, 98–99

Durant, Okla., 126

Duval, Mr., 105

Early, E. B., 176

Early, Elbert, 89, 91–92, 113–14, 121, 126–27, 151, 174–76

Early, John, 132

Early, Mary Anne Dent, 92, 126

Easley, J. M., 122, 162

East End, 29–30, 41–43, 47–48, 50, 54, 57–58, 64, 85, 109, 112–13, 154

East Enders, 30, 43

Edmundson, Turner B., 46–47, 158

Eighth Judicial District: judges of, 117–18, 121–23, 184–85; lawyers of, 108–109, 117–22, 185–86; list of counties in, 107; mentioned, 106, 146; records of, 110–11, 113, 115–16, 118–22, 125, 176, 182–87. *See also* postwar judicial proceedings

Eighth Missouri Cavalry (USA), 82; Co. A, 82

Ellett, W. A., 156

Elliott, Thomas, 167

Ellis County, 12, 46

Ellmore, J. C. C., 159

Elmore, Jim, 50, 64, 159, 164

Elmore, Sarah Ann Helms Leech, 159, 164

Elmore, William and Cyntha, 159
El Paso, Tex., 72
Elter, W. I. (W. J. Etter), 167
Elysian Fields, 97
Emmett, Chris, 187
England, 6, 8, 65
Enloe, Tex., 4
Epperson, B. H., 156
Essy, W. L., 49
Evergreen Cemetery, 127
Evolution of an Elder (Dohoney), 128
Ewing, William M., 181

Fannin County, 3–4, 8–9, 11–12, 14–15, 16–
  18, 20–21, 33–34, 39–40, 48, 59, 69, 71–
  72, 75, 77, 84, 87, 89, 92, 94, 98, 105–107,
  112–13, 126, 147–48, 152, 164–65, 176–77,
  181
farming, 14, 28–30, 42
Fayetteville, Ark., 75–76, 79
Fifteenth Missouri Cavalry (USA): Co. E,
  100
Finney, F. E., 182
fires, 11–12
First Indian Texas Cavalry Regiment, 150
First Methodist Church, Ben Franklin,
  Tex., 41
First Regiment of Arkansas Cavalry,
  168–69
First Regiment of Texas Cavalry (USA),
  169
First Texas Cavalry Regiment (USA), 75–
  76
First Texas Infantry, Hood's Texas
  Brigade: Co. A, 185
First Texas Regiment (USA), 76
Fishing Creek, Ky., 51–52, 60
Fitzgerald, Anderson Lafayette "Fate":
  capture of, 95; escape of, 95, 177; family
  history, 94–95; mentioned, 100; and
  stories about, 100–101
Fitzgerald, Bradford "Brad": family his-
  tory, 92–94; mentioned, 100–101, 179,
  190; stories about, 94–95, 100–101
Fitzgerald, Bud, 179

Fitzgerald, Charity Bailey, 92–93
Fitzgerald, Emaline, 95–96
Fitzgerald, Emeline Bunyan, 168, 170, 178
Fitzgerald, Hiram, 100–101, 179
Fitzgerald, James Star: capture of, 95;
  escape of, 95, 177; family history, 94–
  95; mentioned, 100–101; and stories
  about, 100
Fitzgerald, Lydia D. Bray, 95
Fitzgerald, Malinda Jane, 95
Fitzgerald, Mary Emma Hensen, 100
Fitzgerald, Pleasant "Plez": capture of, 95;
  family history, 93, 95, 151, 168, 170–71;
  hanging of, 96, 177–78; mentioned, 98,
  107, 167; and vigilante trial, 95–96. *See
  also* Fitzgerald-Randolph-Newman
  hanging
Fitzgerald, Sarah E. Stubbs, 94
Fitzgerald, Sarah "Sally," 98, 179
Fitzgerald, Wesley, 94
Fitzgerald, William, 93
Fitzgerald-Randolph-Newman hanging:
  burial site of, 96–97; capture of victims,
  95; hanging of victims, 96, 177; men-
  tioned, 98, 188–90; and vigilante trial,
  95–96
Fitzgeralds: From Tennessee to Texas, 92–93,
  179, 190
Fitzhugh, George, 25
Florida, 8
Forbut, Wm. H., 167
Fore, Frances, 172
Forks, 28, 32, 34, 52–53, 64–65
Forks delta, 28–29, 31, 33–35, 38, 40–41, 46–
  54, 57, 64, 69, 84–86, 88, 92, 97, 106,
  110, 112, 116, 127–28, 154, 163, 178, 182
Forks of Sulphur, 4, 28, 128
Forks watershed, 6–7, 9, 11–15, 21–22, 28,
  30, 34, 38–39, 41, 46, 48, 57, 59, 68, 74,
  81, 118, 127, 129, 145, 149, 152
Four Corners, 105
Fourth Texas Cavalry, 159
Franklin County, 93, 111
Fredericksburg, Tex., 128
Freedmen, 124

Freemasonry, 40–41
Frontier Times, 128
Fort Gipson, 16
Fort Hindman, 93
Fort Lyday, Tex., 92
Fort Smith, Ark., 50, 63, 73, 76, 79–81, 99, 159
Fort Smith (Ark.) New Era, 80, 168
Fort Smith (Ark.) Times, 169–70
Fort Towson, Indian Territory, 81
Fort Worth, Tex., 3, 44
fugitive, 55, 87, 116, 150. *See also* brush men; bush men

Gainesville, Tex., 68, 73, 91, 116, 125–26
Galbraith, Sam. G., 181
Gales, J. N., 167
Galveston News, 132–33
Gambill, William, Jr., 149
Garrett, Jesse C., 183
Garrett, Thomas, 182
Garrett's Bluff, Tex., 84, 173
Gart, W. H., 167
Gaston, Amanda Melvina, 168
Gaston, William, 168
Gates, I. H., 167
George, D. S., 110–11
George, David Simeon "Sim," 58, 108–109, 111, 113, 127, 162
George, Lucinda Nancy, 99, 109
Georgia, 8, 29, 85–86, 126
Gilbreath, Kelly, 167
Giles, Tex., 33, 116
Giles Academy, 33, 48, 111, 164
Giles County, Tenn., 33, 87
Gilspie, I. T. (J. T. Gillespie), 167
Glenn, Ann Speer, 81
Glenn, Austin H., Jr., 82–83, 99, 171–72
Glenn, Austin H., Sr.: capture of, 81–82; family history of, 81–82, 151, 171–72; hanging of, 83; mentioned, 83–84, 99, 107, 171–72, 178; occupation of, 81; and Parson reference, 81, 172. *See also* Glenn-Smith hanging
Glenn, Austin T., 99

Glenn, Charles, 99
Glenn, Elias Turner, 99
Glenn, J. H. (James), 83
Glenn, James H., 82
Glenn, James, 99–100
Glenn, John J., 99
Glenn, Joseph, 82, 99, 100, 171
Glenn, Joseph W., 99
Glenn, Joseph Wilson, 82, 99
Glenn, Lucinda, 99
Glenn, Margaret, 99, 172
Glenn, Mary, 99
Glenn, Mattie, 99
Glenn, Missouri Ann, 82
Glenn, Rhoda, 99, 171–72
Glenn, Rhoda Turner, 87, 99
Glenn, Robert, 82
Glenn, Robert Wilson, 99
Glenn, Thomas, 81
Glenn, Thomas Tyre, 82, 100, 171
Glenn-Smith hanging: burial site of victims, 83, 172; capture of victims, 83, 177–78; hanging of, 83; mentioned, 90, 96, 98, 172, 189
Glewart, J. N., 167
Glewart, Robert E., 167
Gober, J. B., 176
Goff, C. W., 127, 184, 189
Goff, Council, 113, 115, 125, 127, 184, 186–87
Goff, Edward Hill, 127
Goliad County, 132–33
Gonzales County, 131, 135–36
Gould, Nicholas C., 48
Gould's Regiment, 112
Graham (Grayham), Wm., 167
Grant, Ulysses, 124
Gray, B. W., 106–108, 112, 117, 181. *See also* Eighth Judicial District; postwar judicial proceedings
Gray Rock Dragoons, 93–94
Grayson County, 4, 22, 39, 49, 69–72, 77, 105
Great Hanging at Gainesville, 41, 68, 91, 116–17, 122, 125–26, 138, 161–62
Green, Jerry, 83, 97

Greenback party, 127

Green County, Ill., 16

Greenville, Tex., 4, 9, 15, 72–73, 83, 87, 95–96, 106, 115, 146, 165, 172, 189

Greenville Compress, 97

Greenville Guard, 73, 166–67

Greenwood, Ark., 170

Greenwood, Charity, 173

Greenwood, Frances, 173

Greenwood, James, 173

Greenwood, Mary, 173

Greenwood, Sarah A., 173

Greenwood, Thomas: 173; capture of, 87–88, 91; family history, 85–86, 151, 173–74, 176; hanging of, 88–91, 174–76; mentioned, 85, 108, 113, 121, 143; and postwar judicial proceedings, 108–25; and vigilante trial, 88. *See also* Campbell-DeArman-Greenwood-Millsaps hanging; Eighth Judicial District; postwar judicial proceedings

Greg (of Mount Pleasant), 117

Griffin, Charles, 122, 149, 162

Griffith, Joseph McElroy, 155

Griscom, George L., 49

Grothaus, F. E., 133

guerrilla actions, 75–79, 151, 189

Gulivan, Charles A., 167

Gunn, Beth, 92

Hadden, H. B., 149

Hadden, T. H., 149

Hall, Lance, 153–54

Hamblin, A., 10, 59

Hamilton, Andrew Jackson "Jack," 75, 105–106, 117, 122, 168, 182

Hamilton, J. S., 182

Hamilton, L. M., 167

Hancock, John, 156

Handbook of Texas, 129, 148, 185

hangings. *See* Campbell-DeArman-Greenwood-Millsaps hanging; Fitzgerald-Randolph-Newman hanging; Glenn-Smith hanging; Great Hanging at Gainesville; Hart-Hays hanging; Hemby-Howard hanging

Hardin, John Wesley, 134–36

Hargis (found Frank Chamblee), 104

Harmon, Tex., 35

Harney, William S., 31

Harper, Cecil, Jr., 76

Harper, Mr., 154

Harris, "Cap," 99

Harris County, 22

Harrison, W. Walworth, 146, 165–67, 189

Harrison County, 13, 38, 90, 104

Hart, Andrew (Anderson), 167

Hart, Caius, 165

Hart, Carson, 165

Hart, Charles, 165

Hart, Cyrus "Cy," 98, 179

Hart, Dell, 179

Hart, Elvira, 87

Hart, Emeline, 173

Hart, Free Liberty, 72

Hart, Hardin, 69, 72–73, 87, 106, 165–66, 181

Hart, Hugh, 165

Hart, James C., 165, 173, 179

Hart, James C. "Jim," 69, 85, 87, 98–99

Hart, Jim, 84, 173, 180

Hart, Jincy, 165

Hart, John, 69, 89, 165, 167, 174

Hart, John F., 68–69, 71–72, 165

Hart, Jonathan "Fox," 69, 84–87, 98–99, 173

Hart, Jonathan G. "Fox," 165, 169–71, 180

Hart, Jonathan "Jackie," 69, 84, 165, 173

Hart, Josiah (Isiah), 165, 167

Hart, Louisa, 165

Hart, Lyrus, 167

Hart, Martha, 165

Hart, Martha Butt, 180

Hart, Martin D.: accounts about, 72, 74–75, 77–80, 89, 90, 169–71; activities in Ark., 38, 72–74, 75–78, 139; activities in Tex., 72–73, 75; capture of, 78–79, 81; family history of, 69–72, 77, 164–66,

172; hanging of, 79–80, 170; mentioned, 68, 84, 87–89, 95, 106, 156, 167–68, 181, 189; military career of, 73, 167; occupation of, 72–73; and secession views of, 38, 73; trial of, 79. *See also* Hart-Hays hanging

Hart, Mary Green, 72, 165

Hart, Meredith, 165

Hart, Miles H., 165

Hart, Nancy Green, 72

Hart, Prior, 167

Hart, Prior Wallace, 72

Hart, Rebecca, 72

Hart, Sarah "Sally," 98, 179

Hart, Stephen, 173

Hart, Stephen C., 167

Hart, Synthia A., 84–85, 173

Hart, Syrus, 167

Hart, William, 165, 167

Hart, Wilson, 170

Hart-Hays hanging: activities in Ark., 72–78; burial of, 79–80; capture of, 78–79; court martial of, 79; hanging of, 79–80

Hart's Company (Gang), 75–85, 86, 88–90, 92–96, 98, 108, 167–72, 189

Hart's Mounted Men, 69

Havana, Cuba, 39

Hayden, Stephen S., 46–47

Haynes, John L., 125, 156

Hays, J. W. (Hayes): activities in Ark., 74–78, 167–71; capture of, 78–79; court martial of, 79; hanging of, 79–80, 170. *See also* Hart-Hays hanging

Heart, Stephen C., 167

Heart, Syrus, 167

Heart, Wm., 167

heel-flies, 22, 151

"Heel-Fly Time in Texas" (Hunter), 30–31, 128, 141, 154

Hefner, Bill, 96

Helena, Ark., 142

Helms, Charlotte, 41, 127

Helms, G. W. "Pony," 127

Helms, George W., 56, 58, 108, 113, 115–16, 118, 121–23, 125, 127, 140, 151, 162, 186

Helms, John Jack (Helm): death of, 42, 135–36; description of, 42; employee of S. Pierce, 129–31, 184, 187; family history of, 41–42, 49, 58–59, 64, 127, 138, 151, 159; and Hemby-Howard hanging, 56–58, 125, 133; invention of, 42, 135; mentioned, 42–43, 46, 49, 52, 58–59, 108, 112–13, 121–22, 157, 159, 187; military service of, 47–50, 63–64, 66, 159, 163; postwar judicial proceedings, 42, 108–14, 118–24, 162, 186; service as regulator, 131–34; service as sheriff, 42, 134–36; service as State Police, 42, 56–57, 133–34; in Sutton-Taylor feud, 131–36. *See also* Eighth Judicial Court; Hemby-Howard hanging; postwar judicial proceedings

Helms, Margaret Virginia, 159

Helms, Minerva McCown, 41, 50, 64, 159

Helm-Taylor feud, 131

Helper, Hinton Rowan, 38

Hembey, Tom and Kathy, 141, 155, 189–90

Hemby, A. M., 155

Hemby, Amanda, 155

Hemby, Ann, 155

Hemby, Anna M. Pair, 32, 142, 155

Hemby, Elexander (Hembey), 190

Hemby, James, 31

Hemby, James E. (Hembey): capture of, 56–57; family history, 31–33, 141, 143, 151, 154–55, 189–90; hanging of, 61–62; mentioned, 47–48, 50, 55, 85, 88, 108, 119, 122, 160–61; and postwar judicial proceedings, 108–25; and vigilante trial, 58–63. *See also* Eighth Judicial District; Hemby-Howard hanging; postwar judicial proceedings

Hemby, James Wesley, 31–32, 47–48, 62, 112, 119–20, 122–23, 154, 162

Hemby, John, 33

Hemby, John Miller (Hembey), 155

Hemby, John Z., 155

Hemby, Jonathan: capture of, 56–57; family history of, 31–33, 141–42, 151, 154–55; hanging of, 61–62; mentioned, 31, 47–48, 50, 55, 62, 85, 88, 108, 119, 122, 160–61; occupation of, 155; and postwar judicial proceedings, 108–25; and vigilante trial, 58–63. *See also* Eighth Judicial District; Hemby-Howard hanging; postwar judicial proceedings

Hemby, Julien (Hembey), 155

Hemby, Malinda Jane Oldham (Hembey), 33, 141, 155, 189–90

Hemby, Mary (Hembey), 155

Hemby, Miriam, 155

Hemby, Nancy A. (Hembey), 155

Hemby, Sanford, 162–63

Hemby, Silas Wright, 162

Hemby, Thomas (Hembey), 155

Hemby, William, 122

Hemby, William Edward, 155

Hemby, William Henry (Hembey), 155

Hemby, Wm., 155

Hemby, Zachry "Jack," 141

Hemby Crossing, 31, 33

Hemby-Howard hanging: burial site of victims, 62; capture of victims, 56–57; hanging of victims, 61–62, 161, 163; mentioned, 10, 35, 42, 50–51, 54–55, 59–65, 67–68, 96, 106, 108–10, 112–13, 118–20, 126–27, 139–41, 144, 151, 184, 190; postwar judicial proceedings, 108–25; and vigilante trial, 56–63, 110. *See also* Eighth Judicial District; postwar judicial proceedings

Henderson, Tex., 13

Henry, J. E., 156

Henry, Jim, 18

Henslee, Dave, 104

Henson, Mary Emma, 100

Herron, Frances Jay, 75–76

Herron, General, 169

Hickman County, Tenn., 85

Hicks, Harvey, 105

"History of Hopkins County," 139, 156

History of Lamar County (Neville), 137–38, 155–56, 158

Hobbs Thicket, 4

Hockaday, Thomas Hart Benton, 33, 164

Hodges, Robert, 167

Hodges, William, 167

Hoff's Station, 142

Hogeye, Tex., 177

home guard, 22, 47, 114, 132, 164

home militia, 17, 22

Honey Grove, Tex., 12, 14, 34, 98, 149

Hooper, John, 167

Hooten, L. F., Mrs., 155

Hopkins County, 3, 8–9, 12–13, 23–24, 28–30, 34–35, 39, 41, 45, 48, 50, 55, 57, 59, 62–63, 69, 75, 80, 82, 84–91, 93, 97–98, 105–108, 110, 113–16, 118, 120–29, 130, 145, 147–48, 153–54, 162, 165, 174, 176, 178, 181, 184; Militia and Muster Rolls, 47, 85

Hopkins County Eighth Judicial District Court. *See* Eighth Judicial District

Hopper, Erastus "Ras," 50, 55, 88–89, 146, 159–60, 174–76

Hopper, John, 167

horseapples, 112

Horton, Tex., 90, 176

Horton, W. B., 96, 146, 190

Houston, Sam, 35, 144

Houston, Tex., 22, 89

Houston Press, 144, 163, 190

Howard, A. G. W., 29

Howard, Arington (Arrington), 29, 46, 153

Howard, Cornelius, 29

Howard, Eliza, 29, 153

Howard, Elizabeth (Mrs. Arington), 153

Howard, Elizabeth E., 29, 153

Howard, Elizabeth McMahand, 29

Howard, Harriet Young, 30, 154

Howard, Henry T.: capture of, 56–57; family history, 29–31, 46, 142, 151, 153–54; hanging of, 58–63; mentioned, 36, 38, 42–47, 49, 52, 55, 60, 64, 66, 88, 108, 119, 120–22, 143, 156, 160–61; occupation, 30, 60; and postwar judicial proceedings,

108–25; and vigilante trial, 43–45, 58–63. *See also* Eighth Judicial District; Hemby-Howard hanging; postwar judicial proceedings

Howard, Isaac Whitaker, 153

Howard, James K.: capture of, 56–57; family history, 29–31, 153–54; hanging of, 61–63; mentioned, 42–43, 46–47, 55, 60, 88, 108, 119–20, 122, 160–61; and postwar judicial proceedings, 108–25; and vigilante trial, 58–63. *See also* Eighth Judicial District; Hemby-Howard hanging; postwar judicial proceedings

Howard, John, 29

Howard, John Thomas, 153

Howard, Joseph, 29, 153

Howard, Lydia Crabtree, 30, 153

Howard, M., 60, 154

Howard, Martha Jane, 29, 154

Howard, Mary E. J., 154

Howard, Mary Elizabeth, 154

Howard, Sarah, 29

Howard, Thomas: capture of, 56–57; card of, 158; family of, 29–30, 153–54; hanging of, 61–62; mentioned, 42, 45, 47, 55–56, 60, 88, 108, 119, 122, 156, 160–61; and newspaper, 46, 52; and postwar judicial proceedings, 108–25; and vigilante trial, 58–63. *See also* Eighth Judicial District; Hemby-Howard hanging; postwar judicial proceedings

Howard, William Henry, 142–43

Howard, William Henry, Sr., 142–43

Howard, William T., 154

Howell, Alfred, 4, 9, 72–73, 145–46, 166

Huff, Leo E., 75, 77, 79

Hughes, T. P., 156

Hughey, I. M., 167

Hunt County, 3–5, 8–9, 12, 15–18, 23, 38–39, 48, 63, 68–69, 72–73, 75, 77, 80–83, 85–87, 90, 92, 94–100, 105–107, 113–14, 127, 129, 145–47, 165–66, 174, 177, 181–82, 189–90

Hunt County militia, 83

Hunter, John Warren, 30–31, 64, 128, 154

Hunter, Mary Ann Calhoun, 128

Hunter, Richard, 162–63

Hunter family, 154

Hunter's Magazine, 128

Illinois, 6–7, 11, 16, 58, 69, 74, 81, 84, 86, 99–100, 112, 128, 165

"Immortal Eight," 35, 93

impressment laws, 14

Indiana, 6–7, 32, 53, 128–29, 165–66

Indians, 5, 20, 27, 39, 68–69, 71–72, 91–92, 114–15, 145

Indian Territory, 16, 40, 48, 50, 75, 81, 91, 99, 129, 150–51

Ingraham, James (Ingram), 75–76

Ireland, 6

Jack County, 39

Jackson, Josiah "Cy" Hart, 87, 174

Jackson County, Ga., 86

Jameson, S., 157

Janiff, James, 167

Janiff, Richard, 167

Jayhawkers, 97–98

Jefferson, Tex., 12, 34, 93, 156, 184–86

Jefferson County, Ky., 54

Jernigan, Bill, 86–87, 104

Jernigan, Curtis, 5, 69, 86, 146, 165

Jernigan, Elvira, 165, 174

Jernigan, Felix, 104, 165, 181

Jernigan, Frank, 104

Jernigan, Tex., 29, 153

Jernigan, William (Jernigin), 86–87, 104, 165, 181

Jernigan Baptist Church, 153

Jernigan's Thicket, 5, 16, 18, 28–29, 33–34, 55, 61, 69, 84–86, 88, 90, 98, 102–104, 114, 121, 134, 160–61, 171, 178, 181, 189

John Jenkin's Company of Scouts or Spys, 82

Johnson, Andrew, 125

Johnson, J. R., 156

Johnson, Joshua F., 93, 156

Johnson, Mary, 128
Johnson, William H., 35, 105, 119–21, 156, 181, 185
Johnson and Townes Law Firm, 125, 186
Joliff, John James, 167
Joliff, Richard, 167
Jones, Bob, 170
Jones, Dudley W., 66
Jones, Henry, 181
Jones, Mr., 133
Jones, W. E. H. (W. E. M.), 167
Jonesborough, Tex., 69
Jordan, Terry G., 6–8, 14, 28
Jordan, Thomas E., 77
Judge Lynch, 140
Jurnigan, Bill, 104, 180
Jurnigan, Frank, 104, 180

Kansas, 40, 52, 75, 78
Kansas Jayhawker, 78
Karnes County, 131
Kaufman County, 17
Kelly, Bill, 134
Kelly, Henry, 134
Kelly, J. M., 167
Kendall, Mary J., 155
Kentucky, 6–7, 28, 30, 35, 51–52, 54, 60, 70, 83, 85–86, 91, 100, 165
King, G. W., 146, 169, 180, 190
King, L. D., 49
Klondike, Tex., 184
Knights of the Golden Circle, 39, 88, 115, 157
Knights of the Rising Son, 185
Krebs, Okla., 142
Ku Klux Klan, 185

Ladonia Cemetery, 126
Ladonia, Tex., 12, 94
LaFour, Edna Evans, 153
La Grange, Tex., 136
Lake Lodge 255, 40, 65–66, 157, 164
Lamar County, 3, 5, 8–9, 10–13, 15, 20, 24, 28–30, 32–37, 39–40, 45–48, 54, 56, 59–
60, 62–63, 66, 74, 81, 92, 97, 104–108, 110–13, 116, 118, 122–24, 126–29, 141, 147–48, 153–54, 156, 162, 164, 168, 174, 178–79, 181–82, 185
Lamar County, Beat 2, Muster Roll, 47
Lamar County Secession Club, 112
Lamar Rifles, 48
Lamar (Tex.) Enquirer, 10
Lampasas County, 126
Lampasas River, 139
Landreth, S., 45, 119
Landrum, Graham, 72
Lane, Jim, 52
Lane family, 34, 53
Lavaca County, 65
Lawson, Andrew, 167
Lawson, Elby (Elley), 167
Lawson, Zachariah, 175
Lawton, Okla., 129
Layer, Maggie, 163
Leachman, Bill, 180
Leachman, William, 98
Lee, Bob, 106, 116
Lee, Robert E., 188
Leech, A. C. L., 64
Leech, Alonzo, 49, 159
Leech, Jim, 159
Leech, Sarah Ann Helms, 49, 64, 159
Lee-Peacock feud, 105–106, 116
Leonard, Tex., 94, 169
Lewis, A. B., 78, 170–71
Liberty, Tex., 10, 24
Lincoln, Abraham, 13, 60–61, 162
Litchfield, Ill., 168
Little, Henry, 110–11
Little Rock, Ark., 79, 89, 100
Lock, Leander W. P. "Jacob," 164
Lollar, L. A., 181
Lone Oak, Tex., 82–83, 172
Long, William, 167
Long Taw, Tex., 34
Loose Leaves (Patteson), 139–40, 146, 153–54, 163, 183
Los Angeles, Calif., 126, 139

Loughery, R. W., 38, 90

Louisana, 8, 15, 24, 34, 48, 69, 97–98, 100, 120, 122, 180

Lovelace, James, 98–99

Lovelace, Martin, 98–99

Lovelady, W. D., 110–11, 113

Lowe, Richard, 151

Lower South, 7–8, 14, 23, 28, 33, 147–48, 153. *See also* Upper South

Lower Southerners, 8, 14, 23, 57, 147–48. *See also* Upper Southerners

Luckett, Helen Hart, 161

Lunsford, Sam, 157

Lyday, J. T., 59

Lynch, Charles, 57

lynching, 26, 57, 140, 161, 185

Lynch Law, 57

Mabry, Henche Parham, 117–19, 121–25, 184–86

Mabry, Woodford Haywood, 186

McCaslin, Richard B., 41, 44, 68, 118, 138, 161–62, 164

McCloy, O. C., 182

McCokley (McCoulskey), James, 167

McConkley (McCoulskey), Daniel, 167

McCown, Minerva, 41

McCracken Cemetery, 136

McCulloch, Henry, 17–18, 20–21, 107, 150, 168

McFarland, Lena, 104

McFarland, Nancy McGuire, 109, 182

McFarland, Robert, 108–11, 113, 182

McFarlin (McFarland), Nancy, 109, 182

McFarlin, Robert, 111

McGlasson, Anna, 126

McGlasson, James C., 58, 113, 115, 121–22, 126–27, 151, 162

McGlasson Cemetery, 126

McGlasson family, 34

McGlaughlin, Robert, 110–11

McGloflin, Robert, 111

McGoing (one of Martin D. Hart's men), 77, 170

McGrew Creek, 98

McGuire, Cornelius B., 57–58, 109–11, 113, 163

McGuire, Lucinda, 109

McGuire, Salina Duke, 58

McGuire, Thomas Rufus, 58–59, 109, 111, 113, 127, 144, 162, 163, 190

Mackey, George W., 108

McKinney, Tex., 106

McMahan, Bruce, 173

McMinn County, Tenn., 83

Magruder, J. B., 18

Mahan, Bruce, 173

Mainas, Wely N. (Wily N. Manos), 167

Man: His Origin, Nature, and Destiny (Dohoney), 128

Marion County, 12, 34, 93, 107

Marple, Enoch, 10, 59, 107, 129. *See also* Church of God

Marrs, James, 89, 182

Marrs, Margaret Campbell, 182

Marshall, E. I. (E. J.), 167

Marshall, George F., 167

Marshall, Tex., 13, 38, 46, 52, 104

Marshall Texas Republican, 46, 52, 54, 79, 90, 152, 156–58, 172, 176, 181, 185

Martin, James, 164

Marvin, Tex., 63

Mason, Jeff, 89, 146, 175

Mason, Tex., 128, 131

Mason County, 131

Masons, 40–41, 53–54, 65, 115, 164

Massey, I. W. (J. W.), 167

Matamoros, Mex., 65

Mathers, Manuel, 183

Maxey, Marilda, 120

Maxey, Rice, 181, 186

Maxey, Samuel Bell, 48, 99, 116, 119–21, 126, 139, 175–76, 185–86

Menardville, Tex., 128

Mercer County, Ky., 165

Methodist Church, 10, 41

Methodist Church North, 54

Methodist Episcopal Church, 81

Methodist Episcopal Church South, 56

Mexican War, 31, 48, 58, 62

Mexico, 8, 15, 31–31, 39, 64–65, 99, 106, 109, 116, 123, 126, 128

Miles, P., 122, 162

military groups, 15–16, 20–22, 31, 47–50, 52, 63–64, 66, 73–78, 82–83, 85, 91, 93–94, 100, 104, 106, 112, 114–15, 119–20, 150, 158–59, 163–64, 167–70, 180, 183, 185

military impressment laws, 14

military rosters, 47, 85, 158, 166–67, 171, 183

Miller, Ora, 181

Miller, W. B., 164

Millsaps, Algeretta Milholland, 86, 122, 174

Millsaps, Americus, 174

Millsaps, Cicero Franklin: controversy about, 85, 88, 91, 174–75; family history of, 85–86, 174–75; mentioned, 85, 121–22, 174–75

Millsaps, Emeline Chafin, 86, 91, 122, 174–76

Millsaps, Fuller, 174

Millsaps, Jacob, 86, 174

Millsaps, Jacob, Sr., 86

Millsaps, Jake, 175

Millsaps, James M.: capture of, 87–88, 91; family history, 85–86, 151, 153, 174–75; hanging of, 88–90, 91, 174–76; mentioned, 33, 85, 108, 113, 121–22; and postwar judicial proceedings, 91, 108–25; and vigilante trial, 88. *See also* Campbell-DeArman-Greenwood-Millsaps hanging; Eighth Judicial District; postwar judicial proceedings

Millsaps, James Monroe, 29

Millsaps, James Thomas, 33

Millsaps, Jim, 175

Millsaps, Minta (Minky) Vanderford, 86, 91, 121–22, 174–76

Millsaps, Tid, 86, 91, 174–75

Millsaps, William, 174

Mind of the South (Cash), 8, 25–26

Miner, F. W., 119, 152, 181

Miner, W. B., 63

Mississippi, 8, 43, 48, 64, 91, 97, 104

Mississippi River, 16, 37, 69, 93

Missouri, 6–7, 16, 22, 30–31, 33, 41, 47, 73, 75, 79, 82, 85, 87, 100, 118, 124, 151, 182

Monroe County, Tenn., 81

Montague, Daniel, 70–71

Montague County, 39

Montana, 22, 40

Montgomery County Ill., 168

Moody, John F., 71

Moore, Dusen (Duren) A., 167

Moore, Mr., 133

Morgan, Daniel, 110–12

Morgan County, Ala., 29

Morris County, 34, 93

Morrison, Dan, 98

Morton, J. B., 182

Moscoso party, 5, 145–46

Mount, Charles C., 183

Mount Pleasant, Tex., 34, 117

Mt. Carmel, Tex., 177

Mt. Vernon, Tex., 111

Mundine, T. H., 156

Mustang Thicket, 4, 18, 92, 94, 100–101, 189–90

Mustang Thicket gang, 18, 20

Myres, Browne Elizabeth Millsaps, 174–75

Nacogdoches County, 72

Nail family, 181

Nance, James, 167

Napper, Wily, 104

Naud-Burnett Slaughter Barn, 97

Navarro County, 84

Neal, William, 175

Neatherly, Ab., 183

Neathery, Tommy, 50

Neathery, Wesley, 63

Needmore, Tex., 29, 153

Neely, M. S., 110–11

Neil, Emeline, 175

Nelson, John, 70

Nelson County, Ky, 165

Neville, A. W., 30, 137, 146, 183, 189. *See also Paris (Tex.) News* "Backward Glances"

New Orleans, La., 34, 69

New York, 53

Newman, [Martin V.?]: capture of, 95; controversy about, 94–95; hanging of, 96, 177–78; mentioned, 107; vigilante trial, 96. *See also* Glenn-Smith hanging

Nicholson, Old Doc, 92, 176–77

Ninth Texas Cavalry (Sims Regiment), 48–50, 63–64, 66, 74, 104, 106, 159, 163–64, 183; Co. A (Tarrant), 158; Co. B (Fannin), 48; Co. C (Grayson), 158; Co. D (Tarrant), 158; Co. E (Red River), 158; Co. F (Titus), 158; Co. G (Hopkins), 48–50, 63, 112, 159; Co. H (Lamar), 48, 66; Co. I (Titus), 158; Co. K (Hopkins-Hunt), 48, 63, 114, 183

Ninth Texas Infantry Regiment, 15, 48, 64, 158; Co. G (Lamar County), 82. *See also* Lamar Rifles

Noble, John C., 106–107, 112

Norris, Frank B., 176–77, 190

Norris, John G. (W.), 167

North Carolina, 31, 47, 81, 127

Northern Methodist Church, 9–11

Northern Methodist Episcopal Church, 11, 44

Northern Sub-district of Texas (CSA), 107

North Sulphur Academy, 59

North Sulphur River, 4, 28, 31, 33

North Texan, 127

North Texas Regiment, 31

Norton, A. B., 156

Nowell, Bernard Gilbert, 87, 175

Nowell, Hicks, 17, 86–88, 91, 103–104, 146, 171, 174–75

Nueces County, 65

Ober, Benjamin, 10–11, 106–107, 128–29, 154, 163; and Church of God, 59–60, 143, 154; and eyewitness account of Hemby-Howard hanging, 59–63, 118–19, 160, 163; family history, 128–29; mentioned, 33, 143, 160, 163; and witness at Noble trial, 106–107; *The Church Advocate*, 10, 129, 187

Ober, Elizabeth Barnett, 128–29

Ober, Richard, 129

O'Brien, Ben F., 179

Odell, Ruben (Reubin), 167

Odell, Turner, 167

Odell, William, 167

Odom, Fred, 171

Ohio, 6–7, 51, 105

Oklahoma. *See also* Indian Territory

Old Chihuahua Trail, 145

Old Tarrent, Tex. *See* Tarrant, Tex.

Old-timers of Hunt County (Goff), 127

Oliver, Nell, 163

Olsen, Nellie H., 141

Ordinance No. 11, 117–18

Orren, G. G., 139, 156

osage oranges, 112

Owen, W. M., 156

Oxford, Mr., 163

Oxford Bridge, 57, 60, 65, 88, 163

Pace, Alford, 11

pardons, 20

Paris, Tex., 5, 10–13, 15, 20, 29–30, 34–37, 46–48, 74, 81, 105–106, 112, 127–29, 149, 152, 181

Paris Female Seminary, 30

Paris-Tarrant Road, 31

Paris (Tex.) Advocate, 42–43, 157

Paris (Tex.) News "Backward Glances," 146, 149, 158

Paris (Tex.) Press, 12, 46–47, 52, 56, 104, 118, 120, 122–23, 152, 158, 185

Parker County, 53

Paschal, I. A., 156

Pate, O. M., 88

Patterson, J. M., 119, 123

Patterson, James, 34, 53, 58, 140, 182, 184

Patteson, Bernard M., 116, 157

Patteson, Ikie Gray, 6, 139–40, 146, 153, 163

Patteson, James, III, 116, 146, 157, 161–62

Patteson, Myranda Smith, 116

Patteson family, 156

Payne, Wilson M., 35

Peace Party, 68, 73

Pease, Elisha M., 117, 125
Pecan, Tex., 153
Pecan Gap, Tex., 33–34
Peerless, Tex., 111
Peers, J. M., 12–13
Pelts, Wm., 167
Penn, William, 6
Pennsylvania, 6, 10
pension applications, 82, 167, 171–72
Penwell, Eli S., 98–99, 180
Peters, Thomas, 62, 163
Pettigrew, T. A., 79, 146, 169, 171
Petty, William. P., 89–90, 174
Phelps (Unionist), 78
Pierce, Able H. "Shanghai," 115, 129, 184
Pilot Point, Tex., 12
Pine Bluff's, 155
Pine Hills, 155
Pine Woods, 128
Pinson, B. F., 167
Pitts, Wm., 167
Pleasant Hill, La.,
Plow-horse Cavalry (Weddle), 15, 180
Polk County, Mo., 47
Pool, A., 167
Pool, Mr., 133
Posey, Aden, 50, 126, 146, 176, 180
postwar judicial proceedings: arrests of
    men, 108–10; defense witnesses of,
    110–13; grand jury, 110; indictments of
    vigilantes, 113–15; prosecution witnesses
    of, 110–13; trial of, 108–12. *See also*
    Eighth Judicial District
Poteau River, Ark., 78
Poteet, Gibbons, 63
Poteet, T. R. H. "Tommy," 50, 63, 182
Potter, John, 174
prairie matches, 12
Prairie Valley, Tex., 83
Presbyterian Church, 10
Presidio Crossing, 31
Preston Bend, 71
Pridgen, B. J., 133–34
Primm, B. F., 167
Prohibition party, 127

pro-South, 53
Protestants, 6
Purcell, P. B., 167

Quantrill, William Clark, 22, 124, 151
Quantrill's Raiders, 21–22

Rains, Emory, 156
Rains, John D., 156
Rains County, 156
ranching, 28–29, 84
Rancho Grande, 129, 131
Randolph, Clay, 176
Randolph, Malinda Jane Fitzgerald, 95
Randolph, Thomas: capture of, 95; family
    history of, 94–95, 142, 151, 190; hanging
    of, 96, 177–78; mentioned, 107; and vigi-
    lante trial, 95. *See also* Fitzgerald-
    Randolph-Newman hanging
Ratton, V. C., 182
Reconstruction: in Central and South
    Texas, 131–33; in Fannin County, 105–
    106; in Hopkins County, 105, 109–10,
    118–22, 124; in Lamar County, 105–106,
    116, 124, 181; in Northeast Texas, 105,
    117–18, 125; and President Johnson, 125;
    in Texas, 104–105, 117–22, 124–26,
    185–86
Redgate, Sam J., 156
Redman Boyd Toll Bridge, 163
Red River, 5, 13, 34, 68, 81, 91, 93, 156
Red River Campaign, 48, 180
Red River County, 5, 12, 39, 69, 107, 181
Red River Landing, 120
Red River Raft, 34, 36, 156
Reed, J. M., 139
regulators, 131–32
Reiff, A. V., 78, 170–71
Republic of Texas, 5, 34, 81
Reynolds, Donald E., 13, 25–26, 149
Reynolds, Joseph Jones, 131
Richardson, E. M., 169–70
Richardson, Edward, 76–78
Riley, J. W., 167
Ringo Lake, 111

Ringo, C. R., 110–11
Ringo, E. F., 110–11
Rio Grande River, 11, 31, 39
Rise and Fall of Mission San Saba
    (Hunter), 128
Roberts, I. F. (J. H.), 167
Roberts, O. M., 18
Robinson, I. W. (J. M.), 167
Rockcastle County, Ky., 83
Rocky Comfort, Ark., 46
Rogers, F. M., 182
Rome, Ga., 126, 139
Rose, Victor, 42
Ross, Sullivan R. "Sul Ross," 164
Ross Texas Brigade, 164
Round Rock (Tex.) Sentinel, 187
Roxton, Tex., 34, 40, 45, 63, 113, 126
Rush, Bud, 181
Rusk County, 13
Rutherford, Jack, 99, 180

Sabine County, 4
Sabine River, 4, 97
San Angelo, Tex., 128
San Angelo (Tex.) Daily Standard, 128
San Antonio, Tex., 9, 31–32, 39
Sanders, David, 110–11
Sanders, Joseph, 110–12
San Jacinto, 69
San Patricio, Tex., 65
San Patricio County, 132
Sawyer, William E., 77
Scots-Irish, 6. *See also* Lower South;
    Upper South
Scott, R. H., 167
Scott, Tom, 148
Scott County, Ark., 99, 180
Scroggins, Sterling Rodney, 17, 102, 104,
    180
Searls, Bob, 113–14, 116
Searls, Thomas (Searles), 113–15, 126–27,
    151, 186
Sebastian County, Ark., 169
secession: and anti-secession, 15, 17–18, 20–
    21, 35–40, 42–45, 58, 68, 73, 75, 93, 98,
105–106, 117, 156–57, 168, 181–82; conven-
    tion, 35, 40, 92–93; debate, 35–38, 45;
    Lamar County Secession Club support
    of, 112, 116; meetings, 35–36; men-
    tioned, 13, 35, 39, 105; and ordinance
    No. 11, 117–18; referendum and, 35;
    secessionists and, 35–40, 45, 50, 52, 58,
    77, 93, 116, 117–18; and vote on, 35,
    38–39, 92–93, 157
Sellers, John, 89, 175–76
Settle, M. G., 56, 58, 64, 112–13, 115–16,
    120–21, 126, 139, 151, 162
Shanklin, William, 98–99
Shelby, Gen., 124
Sheppard (Shepherd), B. C., 167
Sheridan, Philip Henry, 122, 124 25
Sherman, Tex., 22, 49, 114
Shiloh, Tex., 90, 176
shipping. *See* cotton
Shrade, H. W., 182
Shreveport, La., 34
Shuford, A. P., 156
Simmons, Ben Franklin, 33
Sims, William B., 114
Skidmore, F. O., 132
Slaughter, Mrs., 97
slavery, 8–14, 16, 26, 33–34, 37–41, 43–45,
    59 60, 70 72, 77, 81, 92, 97, 112, 115,
    147–48, 153, 178
slaves: and anti-slavery, 10, 14–15, 23, 39,
    43–44, 54, 81; attitude on, 37–41, 137–38,
    147–48; and church, 9–10, 44, 54, 56,
    59–60, 81–82; and insurrections, 9, 11–
    13, 39; mentioned, 39, 44, 76, 147–48;
    numbers of, 9, 38–39, 148, 178; owners
    of, 8, 10, 14, 33–34, 38, 40–42, 44, 53, 56,
    68, 70, 91–92, 97, 112, 116, 147–48, 153,
    178; proslavery, 10–12, 14, 23, 38, 43–44,
    92; speeches on, 37–38, 40, 44; and sto-
    ries about, 11–12, 33
Smith, Benjamin, 179
Smith, Billie Rhodes (Mrs. Dale), 136, 187
Smith, Charles H., 179
Smith, David Paul, 20–21, 91
Smith, Edmund Kirby, 21

Smith, G., 113, 115
Smith, Gilbert, 164
Smith, Gilford, 179
Smith, Greenville, 34, 40, 48, 52, 58, 66, 113–16, 118, 122–23, 126–27, 139, 151, 157, 162, 164, 178, 184
Smith, Henry, 179
Smith, "Honey," 179
Smith, J. K. P., 48
Smith, Josiah, 181
Smith, Mira J., 179
Smith, Moses, 179
Smith, Mr., 97, 178
Smith, Sam W., 182
Smith, Thomas, 83
Smith, Trace Chain: capture of, 83; hanging of, 83; mentioned, 98, 107, 172. *See also* Glenn-Smith hanging
Smith County, 89, 96
Smoot, Charles, 89
Socatino, 5
Sonnichsen, C. L., 129
Sons of Liberty, 53
Sons of the South, 53
Sons of Washington, 23, 40, 53–54, 56–57, 61–62, 65, 113, 182
South Carolina, 28
Southerland, Charles H., 47, 58–59, 108, 113, 115–16, 118–27, 140, 151, 161–62, 186
Southerland, Rachel, 127
Southern Honor: Ethics and Behavior in the Old South (Wyatt-Brown), 25
"Southern Marseillaise, The," 53
South's "Great Fear," 11
South Sulphur River, 4, 28, 34, 57, 62, 154, 161
South Texas, 28
Sparks, A. W., 12, 49
Speight, Joseph W., 76
Springfield, Mo., 73, 100, 168
Stafford, William, 174
Stansbury, Captain, 113, 182
Stansbury, J. W., 58–59, 113, 115, 162
State Police, 42, 56–57, 133–34
State (Tex.) Journal, 133

Steele, Frederick, 76, 100
Steele, William, 76
Steen, A. M., 111
Stein, Alfred M., 110–12
Stell, Aubrey, 111
Stell, George Washington, 111
Stell, James Wynne, 110–12
Stell, Wilson Wynne, Dr., 12, 112
Stevens, James G., 150
Steven's Regiment of Texas Dismounted Cavalry, 16, 150
Stewart, J. W., 167
Stewart, Robert E., 167
St. Louis, Mo., 75, 168, 179
Stone, Amanda, 97, 178
Stone, Amanda Rebecca, 178
Stone, Coleman, 178
Stone, Cornelia Branch, 137
Stone, Jimmy, 178
Stone, Johnny, 178
Stone, Kate, 24, 51–52, 97–98, 152, 178–79
Stone, Walter, 178
Stone, William, 178
Stout, Henry, 183
Stuart, Charles S. (Stewart), 49
Stubbs, John and Elizabeth, 94, 177
Stubbs family, 94, 177
Sullman, Charles A., 167
Sulphur Bluff, Tex., 41, 154
Sulphur Forks, 28, 147
Sulphur Forks of Red River, 28, 36
Sulphur Forks watershed, 3–5, 7–9, 21, 23–25, 39, 68–69, 80, 97, 126, 148, 178
Sulphur River, 17
Sulphur Springs, Tex., 12–13, 29, 39, 82, 88–89, 105, 113–14, 121, 126, 152, 175–76, 189
Surry County, N. C., 81
Sutton, Bill, 131, 135
Sutton-Taylor feud: 131; and John Jack Helms, 131–36; and John Wesley Hardin, 134–36; mentioned, 131; State Police involvement in, 133–34. *See also* Helms, John Jack
Swamp Fox of the Sulphur, 105
Sweet Home, Tex., 134

Tainted Breeze: The Great Hanging at Greenville, Texas 1862 (McCaslin), 161–62, 164

Tarrant, Tex., 24, 107, 110, 115, 118, 120, 152, 175, 184

Tarrant County, 3, 29, 34, 43

Tart, W. H., 167

Taylor, Buck, 131

Taylor, Creed, 131, 134

Taylor, Doby (Doboy), 131

Taylor, Hays, 131

Taylor, Jim, 135–36

Taylor, Pitkin, 131, 134

Taylor, Robert, 167

Taylor, Robert H., 20, 105, 150, 156, 181

Taylor, T. U., 18

Taylor, William, 131

Templeton, Howard, 111

Templeton, Robert, 62, 163

Tennessee, 6, 7, 9, 28–31, 33, 41, 43, 51, 53, 57, 64, 71, 81, 83–85, 87, 91–95, 106, 111, 115, 118–19, 123, 126

Tennessee River, 93

Tennile, George, 135

Ten Stitchers, 23, 92, 94, 96, 176, 178

Terrell, Judge, 71

Terrell, Z. R., 110–12, 182

Terry, James, 177

Terry, James L., 149

Terry, Joseph, 15

Terry, Thomas Henderson, 15, 149

Texarkana, Tex., 9

Texas Advocate, 11

Texas Constitutional Convention of 1866, 117

Texas First Cavalry Regiment, Partisan Rangers, 78; Texas First Cavalry Battalion, 170

Texas Loyal League of Union Citizens, 125

Texas News, 128

Texas Republican, 38, 171

Texas Revolution, 28, 69

Texas Second Cavalry Regiment, Partisan Rangers, 180

Texas State Historical Association, 138

Texas Troubles, 11–13, 40

Texas Twenty-Second Cavalry Regiment, 150

thickets: animals, 5; description of, 3–5, 28, 145–46; mentioned, 55–57, 69, 84–87, 100, 104, 160; warning system in, 55. *See also* Big Creek Thicket; Black Cat Thicket; Hobbs Thicket; Jernigan's Thicket; Mustang Thicket; Tidwell Thicket; Wildcat Thicket

Third Regiment of Texas Mounted Volunteers, Co. G (North Texas Regiment), 31

Third Texas Cavalry Regiment, Co. G, 185

Thirty-First Cavalry Regiment (CSA), 77

Thirty-Second Texas Cavalry Regiment, 52, 66; Co. G (Lamar Cavalry), 52

Thomason, E., 156

Thrasher, W., 182

Throckmorton, J. W., 20, 117–18, 124–25, 156

ticks, 146

Tidwell Thicket, 4

Timber Creek, 11

Tingley, Sharon Jernigan, 165, 174, 181

Tittle, Henry, 111

Titus County, 12, 34, 49, 107, 111, 113, 156, 168, 181

Todd, George T., 117–25, 185–86

Todd, William Smith, 117, 123

Torbert, Wm. H., 167

Townes, Nathan W., 66, 185

Tranquil, Tex., 112

Traveler's Inn, 46

Travelstead, Anthony, 30

Travis County, 22, 34, 39, 52, 117, 125, 131, 153

Trevilion, John A., 157

Trinity River, 69, 92

Tri-Weekly Telegraph, 89

TST Second Cavalry Regiment, Co. I, 114–15, 183

Tuck, June E., 139, 141

Tucker, George, 25

Twenty-Second Cavalry Regiment, 180

Twenty-Third Regular Texas Dismounted Cavalry, 15, 163; Co. G, 163
Twenty-Third Texas Cavalry Regiment, (Gould's Regiment), 48, 112, 119–20; Co. G, 48
Tyler, Tex., 89, 96, 174

Union Academy, 35
Unionists, 8, 11, 13–15, 22, 43, 45, 47–48, 50, 52, 57, 60, 64, 68–69, 75, 78–79, 88, 93, 96–98, 107, 116–18, 122, 124–25, 130, 132, 137, 139, 157, 168, 189. *See also* brush men; bush men; deserters
"United Daughters of the Confederacy Catechism for Children," 137
Upper South, 8, 14, 23, 30, 33, 39, 70, 93, 147–48, 153. *See also* Lower South
Upper Southerners, 6, 8, 14, 23, 28, 31, 41, 57, 83, 85, 88, 147–48. *See also* Lower Southerners

Van Buren, Ark., 159
Vancil, James, 110–12
Vaughn, Mrs., 178–79
Vaughn family, 178–79
Vick, M., 181
Vicksburg, Miss., 97, 178
Victoria (Tex.) Advocate, 132–33
vigilantes: 13; actions of, 11–13, 23–27, 43–45, 53–58, 63, 68, 82–83, 86, 88–90, 92–97, 98, 119, 139–40, 149, 152, 161–62, 164, 174, 177–78, 180–81, 184; committees of, 9, 25, 40–41, 43, 45; and courts, 11–13, 44–45, 108, 162; groups, 11–13, 23, 25–27, 41, 53, 58–59, 82–83, 148, 176–77, 185; hangings of, 38, 56, 83, 88–90, 96, 146, 174; and Knights of the Golden Circle, 39, 88, 115, 157; and Knights of the Rising Son, 185; and Ku Klux Klan, 185; leaders of, 17–23, 40, 44–45, 52–54, 56–59, 61–62, 64–66, 86–87, 89, 91–92, 94, 96, 108–10, 113, 118–19, 122–27, 129–34, 136, 140, 162, 176, 184, 186–87; memberships of, 23, 25, 27, 40, 52, 58–60; men-

tioned, 49, 65, 116; movements, 25–27, 40, 57; and Sons of the South, 53; and Sons of Washington, 23, 40, 53–54, 56–57, 61–62, 65, 113, 182; and Ten Stitchers, 23, 92–97, 177–78; and vigilantism, 24–27, 50, 97–98, 152
Village Creek, 92
Virginia, 4, 8, 41, 72, 145, 165

Waco, Tex., 149
Wadson, Hugh, 167
Wardlon, I. W. (J. W. Wardlow), 167
Warren, John Wesley, 22
Warren, Rice, 58–59, 113, 121–22, 162
Warren, Tex., 69–71
Washington, George, 53–54
Watson, William C., 167
Waxahachie, Tex., 12, 46
Weatherford, Jackson, 167
Weatherford, Money, 167
Weaver, William T. G., 122, 125
Webster, W. H., 110
Weddle, Robert S., 14–15, 180
Welbanks (Wilbanks), James, 167
West Point, 48
Wharton County, 9, 129, 131
Whiskey Rebellion, 53
White, Matt, 145
White Oak Creek, 116
Whitmore, G. W., 156
Wieland, Tex., 69
Wildcat Thicket, 4, 18
William, Winnfield, 157
Williams, G. W., 157
Williams, James P., 183
Williams, Lemuel H., 156
Williamson County, 156
Wilson, George, 167
Wilson, Hugh, 167
Wilson, Jason, 167
Wilson County, 132, 135–36
Wise County, 39
Wood, James, 167
Wood County, 156

Woods, I. L., 176
Woody, H. W. (H. S.), 110–11
Worsley, P. S., 188
Wright, George W., 35, 105, 156, 181
Wright, Leander, 110–11
Wright, M. H., 166, 181
Wright, T. G., 181
Wright, W. B., 35–36, 119–21, 185
Wright's Landing, 155

Writ of Habeas Corpus, 14, 107, 112
Wyatt-Brown, Bertram, 25–26

Yates, John, 56, 161
Yost, W. C., 167
Young, Harriet, 30
Young Man, 80–81, 88
Yowell, Tex., 153

Zollicoffer, Felix Kirk, 51–52